THE HISTORY OF NORTHERN AFRICA

THE BRITANNICA GUIDE TO AFRICA

THE HISTORY OF NORTHERN AFRICA

EDITED BY AMY MCKENNA, SENIOR EDITOR, GEOGRAPHY AND HISTORY

Britannica Educational Publishing
IN ASSOCIATION WITH
ROSEN
EDUCATIONAL SERVICES

Published in 2010 by Britannica Educational Publishing
(a trademark of Encyclopædia Britannica, Inc.)
in association with Rosen Educational Services, LLC
29 East 21st Street, New York, NY 10010.

Distributed exclusively by Rosen Educational Services.
For a listing of additional Britannica Educational Publishing titles, call toll free (800) 237-9932.

First Edition

Britannica Educational Publishing
Michael I. Levy: Executive Editor
Marilyn L. Barton: Senior Coordinator, Production Control
Steven Bosco: Director, Editorial Technologies
Lisa S. Braucher: Senior Producer and Data Editor
Yvette Charboneau: Senior Copy Editor
Kathy Nakamura: Manager, Media Acquisition
Amy McKenna: Senior Editor, Geography and History

Rosen Educational Services
Hope Lourie Killcoyne: Senior Editor
Nelson Sá: Art Director
Cindy Reiman: Photography Manager
Matthew Cauli: Designer, Cover Design
Introduction by Shalini Saxena

Library of Congress Cataloging-in-Publication Data

The history of northern Africa / edited by Amy McKenna. — 1st ed.
p. cm. — (The Britannica guide to Africa)
"In association with Britannica Educational Publishing, Rosen Educational Services."
Includes bibliographical references and index.
ISBN 978-1-61530-318-2 (library binding)
1. Africa, North—History. I. McKenna, Amy, 1969-
DT167.H58 2011
961—dc22

2010021702

Manufactured in the United States of America

On the cover: A Berber man stands in southeastern Morocco, surrounded by the wind-rippled sands of the Sahara desert. The largest desert in the world, the Sahara fills nearly all of Northern Africa. *Herman du Plessis/Gallo Images/Getty Images*

On pages 1, 21, 38, 58, 63, 83, 100, 109, 126, 156, 166: Pictured here in 1961, these Berber women of Aït Ben Haddou, Morocco, wear traditional dress for a marriage market, where they may choose a husband. *Ingebore Lehmann/Hulton Archive/Getty Images*

CONTENTS

Introduction x

Chapter 1: Early History 1

- Early Humans and Stone Age Society 3
- *Arab* 4
- The Carthaginian Period 6
  - The Phoenician Settlements 6
  - Carthaginian Supremacy 7
  - Trade 9
  - Wars Outside Africa 10
  - Treatment of Subject Peoples 11
  - Political and Military Institutions 12
- The City 13
  - Religion and Culture 13
  - Carthage and Rome 14
  - *Human Sacrifice* 15
  - The Greeks in Cyrenaica 16
- The Rise and Decline of Native Kingdoms 18

Chapter 2: Roman North Africa 21

- Administration and Defense 21
- The Growth of Urban Life 23
- Economy 25
- Later Roman Empire 27
- Christianity and the Donatist Controversy 29
- Extent of Romanization 32
- The Vandal Conquest 33
- The Byzantine Period 34
- *Arianism* 35
- Roman Cyrenaica 37

Chapter 3: From the Arab Conquest to 1830 38

- Khārijite Berber Resistance to Arab Rule 41
- The Maghrib Under Muslim Dynasties in the 8th–11th Centuries 42
  - The Rustamid State of Tāhart 43
  - The Banū Midrār of Sijilmāssah 43
  - The Idrīsids of Fez 44
  - The Aghlabids 44
  - The Fāṭimids and Zīrids 46

16

17

26

The Maghrib Under the Almoravids and the Almohads 48
Political Fragmentation and the Triumph of Islamic Culture (*c.* 1250–*c.* 1500) 51
The Maghrib from About 1500 to 1830 53
Morocco Under Sharifian Dynasties 54
Ottoman Rule in the Maghrib 55

Chapter 4: North Africa After 1830 58
Advent of European Colonialism 58
Nationalist Movements 61
Sanūsiyyah 62

Chapter 5: Algeria 63
Early History 63
French Algeria 63
The Conquest of Algeria 64
Colonial Rule 66
Nationalist Movements 68
World War II and the Movement for Independence 70
The Algerian War of Independence 71
Independent Algeria 75
From Ben Bella to Boumedienne 76
Bendjedid's Move Toward Democracy 77
Civil War: the Islamists Versus the Army 78
Foreign Relations 81

Chapter 6: Egypt 83
Early History Through the 19th Century 83
British Occupation 84
Constitutional Monarchy 88
The Republic 92
The First Decades 92
The Republic in the 1970s and '80s 95
The Republic Since the 1980s 97

Chapter 7: Libya 100
Early History 100
Ottoman Rule 102
Italian Colonization 103
Independence 103

56

74

101
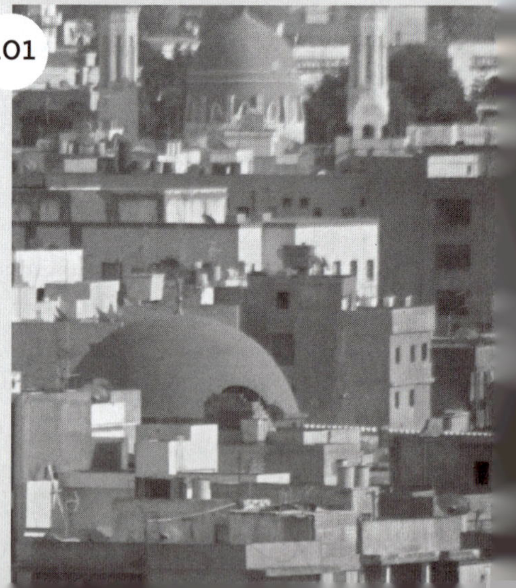

The Discovery of Oil 103
Muammar al-Qaddafi *105*
The Qaddafi Regime 106

CHAPTER 8: MOROCCO **109**
Early History 109
'Abīd al-Bukhārī *111*
Decline of Traditional Government 111
The French Protectorate 113
World War II and Independence 115
The French Zone 115
The Spanish Zone 117
Independent Morocco 120
Foreign Policy 122
Western Sahara 122
Hassan's Last Years 123
Into the 21st Century 125

CHAPTER 9: SUDAN **126**
Ancient Nubia 126
Egyptian Influence 126
The Kingdom of Kush 127
Darfur *128*
Christian and Islamic Influence 129
Medieval Christian Kingdoms 131
Islamic Encroachments 132
The Funj 133
The Spread of Islam 134
Egyptian-Ottoman Rule 135
Muḥammad 'Alī and His Successors 135
Ismā'īl Pasha and the Growth of European Influence 136
The Mahdiyyah 139
The Reign of the Khalīfah 140
The British Conquest 142
The Anglo-Egyptian Condominium 143
The Early Years of British Rule 143
The Growth of National Consciousness 144
The Republic of The Sudan 146
The 'Abbūd Government 147
Sudan Since 1964 148

110

130

141

CHAPTER 10: TUNISIA **156**

Early History 156

The Growth of European Influence 157

The Protectorate 158

Young Tunisians *160*

World War II 160

Independence 162

Domestic Development 162

Foreign Relations 164

CHAPTER 11: WESTERN SAHARA **166**

CONCLUSION **170**

GLOSSARY **171**

BIBLIOGRAPHY **173**

INDEX **175**

168

169

INTRODUCTION

Serving as an interface between African, European, and Arab cultures, northern Africa has been a crucible of both conflict and exchange. The region, which encompasses the Maghrib countries of Morocco, Tunisia, and Algeria as well as Libya, Egypt, and Sudan, has in many ways been insulated from the crises that have plagued much of the African continent. However, as the histories recounted in this volume will attest, these countries have been subject to their own share of turbulence over the centuries. Still, amidst the volatility, northern Africans have displayed their remarkable adaptability and enduring import to Africa, the Middle East, and the world.

Prehistoric evidence of Paleolithic and Neolithic cultures suggests that the early societies of the Maghrib and Libya supported themselves initially by hunting and gathering and later by rearing animals and cultivating food production techniques. The region began to thrive after the arrival of the Phoenicians from the area that is now present-day Lebanon.

By establishing numerous communities around the Mediterranean in the 1st millennium BCE, Phoenician traders instituted an enduring link between northern Africa and Europe. After successfully staving off hostile Greek forces that threatened their Sicilian settlements in 580 BCE, the Phoenicians secured their footing in parts of Sardinia, Corsica, and southern Spain as well. With large stores of wealth accumulated via the extensive trading networks it had instituted, the city of Carthage, located in present-day Tunisia, proved to be the most powerful Phoenician settlement and became the centre of western Phoenician power.

By the 3rd and 2nd centuries BCE, Carthaginian success foundered as Carthage and Rome were involved in territorial disputes in Sicily and Spain that led to the three Punic Wars. The destruction of Carthage marked the end of the Third Punic War in 146 BCE, and propelled the ascendancy of Roman influence in northern Africa. After Carthage was reconstituted as a Roman colony, the region witnessed an influx of migrants from Italy who influenced the administration, infrastructure, and culture of the land.

Even as native settlements retained much of their autonomy under Roman authority, Roman culture pervaded Tunisia as well as parts of Algeria and Morocco, many areas of which were highly urbanized. The Romanization of the Maghrib was accompanied by the proliferation of Christianity, which attracted a substantial following among both the wealthy and poor. Following a schism over doctrine and social issues, the Christian community of northern Africa was divided between orthodox Christians, who typically were

The Medersa Slimania in Tunisia, shown here around 1895, was at that time a Qur'ānic school for girls. The stucco and tile building was built in the mid-1700s. /Roger Viollet/Getty Images

wealthier than the general population, and Donatists, who tended to be among the poor. While the Donatist movement was largely suppressed beginning in 411 CE, the controversy generated by this schism weakened Roman administration.

Still, the Roman grip on northern Africa outlasted the rest of the Roman Empire. However, nearly two decades after the Visigoths captured Rome in 410 CE and opened the floodgates to other Germanic invaders, the Maghrib fell to the Vandals as well. Eventually the Vandals were defeated by the Byzantine emperor Justinian's forces in 533–34, and they were supplanted, in turn, by the Arabs in the 7th century.

The Arab conquests marked a new phase in the history of the Maghrib. As the locus of power shifted to Damascus—the seat of the Umayyad caliphate—and Islam began to spread throughout the region, the hegemony once enjoyed by the Christians there dissolved. The early stages of Arab power were characterized by constant struggles with the native Berbers (now known by their preferred name, Imazighen), who despite their conversion to Islam, were classified as inferior to their Arab conquerors. After the Abbāsids assumed caliphal authority, the Berbers allied with other Muslims who opposed caliphal rule. As a result, four Muslim states were created, each ruled from the 8th until 11th centuries by Muslim dynasties with either weak ties to the caliphate or none at all. In the 11th century, the Maghrib was finally unified under Berber Muslims by the Almoravids.

In the centuries that followed, the Maghrib was variously divided by its different rulers, experiencing a series of internal and international conflicts. Tensions between the Muslims of the region and Iberian Christians led to the establishment of Spanish and Portuguese strongholds on the Maghribi coast. In the early 16th century, the clash between the Muslims and Christians drew the attention of the Ottoman Turks, who had recently occupied Egypt. As the Ottomans proceeded to capture much of Algeria, Tunisia, and Libya, Muslims retained primacy in the region, and European threats receded until 1830.

After ousting the Ottoman ruler of Algeria in 1830—and ending three centuries of Ottoman authority there—the French would go on to sustain more than a century of colonial rule in the Maghrib. As such, they were critical in shaping the region as it stands today. The French went on to colonize Tunisia, while Libya became a province of the Ottoman Empire and Morocco was able to retain its independence in the 19th century. By 1939, however, the French and Italians had settled Tunisia, Morocco, and Libya. Only after World War II did nationalist movements in each of the four countries become strong enough to finally shake foreign rule.

When the Algerian city of Algiers succumbed to French advances in 1830, the rulers of northern Africa effectively lost the hope of regaining their power in the Maghrib. Massive miscommunication between the French and the Algerians they ruled as well as excessive violence cost many Algerians their livelihoods, if not their lives. With resources and infrastructure disproportionately available to the wealthier European settlers, native Algerians residing in rural areas, who were largely Muslim, often remained unemployed.

In 1947 Algerians were finally granted French citizenship with the right to maintain their personal status under Islamic law as well as the opportunity to work in France. Dissatisfied with the enforcement of these rights and vying for full independence from the French, the National Liberation Front waged the Algerian War of Independence in 1954. The war ended in 1962 when an agreement was reached to hold a referendum on independence for Algeria that would allow French aid to continue and would provide European residents with the option to remain, either with foreigner status or by requesting Algerian citizenship, or leave Algeria; the referendum was overwhelmingly approved.

A stable government, however, did not necessarily accompany independence. Although unstable leadership was eventually followed by a move towards democracy, a civil war launched in 1992 between Islamists and the army renewed violence in the country. Algeria's often contentious foreign policies have also strained its relations with the international community. By partnering with the European Union, the United Nations, and other international organizations in recent years, however, Algeria continues to move forward by seeking peaceful and mutually beneficial solutions to its problems.

The history of Egypt has followed a different trajectory than the countries of the Maghrib. Despite the differences, however, it too was variously held by the Romans, Byzantines, and Ottomans, and was later subject to European imperialism. Resistance to British occupation, which began in 1882, culminated in independence in 1922. The British retained certain powers with respect to Egypt's foreign relations, however, which created tension between the British and the Egyptian monarchs who assumed power after independence. Egyptian independence consequently remained tenuous for the next few decades.

Following World War II, Egypt began assuming a greater role in the Arab world. With its support of Arab opposition to the creation of the Jewish state of Israel in Palestine, Egypt gained new international commitments that would become central to the leaders of the next half century and beyond. After the monarchy was toppled in a 1952 coup by military forces, Egypt came under the leadership of three powerful men: Col. Gamal Abdel Nasser, Anwar el-Sādāt, and Hosnī Mubārak. Despite the turbulence of their regimes and the various economic, political, and international issues that wracked Egypt in the latter half of the 20th century and into the 21st century, Egypt has become a powerful player in the Middle East and on the world stage.

Although it borders Algeria and Tunisia and has much in common with its neighbours, Libya, like Egypt, is not considered part of the Maghrib. Italy invaded Libya in 1911, unseating the Ottomans who had ruled there since the 16th century. With an influx of Italian settlers into Libya, the Italian government developed the region's infrastructure to accommodate them. However, much of the newly developed towns, roads, and agricultural communities were destroyed during World War II and the country was left divided and impoverished.

Libya obtained independence in 1951, and through 1969 Libya retained close ties to the West. However, with the discovery of its oil reserves in 1959 and its subsequent decreasing reliance on international aid, Libya began to pursue large-scale development without much Western influence, and a coup led by Col. Muammar al-Qaddafi in 1969 officially severed Libya's relations with the United States and Britain and transformed Libya from a monarchy to a republic. Under Qaddafi, Libya has alienated a number of Arab and Western countries, but in an effort to become more integrated into the international community, it has begun taking measures to increase business opportunity and tourism.

Unlike the other countries of the Maghrib, Morocco was able to resist colonial authority and survived through the 19th century as an independent Islamic monarchy. However, in the early 20th century, it too came within the grasp of the French. Although the French and Spanish had already established a presence at Moroccan ports, Morocco's status as a French protectorate resulted less from aggressive French designs on the region and rather as a consequence of the sultan Abd al-Aziz's need for French protection. France granted Spain protectorate status over areas of Morocco as well. Both countries largely controlled their respective territories and Moroccans held only nominal sway over the administration and governance.

As with other colonies, Morocco birthed nationalist movements that demanded liberation from European rule. In 1956 France finally agreed to restore power to the sultan, and an agreement was reached with the Spanish authorities as well. In the years following independence, Morocco has often differed from the Arab world with respect to its foreign relations. Rejecting alliances with volatile states and encouraging peace talks and compromise in the Middle East, Morocco positioned itself closer to the United States and the West than have most other Arab states. The country has, however, been subject to criticism regarding its stance on the adjacent territory known as the Western Sahara. Although Morocco claims this territory, its claim is not internationally recognized. The inhabitants of Western Sahara, known as Saharawis, have advocated and fought for their independence, but the situation remained unresolved into the 21st century.

The centrality of Islam to the recent centuries of Sudan's history as well as its close ties to Egypt dating back to before the Common Era has bound Sudan to the other countries of northern Africa. Eventually subject to Ottoman rule by way of its Egyptian neighbour, Sudan, like Egypt, also eventually became subject to British rule. In the case of Sudan, however, the British ruled alongside the Egyptians, even as they often dominated the Egyptians in decision-making and administration. Colonial rule here, as elsewhere, eventually ended, producing a state that would be fractured along ethnic and religious lines and be embroiled in lengthy civil war.

Today, the population of northern Sudan is predominantly Arab and Muslim, while southern Sudan's population is predominantly African peoples who adhere to either animist or Christian beliefs. The country continues to struggle to achieve stability after decades of civil war, as well as deal with the devastating conflict of the Darfur region that was launched in 2003.

The history of the final Maghrib country, Tunisia, in ways parallels that of Algeria. Both were French colonial subjects, although Tunisia was designated a protectorate by treaty after years of French aggression rather than by outright French capture. Following its independence from French rule in 1956, Tunisia established a republic, whose relative stability and commitment to reform distinguished it from its neighbours. While reform has been stymied considerably under Pres. Zine al-Abidine Ben Ali, the country continues to align itself more closely with the West than some other Arab states on a number of international matters.

Northern Africa is a region that has constantly been forced to confront adversity and adjust accordingly. Although it has its own long history with slavery, it has been spared the legacy of the Atlantic slave trade, which came to devastate numerous regions and communities throughout the African continent. Still, it is bound in other ways to its sub-Saharan African neighbours. Likewise, although it remains physically separated from the countries of the Middle East, it has experienced many of the same challenges that have faced those countries. While dogged by conflict for centuries, the countries of northern Africa have proven also that coexistence does not require absolute uniformity.

CHAPTER 1

EARLY HISTORY

The northern region of the African continent is subject to various methods of definition. It has been regarded by some as stretching from the Atlantic shores near Morocco in the west to the Suez Canal and the Red Sea in the east. This region is commonly referred to as northern Africa and comprises the modern countries of Morocco, Algeria, Tunisia, Libya, Egypt, and Sudan, as well as the territory of Western Sahara—all of which are included in this book.

The designation North Africa is also associated with this region of the continent. It refers to a smaller geographical area than that embraced by the term northern Africa—namely the countries of Morocco, Algeria, and Tunisia, a region known by the French during colonial times as Afrique du Nord and by the Arabs as the Maghrib ("West"). The most commonly accepted definition of North Africa, and one that is also used in this book, includes the three above-mentioned countries as well as Libya. The regions here designated North Africa, however, have also been called Northwest Africa.

The ancient Greeks used the word Libya (derived from the name of a tribe on the Gulf of Sidra) to describe the land north of the Sahara, the territory whose native peoples were subjects of Carthage, and also as a name for the whole continent. The Romans applied the name Africa (of Phoenician origin) to their first province in the northern part of Tunisia, as well as to the entire area north of the Sahara and also to

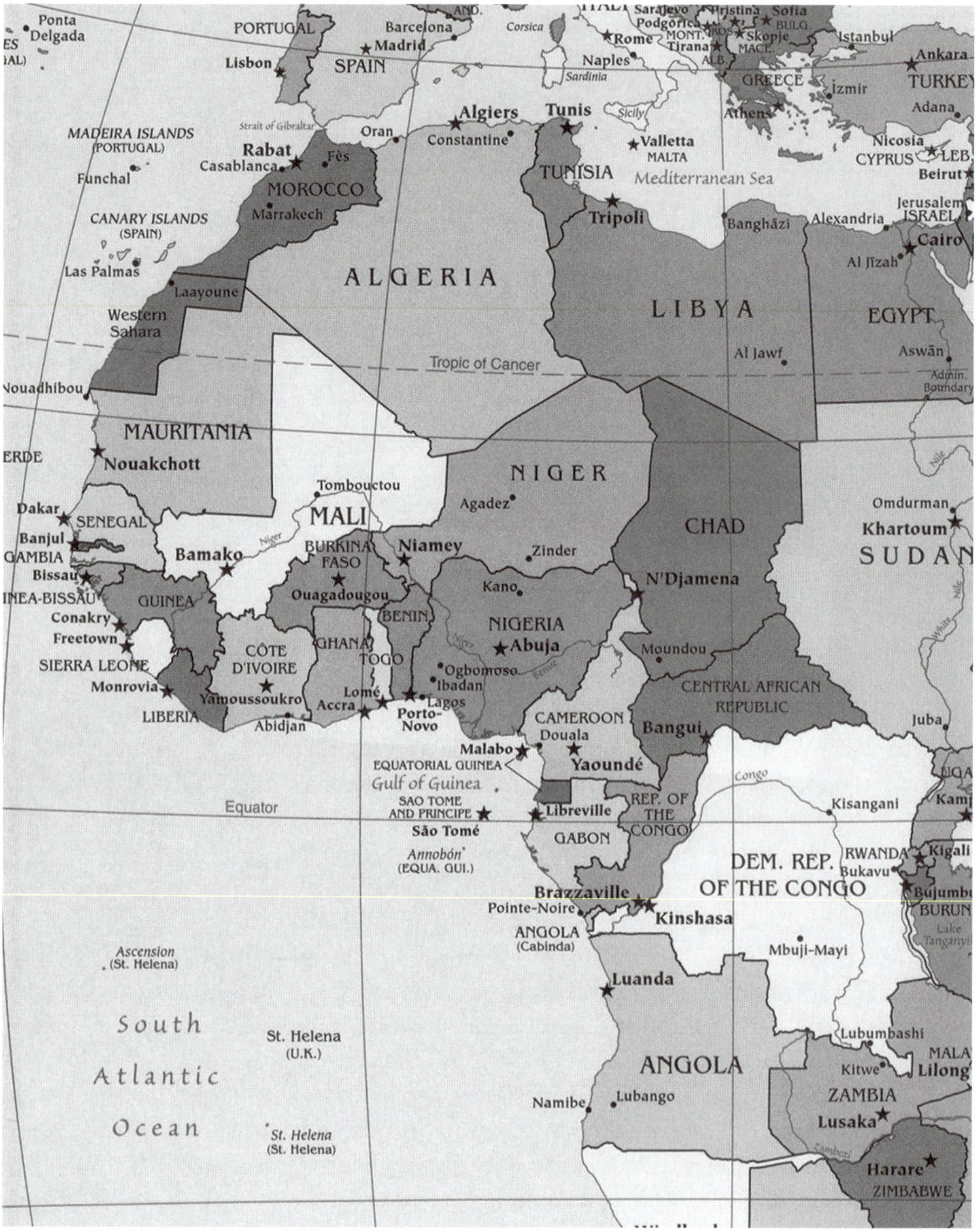

2008 map produced by the U.S. Central Intelligence Agency, highlighting the northern region of Africa. Courtesy of the University of Texas Libraries, The University of Texas at Austin

the entire continent. The Arabs used the derived term Ifrīqiyyah in a similar fashion, though it originally referred to a region encompassing modern Tunisia and eastern Algeria.

In all likelihood, the Arabs also borrowed the word Barbar (Berber) from the Latin *barbari* to describe the non-Latin-speaking peoples of the region at the time of the Arab conquest, and it has been used in modern times to describe the non-Arabic-speaking population called Berbères by the French and known generally as the Berbers (although their term for themselves, Amazigh [plural: Imazighen], is now preferred). As a result, Europeans have often called North Africa the Barbary States or simply Barbary. (A frequent usage refers to the non-Phoenician and non-Roman inhabitants of classical times, and their language, as Berber. It should be stressed, however, that the theory of a continuity of language between ancient inhabitants and the modern Imazighen has not been proved; consequently, the word Libyan is used here to describe these people in ancient times.)

The countries of Morocco, Algeria, and Tunisia have also been known as the Atlas Lands, for the Atlas Mountains that dominate their northern landscapes, although each country, especially Algeria, incorporates sizable sections of the Sahara. Farther east in Libya, only the northwestern and northeastern parts of the country, called Tripolitania and Cyrenaica respectively, are outside the desert.

Although geographically proximate to the other countries of northern Africa, Egypt's ancient civilization and long historical continuity—one marked by the ebb and flow of major religions, cultural trends, and foreign powers—is traditionally treated as a separate entity, one ultimately closer in distance and culture to the countries of the Middle East than to the countries to its west. Its role in this region of Africa, however, is undeniable. Sudan too is a place traditionally treated as atypical within its immediate geographic context, with its northern regions, today dominated by Islam and the Arabic language, closer to the Mediterranean world than its southern parts, where African languages and cultures hold the greatest sway. Sudan and Egypt are places where multifarious cultures have met, mixed, and clashed; they are the crossroads of the cultures and regions surrounding them. The histories of the two countries are also tightly bound. They may be *in* northern Africa, but they are not comfortably *of* that region. Their presence in this book, however, helps to underscore their often overlooked connections to the African countries nearby to them.

EARLY HUMANS AND STONE AGE SOCIETY

Although there is uncertainty about some factors, Aïn el-Hanech (in Algeria) is the site of one of the earliest traces of hominin occupation in the Maghrib. Somewhat later but better-attested are

Arab

Before the spread of Islam and, with it, the Arabic language, Arab referred to any of the largely nomadic Semitic inhabitants of the Arabian Peninsula. In modern usage, it embraces any of the Arabic-speaking peoples living in the vast region from Mauritania, on the Atlantic coast of Africa, to southwestern Iran, including the entire Maghrib of North Africa, Egypt and Sudan, the Arabian Peninsula, and Syria and Iraq.

This diverse assortment of peoples defies physical stereotyping, because there is considerable regional variation. The early Arabs of the Arabian Peninsula were predominantly nomadic pastoralists who herded their sheep, goats, and camels through the harsh desert environment. Settled Arabs practiced date and cereal agriculture in the oases, which also served as trade centres for the caravans transporting the spices, ivory, and gold of southern Arabia and the Horn of Africa to the civilizations farther north. The distinction between the desert nomads, on the one hand, and town dwellers and agriculturists, on the other, still pervades much of the Arab world.

Islam, which developed in the west-central Arabian Peninsula in the early 7th century CE, was the religious force that united the desert subsistence nomads—the Bedouins—with the town dwellers of the oases. Within a century, Islam spread throughout most of the present-day Arabic-speaking world, and beyond, from Central Asia to the Iberian Peninsula. Arabic, the language of the Islamic sacred scripture (the Qur'an), was adopted throughout much of the Middle East and North Africa as a result of the rapidly established supremacy of Islam in those regions. Other elements of Arab culture, including the veneration of the desert nomad's life, were integrated with many local traditions. Arabs of today, however, are not exclusively Muslim; some of the native speakers of Arabic worldwide are Christians, Druzes, Jews, or animists.

Traditional Arab values were modified in the 20th century by the pressures of urbanization, industrialization, detribalization, and Western influence. This is particularly evident with Arabs who live in cities and towns, where family and tribal ties tend to break down, and where women, as well as men, have greater educational and employment opportunity. It is not as evident with Arabs who continue to live in small, isolated farming villages, where traditional values and occupations prevail, including the subservience and home seclusion of women.

sites at Ternifine (near Tighenif, Alg.) and at Sidi Abd el-Rahmane, Mor. Hand axes associated with the hominin *Homo erectus* have been found at Ternifine, and Sidi Abd el-Rahmane has produced evidence of the same hominin dating to at least 200,000 years ago.

Succeeding these early hand ax remains are the Levalloisian and Mousterian industries similar to those found in the Levant. It is claimed that nowhere did the Middle Paleolithic (Old Stone Age) evolution of flake tool techniques reach a higher state of development than in North Africa. Its high point in variety, specialization, and standard of workmanship is named Aterian for the type site Bi'r al-'Atir in Tunisia; assemblages of Aterian material occur throughout the Maghrib and the Sahara. Radiocarbon testing from Morocco indicates a date of about 30,000 years ago for early Aterian industry. Its diffusion over the region appears to have taken place during one of the periods of desiccation, and the carriers of the tradition were clearly adept desert hunters. The few associated human remains are Neanderthal, with substantial differences between those found in the west and those in Cyrenaica. In the latter area a date of about 45,000 years ago for the Levalloisian and Mousterian industries has been obtained (at Haua Fteah, Libya). The tools and a fragmentary human fossil of Neanderthal type are almost identical to those of Palestine.

The earliest blade industry of the Maghrib, associated as in Europe with the final supersession of Neanderthals by modern *Homo sapiens*, is named Ibero-Maurusian or Oranian (type site La Mouilla, near Oran in western Algeria). Of obscure origin, this industry seems to have spread along all the coastal areas of the Maghrib and Cyrenaica between about 15,000 and 10,000 BCE. Following the Ibero-Maurusian was the Capsian, the origin of which is also obscure. Its most characteristic sites are in the area of the great salt lakes of southern Tunisia, the type site being Jabal al-Maqta' (El-Mekta), near Gafsa (Capsa, or Qafṣah). The climate during both Ibero-Maurusian and Capsian times appears to have been relatively dry and the fauna one of open country, ideal for hunting. Between about 9000 and 5000 BCE upper Capsian industry spread northward to influence the Ibero-Maurusian and also eastward to the Gulf of Sidra. Since there is much evidence that the Neolithic culture of the Maghrib was introduced not by invasion but through the acceptance of new ideas and technologies by the Capsian peoples, it is probable that they were the ancestors of the Libyans known in historic times.

The spread of early Neolithic culture in Libya and the Maghrib occurred during the 6th and 5th millennia BCE and is characterized by the domestication of animals and the shift from hunting and gathering to self-supporting food production (often still including hunting). The pastoral economy, with cattle the chief animal, remained dominant in North Africa until the classical period. Although the new type of economy may have originated in Egypt or the Sudan, the character of the flint-working tradition of the Maghribian Neolithic argues in favour of the survival of much of the earlier culture, which has been called Neolithic-of-Capsian tradition. Accordingly, the technology of the transition, if not of independent local origin, is best explained by the gradual diffusion of new techniques rather than by the immigration of new peoples.

The Neolithic-of-Capsian tradition in the Maghrib persisted at least into the 1st millennium BCE with relatively little change and development; there was no great flourishing of late Neolithic culture and little that can be described as a Bronze Age. North Africa was wholly lacking in metallic ores other than iron, hence most tools and weapons continued to be made of stone until the introduction of ironworking techniques.

Prehistoric rock carvings have been found in the southern foothills of the Atlas Mountains south of Oran and in the Ahaggar and Tibesti ranges. While some are relatively recent, the great majority appear to be of the Neolithic-of-Capsian tradition. Some show animals now locally or even totally extinct, such as the giant buffalo, elephant, rhinoceros, and hippopotamus, in areas now covered by desert. While Egyptian-like patterns may be discerned, the character of the rock art is so different from that of Egypt that it can hardly be said to derive from it. On the other hand, it is very much later than the rock paintings of Paleolithic times in southwestern Europe, and an independent development is probable. The art is primarily that of a culture that continued to depend largely—though not exclusively—on hunting and that survived on the Saharan fringes until historical times.

There are many thousands of large, stone-built surface tombs in North Africa that appear to have no connection with earlier megalithic structures found in northern Europe, and it is unlikely that any of them is earlier than the 1st millennium BCE. Large structures in Algeria such as the tumulus at Mzora (177 feet [54 metres] in diameter) and the mausoleum known as the Medracen (131 feet [40 metres] in diameter) are probably from the 4th and 3rd centuries BCE and show Phoenician influence, though there is much that appears to be purely Libyan.

THE CARTHAGINIAN PERIOD

North Africa (with the exception of Cyrenaica) entered the mainstream of Mediterranean history with the arrival in the 1st millennium BCE of Phoenician traders, mainly from Tyre and Sidon in modern Lebanon. The Phoenicians were looking not for land to settle but for anchorages and staging points on the trade route from Phoenicia to Spain, a source of silver and tin. Points on an alternative route by way of Sicily, Sardinia, and the Balearic Islands also were occupied. The Phoenicians lacked the manpower and the need to found large colonies as the Greeks did, and few of their settlements grew to any size. The sites chosen were generally offshore islands or easily defensible promontories with sheltered beaches on which ships could be drawn up. Carthage (its name derived from the Phoenician Kart-Hadasht, "New City"), destined to be the largest Phoenician colony and in the end an imperial power, conformed to the pattern.

The Phoenician Settlements

Tradition dates the foundation of Gades (modern Cádiz; the earliest known Phoenician trading post in Spain) to

1110 BCE, Utica (Utique) to 1101 BCE, and Carthage to 814 BCE. The dates appear legendary, and no Phoenician object earlier than the 8th century BCE has yet been found in the west. At Carthage some Greek objects have been found, datable to about 750 or slightly later, which comes within two generations of the traditional date. Little can be learned from the romantic legends about the arrival of the Phoenicians at Carthage transmitted by Greco-Roman sources. Though individual voyages doubtless took place earlier, the establishment of permanent posts is unlikely to have taken place before 800 BCE, antedating the parallel movement of Greeks to Sicily and southern Italy.

Material evidence of Phoenician occupation in the 8th century BCE comes from Utica and in the 7th or 6th century BCE from Hadrumetum (Sousse, Sūsah in Tunisia), Tipasa (east of Cherchell, Alg.), Siga (Rachgoun, Alg.), Lixus, and Mogador (Essaouira, Mor.), the last being the most distant Phoenician settlement so far known. Finds of similar age have been made at Motya (Mozia) in Sicily, Nora (Nurri), Sulcis, and Tharros (San Giovanni di Sinis) in Sardinia, and Cádiz and Almuñécar in Spain. Unlike the Greek settlements, however, those of the Phoenicians long depended politically on their homeland, and only a few were situated where the hinterland had the potential for development. The emergence of Carthage as an independent power, leading to the creation of an empire based on the secure possession of the North African coast, resulted less from the weakening of Tyre (the chief city of Phoenicia) by the Babylonians than from growing pressure from the Greeks in the western Mediterranean; in 580 BCE some Greek cities in Sicily attempted to drive the Phoenicians from Motya and Panormus (Palermo) in the west of the island. The Carthaginians feared that, if the Greeks won the whole of Sicily, they would move on to Sardinia and beyond, isolating the Phoenicians in North Africa. Their successful defense of Sicily was followed by attempts to strengthen limited footholds in Sardinia; a fortress at Monte Sirai is the oldest Phoenician military building in the west. The threat from the Greeks receded when Carthage, in alliance with Etruscan cities, checked the Phocaeans off Corsica about 540 BCE and succeeded in excluding the Greeks from contact with southern Spain.

Carthaginian Supremacy

By the 5th century BCE active military participation in the west by Tyre had doubtlessly ceased; from the latter half of the 6th century Tyre had been under Persian rule. Carthage thus became the leader of the western Phoenicians and in the 5th century formed an empire of its own, centred on North Africa, which included existing Phoenician settlements, new ones founded by Carthage itself, and a large part of modern Tunisia. Nothing is known of resistance from the indigenous North African populations, but it was probably limited because of the scattered nature of local societies and the lack of state formation. The actual stages of the growth of Carthaginian power are not known, but the process was largely completed by the beginning of the 4th century. The whole of the Sharīk (Cap Bon) Peninsula was occupied early, ensuring Carthage a fertile and secure hinterland. Subsequently it extended its control southwestward as far as a line running roughly from Sicca Veneria (El-Kef) to the coast at Thaenae (Thyna, or Thīnah; now in ruins). Penetration occurred south of this line later, Theveste (Tbessa, Tébessa) being occupied in the 3rd century BCE. In the Sharīk Peninsula, where the Carthaginians developed a prosperous agriculture, the native population may have been enslaved, while elsewhere they were obliged to pay tribute and furnish troops.

Carthage maintained an iron grip on the entire coast, from the Gulf of Sidra to the Atlantic coast of Morocco, establishing many new settlements to protect its monopoly of trade. These were mostly small, probably having only a few hundred inhabitants. The Greeks called them emporia, markets where native tribes brought articles to trade, which could also serve as anchorages and watering places. Permanent settlements in modern Libya were few and date to after the attempt by the Greek Dorieus to plant a colony there. Though in time fishing and agriculture played a part in their wealth, Leptis Magna with its neighbours Sabratha and Oea (Tripoli) became wealthy through trans-Saharan trade; Leptis Magna was the terminus of the shortest route across the Sahara linking the Mediterranean with the Niger River. A Carthaginian named Mago is said to have crossed the desert several times, but doubtless much of the trade (in precious stones and other exotics) came through intermediate tribes. Other stations on the Gulf of Gabes included Zouchis, known for its salted fish and purple dye, Gigthis (Boughrara, or Bū Ghirārah), and Tacape (Gabès, or Qābis). North of Thaenae were Acholla, traditionally an offshoot of the Phoenician settlement on Malta, Thapsus (near Ṭabulbah, Tun.), Leptis Minor, and Hadrumetum, the largest city on the east coast of Tunisia. From Neapolis (Nābul, or Nabeul) a road ran direct to Carthage across the base of the Sharīk Peninsula.

West of Carthage there have been changes in the course of the Majardah River; as a result, Utica, a port in Carthaginian and Roman times, is now some 7 miles (11 km) from the sea. Utica was second only to Carthage in importance among the Phoenician settlements and always maintained at least a nominal independence. Beyond Cape Sidi Ali el-Mekki (Farina) as far as the Strait of Gibraltar, the coast offered a number of anchorages, but few of the stations reached anything like the prosperity of those on the Gulf of Gabes and the east coast of Tunisia. One of the more important was Hippo Diarrhytus (Bizerte, Banzart), whose natural advantages as a port were utilized at an early date; another Hippo, later called Hippo Regius (Bône; modern Annaba, Alg.), was also probably of Carthaginian origin. Along the same stretch of coast were Rusicade (Skikda, or Philippeville) and Collo. Still farther west a number of place-names known from the Roman period show an earlier Phoenician interest, through the incorporation of a Phoenician linguistic element, *rus*, meaning "cape"—e.g., Rusuccuru (Dellys) and Rusguniae (Borj el-Bahri). Tingis (Tingi, or Tangier, Mor.) was already settled in the 5th century BCE.

TRADE

Ancient sources agree that Carthage had become perhaps the richest city in the world through its trade, yet few traces of its wealth have been discovered by archaeologists. This is because most of it was in perishables—textiles, unworked metal, foodstuffs, and slaves; its trade in manufactured goods was only a part of the whole. There can be no doubt that the most profitable trade was that inherited from the Phoenicians in the western Mediterranean, in which tin, silver, gold, and iron were obtained in exchange for manufactures and consumer goods of small value. Carthage ruthlessly maintained its monopoly of this trade from the late 6th to the end of the 3rd century BCE by sinking the vessels of intruders and exacting recognition of its position from other states. Its wealth is attested by the vast mercenary armies it was able to maintain with a mintage of gold coins in the 4th century far in excess of that known for other advanced states.

It was apparently in connection with this trade that during the 5th century there occurred two voyages of exploration and trade, evidently of particular importance since reports of them were known to later generations of Greeks and Romans. One was along the Atlantic coast of Morocco, the other northward along the Atlantic coast of Spain. They were led by Hanno and Himilco, respectively, both members of a leading family in Carthage.

Hanno's voyage is generally associated with Herodotus's account, written about 430 BCE, of Carthaginian trade on the Atlantic coast of Morocco. Herodotus describes a system of dumb barter with the coastal peoples, by which the Carthaginians exchanged manufactured goods for gold. It is not known where the exchanges took place; the Río de Oro is a possibility, and it is probable that Hanno's expedition went beyond Cape Verde. Nevertheless, the "gold route" did not survive the fall of Carthage and was not exploited by the Romans. This has led some scholars to argue that the Carthaginians' interest in the Atlantic coast of Morocco was stimulated by the more prosaic attraction of abundant fish stocks there.

Himilco's voyage also was known to the Greeks and Romans. He sailed north along the Atlantic coast of Spain, Portugal, and France and reached the territory of the Oestrymnides, a tribe living in Brittany. The purpose of this voyage was apparently to consolidate control of the trade in tin along the Atlantic coast of Europe. It followed the route used by the Tartessians, a people of southern Spain (in the area where Cádiz had been founded) who knew of Ireland and Britain. This trade was no doubt the latest phase of contact between the various areas of the Atlantic seaboard that went back to late Neolithic times. There is no evidence that Himilco reached Britain, nor indeed has any Phoenician object ever been found on the island, but probably Cornish tin was obtained through the tribes of Brittany. Tin was also obtained from northwestern Spain. It is notable that the Carthaginian tombs at Cádiz, found at intervals since 1900, have produced nothing earlier than the 5th century BCE, which would indicate that it was not until that date that Cádiz became a large and permanent base for the exploitation of trading opportunities in the west.

Trading contacts with the Greek world had been substantial from the earliest period of Phoenician colonization, in spite of the intermittent wars with the Greeks of Sicily. Pottery from Corinth, Athens, Ionia, Rhodes, and other Greek centres has been found at Carthage, Utica, and many other sites, as well as imports from Phoenicia itself and from Egypt. It is known that Selinus, a Greek city in Sicily, grew wealthy from trade with Carthage, probably in foodstuffs, before Carthage enlarged its Sicilian territory. During the 5th century BCE imports from the Greek world seem to have declined. One factor that may have inhibited trade was the lack of a Carthaginian coinage before the early 4th century, though most important Greek states had had their own coinages for at least a century before that. Carthaginian merchants, however, did not cease to frequent Greek ports, and a number of them were established at Syracuse in 398. From that date economic contacts with advanced states seem to have revived, especially after the conquests of Alexander the Great in the eastern Mediterranean created a new market for the cheap Carthaginian manufactured goods. The Carthaginian merchant became a familiar figure in such economic centres of the Greek world as Athens and Delos, so much so that there were Greek comedies in which the central figure was the Carthaginian trader.

Wars Outside Africa

Except in politically backward or thinly populated areas, Carthage's foreign policy was nonexpansive. One major departure from this policy was a disaster: in 480 BCE Carthage intervened in intercity struggles among the Greeks of Sicily and suffered a heavy defeat at Himera. After a long period of peace, it went in 410 to the aid of Segesta, an ally in Sicily, and turned the war into one of revenge for the earlier defeat. After initial successes, including the destruction of Himera, a treaty confirmed Carthage's control of the west of the island. During the 4th century most of the region's wars were caused by the attempts of various rulers of Syracuse to drive the Carthaginians out of Sicily; three of these (398–392, 382–375, and 368) were with Dionysius I of Syracuse. Most of the time the eastern limit of Carthaginian power in the island was recognized as the Halycus (Platani) River. The only occasion in which Carthage suffered directly (since its armies were largely mercenary) was in 310, when the ruler of Syracuse, Agathocles, under heavy pressure in Sicily, launched a daring invasion of Africa, the first experienced by Carthage. Over a period of three years he caused great devastation in Carthaginian territory in eastern Tunisia, but in the end he was defeated.

TREATMENT OF SUBJECT PEOPLES

Carthage was accused by its enemies in antiquity of oppressing and exacting excessive tribute from its subjects. There were, however, different categories of subject communities, the most-favoured being the original Phoenician settlements and the colonies of Carthage itself. There is little evidence of opposition among them to Carthaginian control. Similar institutions and laws may be attributed to a common cultural background rather than to an attempt to impose uniformity. Carthage exacted dues on imports and exports and levied troops and probably sailors. Carthaginian subjects of various nationalities in Sicily also received favourable treatment, at least in economic matters. Relatively free trade was allowed until the end of the 5th century BCE, and a number of cities had their own coinage. In the 4th century some Sicilian Greek states became subject to Carthage, paying a tribute amounting apparently to one-tenth of their produce. It was the Libyans of the interior who suffered most, though few were reduced to slavery. During the First Punic War (264–241 BCE) Libyans are said to have had to pay half their crops as tribute, and it is supposed that the normal exaction was one-fourth—still a burdensome imposition. They were also required to provide troops, and from the early 4th century they formed the largest single element in the Carthaginian army; it is unlikely that they received pay except in booty before the Punic Wars. The Carthaginians are said to have "admired not those governors who treated their subjects with moderation but those who exacted the greatest amount of supplies and treated the inhabitants most ruthlessly." This hostile judgment (by the Greek historian Polybius) was made in connection with the Libyans and a destructive revolt—one of a number known—that followed the First Punic War. In that revolt (241–237 BCE) mercenaries, unpaid after the Carthaginian defeat in the First Punic War, revolted and for a while controlled much of Carthage's North African territory. Great atrocities were committed on both sides during the fighting, and the Libyans were among the most fervent of the rebels. They even issued coins on which the name Libyan appears (in Greek), which probably indicates a growing ethnic consciousness. Notwithstanding this relationship, Carthaginian civilization had profound effects on the material culture of the Libyans.

Political and Military Institutions

Hereditary kingship prevailed in Phoenicia until Hellenistic times, and Greek and Roman sources refer to kingship at Carthage. It appears to have been not hereditary but elective, though in practice one family, the Magonid, dominated in the 6th century BCE. The power of the kingship was diminished during the 5th century, a development that has its parallels in the political evolution of Greek city-states and of Rome. Roman sources directly transcribe only one Carthaginian political term—*sufet*, etymologically the same as the Hebrew *shofet*, generally translated as "judge" in the Hebrew Bible but implying much more than merely judicial functions. At some stage, probably in the 4th century, the *sufet*s became the political leaders of Carthage and other western Phoenician settlements. Two *sufet*s were elected annually by the citizen body, but all were from the wealthy classes. Real power rested with an oligarchy of the wealthiest citizens, who were life members of a council of state and decided all important matters unless there was serious disagreement with the *sufet*s. A panel of judges chosen from among its members had obscure but formidable powers of control over all organs of government.

During the 6th and 5th centuries BCE most military commands were held by kings, but later the generalship was apparently dissociated from civil office. Even in the time of the kings, military authority appears to have been conferred upon the kings only for specific campaigns or in emergencies. The generals are said to have been regarded as potential overthrowers of the legal government, but in fact there is no record that any army commander attempted a coup d'état.

Until the 6th century BCE the armies of Carthage were apparently citizen levies similar to those of all city-states of the early classical period. But Carthage was too small to provide for the defense of widely scattered settlements, and it turned increasingly to mercenaries, who were under the command of Carthaginians, with citizen contingents appearing only occasionally. Libyans were considered particularly suitable for light infantry and the inhabitants of the later Numidia and Mauretania for light cavalry; Iberians and Celtiberians from Spain were used in both capacities. In the 4th century the Carthaginians also hired Gauls, Campanians, and even Greeks. The disadvantages of mercenary armies were more than outweighed by the fact that Carthage could never have stood the losses incurred in a whole series of wars in Sicily and elsewhere. Little is known about how the Carthaginian fleet was operated; technically, it was not overwhelmingly superior to those of the Greeks, but it was larger and had the benefit of experienced sailors from Carthage's maritime settlements.

THE CITY

The Romans completely destroyed Carthage in 146 BCE and a century later built a new city on the site, so that little is known of the physical appearance of the Phoenician city. The ancient artificial harbour—the Cothon—is represented today by two lagoons north of the bay of Al-Karm (El-Kram). In the 3rd century BCE it had two parts, the outer rectangular part being for merchant shipping, with the interior, circular division reserved for warships; sheds and quays were available for 220 warships. The harbour's small size probably means that it was used chiefly in winter when navigation almost ceased. The city walls were of great strength and were 22 miles (35 km) in length; the most vulnerable section, across the isthmus, was more than 40 feet (12 metres) high and 30 feet (9 metres) thick. The citadel on the hill called Byrsa was also fortified. Between Byrsa and the port was the heart of the city: its marketplace, council house, and temples. In appearance it may have been not dissimilar to towns in the eastern Mediterranean or Persian Gulf before the impact of modern civilization, with narrow winding streets and houses up to six stories high. The exterior walls were blank except for a solitary street door, but they enclosed courtyards. A figure of 700,000 for the city population is given by the geographer Strabo, but this probably included the population of the Sharīk Peninsula. A more reasonable figure could be about 400,000, including slaves, a size similar to that of Athens.

Religion and Culture

The Carthaginians were notorious in antiquity for the intensity of their religious beliefs, which they retained to the end of their independence and which in turn influenced the religion of the Libyans. The chief deity was Baal Hammon, the community's divine lord and protector, who was identified by the Greeks with Cronus and by the Romans with Saturn. During the 5th century BCE a goddess named Tanit came to be widely worshiped and represented in art. It is possible that her name is Libyan and that her popularity was connected with land acquisition in the interior, as she is associated with symbols of fertility. These two overshadow other deities such as Melqart, principal deity of Tyre, identified with Heracles, and Eshmoun, identified with Asclepius. Human sacrifice was the element in Carthaginian religion most criticized; it persisted in Africa much longer than in Phoenicia, probably into the 3rd century BCE. The child victims were sacrificed to Baal (not to Moloch, an interpretation based on a misunderstanding of the texts) and the burned bones buried in urns under stone markers, or stelae. At Carthage thousands of such urns have been found in the Sanctuary of Tanit, and similar burials have been discovered at Hadrumetum, Cirta (Constantine, Alg.), Motya, Caralis (modern Cagliari, Italy),

Nora, and Sulcis. Carthaginian religion appears to have taught that human beings are weak in the face of the overwhelming and capricious power of the gods. The great majority of Carthaginian personal names, unlike those of Greece and Rome, were of religious significance—e.g., Hannibal, "Favoured by Baal," or Hamilcar, "Favoured by Melqart."

In comparison with the extent of its power and influence, the artistic and intellectual achievements of Carthage are small. What limited remains of buildings survive—mostly in North Africa and Sardinia—are utilitarian and uninspired. In the decorative arts—pottery, jewelry, metalwork, terra-cotta, and the thousands of carvings on stelae—a similar lack of inspiration may be felt. The influence of Phoenician, Egyptian, and Greek artistic traditions can be observed, but they failed to stimulate as they did, for example, in Etruria. There is no evidence that Greek philosophy and literature made much impact, though certainly many Carthaginians in the city's later history knew Greek and there were libraries in the city. One written work is known, a treatise on agriculture by a certain Mago, but this may have been based on Hellenistic models. On the whole, the Carthaginians adhered to traditional modes of thought, which no doubt gave them a sense of solidarity amid more numerous and hostile peoples. Their fanatical patriotism enabled them to offer a more prolonged resistance to Rome than any other power. Their influence on North African history was, in the first place, to bring it into the mainstream of the advancing civilization of the Mediterranean world; more particularly, it introduced into North Africa advanced techniques leading to agricultural progress, which implied, in turn, a change by many Libyans from a seminomadic to a stable way of life and the possibilities of urbanization, which were fully realized in the Roman period.

Carthage and Rome

In the 3rd and 2nd centuries BCE Carthage was weakened and finally destroyed by Rome in the three Punic Wars. Treaties between Carthage and Rome had been made in 508, 348, and 279, and for a long period the two powers had no conflicting interests. But by the 3rd century Rome dominated all of southern Italy and thus approached the Carthaginian sphere in Sicily. In 264 Rome accepted the submission of Messana (Messina), though this state had previously had a Carthaginian garrison, partly because it had exaggerated fears of a possible Carthaginian threat to Italy and partly because it hoped to gain a foothold in Sicily. For Carthage a Roman presence in Sicily would upset the traditional balance of power on the island. The ensuing First Punic War, which lasted until 241, was highly costly in human life, with losses of tens of thousands being recorded in some naval engagements. Contrary to expectation, the Carthaginian fleet was worsted on several occasions by the newly built Roman navy; on land the Romans failed to drive the Carthaginians out of Sicily,

Human Sacrifice

The offering of the life of a human being to a deity is referred to as human sacrifice. The occurrence of human sacrifice can usually be related to the recognition of human blood as the sacred life force. Bloodless forms of killing, however, such as strangulation and drowning, have been used in some cultures. The killing of a human being, or the substitution of an animal for a person, has often been part of an attempt to commune with a god and to participate in divine life. Human life, as the most valuable material for sacrifice, has also been offered in an attempt at expiation.

There are two primary types of human sacrifice: the offering of a human being to a god and the entombment or slaughter of servants or slaves intended to accompany the deceased into the afterlife. The latter practice was more common. In various places in Africa, where human sacrifice was connected with ancestor worship, some of the slaves of the deceased were buried alive with him, or they were killed and laid beneath him in his grave. The Dahomey of western Africa instituted especially elaborate sacrifices at yearly ceremonies related to the cult of deceased kings. Excavations in Egypt and elsewhere in the ancient Middle East have revealed that numerous servants were at times interred with the funerary equipment of a member of the royal family in order to provide that person with a retinue in the next life. The Chinese practice of burying the emperor's retinue with him continued intermittently until the 17th century.

and a Roman invasion of Tunisia ended in catastrophe. Carthage made peace after a final naval defeat off the Aegates (Egadi) Islands, surrendering its hold on Sicily. Sardinia and Corsica fell to Rome in 238.

In response to the defeat, Carthage, under the leadership of Hamilcar Barca and his successors (usually described as the Barcid family), set about establishing a new empire in Spain. The object appears to have been to exploit the mineral wealth directly rather than through intermediaries and to mobilize the manpower of much of Spain into an army that could match that of Rome. Hamilcar and his son-in-law Hasdrubal built up an army of more than 50,000 Spanish infantry and occupied half of the Iberian Peninsula. Finally, in 219, Hannibal, Hamilcar's son, ignored Roman threats designed to prevent the consolidation or extension of the new empire. His invasion of Italy and the crushing defeats he inflicted on the Romans at Lake Trasimene (217) and the Battle of Cannae (216) were the gravest danger Rome had ever faced. The majority of Rome's allies and subjects in Italy remained loyal, however, and Hannibal found it increasingly difficult to get supplies and reinforcements. After clearing Spain of the Carthaginians (209–206), Scipio Africanus the Elder landed near Utica in 204 with a Roman army. In 203 Hannibal was recalled from Italy, but he was defeated by Scipio at the Battle of Zama (in the vicinity of present-day Sakiet Siddi Youssef, Tun.) in 202. Carthage made peace soon afterward, surrendering its fleet, its overseas possessions, and some of its African territory, thus bringing an end to the Second Punic War (218–201). During the next 50 years it retained some measure of prosperity, although frequently under pressure from the Numidians under King Masinissa. From 155 irrational fears of a Carthaginian revival were stimulated at Rome by Cato the Elder, and in 149, on flimsy pretexts, the Carthaginians were forced to choose between evacuating their city and settling inland or a doomed resistance. They chose the latter, and, after a three-year siege, termed the Third Punic War (149–146), the city was destroyed and its site ceremonially cursed by Scipio Africanus the Younger.

The Greeks in Cyrenaica

The natural contacts of Cyrenaica were northward with Crete and the Aegean

Eighteenth-century engraving by J.A. Pierron after S. de Mirys depicting the Battle of Zama, 202 BCE. The decisive Roman victory, led by Scipio Africanus the Elder over Hannibal and the Carthaginian army, ended the Second Punic War. Hulton Archive/Getty Images

world. In the late 12th century BCE Sea Peoples landing in Cyrenaica armed the Libyans and with them attempted unsuccessfully an invasion of Egypt. Cyrenaica's coast was visited by Cretan fishermen in the 7th century, and the Greeks became aware that it was the only area in North Africa still available for colonization. Severe overpopulation on the small Cyclades island of Thera (Thíra Santorini) led to Cyrene being founded (*c.* 630) on a site within easy reach of the sea, well watered, and in the fertile foothills of the Akhḍar Mountains. The founder's name was, or was changed to, Battus, a Libyan word meaning king. For some time friendly relations existed with the local peoples, and there was more intermarriage between Greek men and non-Greek women than was usual in Greek colonies. Later, when more colonists were attracted by Cyrene's increasing prosperity, hostilities broke out in which the settlers were successful. Cyrene also repulsed an invasion by the Egyptians (570) but in 525 submitted to Persia. Meanwhile,

Ruins at the ancient Greek city of Apollonia on the coast of Cyrenaica, modern Libya. Horace Abrahams/Hulton Archive/Getty Images

Cyrene had established other Greek cities in the area of modern Libya—Barce (Al-Marj), Taucheira (Al-ʿAqūriyyah), and Euhesperides (Banghāzī), all of which were independent of their founding city. During the 6th century Cyrene rivaled the majority of other Greek cities in its wealth, manifested in part by substantial temple building. Prosperity was based on grain, fruit, horses, and, above all, a medicinal plant called *silphium* (apparently an extinct species of the genus *Ferula*).

The dynasty of Battus ended about 440 BCE with the establishment of a democratic constitution like that of Athens, and the general prosperity of Cyrenaica continued through the 4th century in spite of some political troubles. Cyrenaica submitted to Alexander the Great in the late 4th century and subsequently became subject to the Ptolemies of Egypt. The cities, nevertheless, enjoyed a good deal of freedom in running their own affairs. The constitution of Cyrene elaborated a fairly liberal oligarchy, with a citizen body of 10,000 and two councils. During the 3rd century a federal constitution for all the Cyrenaican cities was introduced. Apollonia, the port of Cyrene, became a city in its own right; Euhesperides was refounded as Berenice, and a new city, Ptolemais (Ṭulmaythah), was founded, while Barce declined; the term Pentapolis came to be used for the five cities Apollonia, Cyrene, Ptolemais, Taucheira, and Berenice.

In 96 BCE Ptolemy Apion bequeathed Cyrenaica to Rome, which annexed the royal estates but left the cities free. Disorders led Rome to create a regular province out of Cyrenaica in 74 BCE, to which Crete was added seven years later. After the Roman general Mark Antony temporarily granted the province to his daughter (by the Egyptian queen Cleopatra) Cleopatra Selene, the emperor Augustus reestablished it, together with Crete, as a senatorial province.

THE RISE AND DECLINE OF NATIVE KINGDOMS

Between the destruction of Carthage and the establishment of effective Roman control over the Maghrib, there was a brief period in which native kingdoms flourished. Amid the shifting tribal nomenclature used in the sources of various periods, two main groups of relatively sedentary tribes may be distinguished: the Mauri, living between the Atlantic Ocean and the Moulouya or perhaps the Chelif River, who gave their name to Mauretania; and the Numidae, for whom Numidia was named, in the area to the west of that formerly controlled by Carthage. A third group, the Gaetuli, was a largely nomadic people of the desert and its fringe. The various tribes first emerge into history in the late 3rd century BCE, after a period of social evolution resulting from contact with Carthaginian civilization. This is difficult to trace, as Carthaginian products were scarce in the interior of the Maghrib before the 2nd century BCE, but the large tumuli at Mzora, Sīdī Sulaymān, Souk el-Gour, and the Medracen, apparently royal tombs of the 4th and 3rd centuries BCE, testify to a developing economy and society. No doubt service in the Carthaginian mercenary armies was a major stimulus to change.

This was most noticeable in Numidia and reached a high point under Masinissa. The son of a chief of the Massyli, a tribe dominating the area between Carthaginian territory and the Ampsaga River (Wadi al-Kabīr), he had been brought up at Carthage and was 20 years old at the outbreak of the Second Punic War. At first his tribe was at variance with Carthage, but in 213 BCE it became reconciled when its powerful western neighbours, the Masaesyli, under Syphax, deserted Carthage. From 213 to 207 BCE Masinissa commanded Numidian cavalry in Spain for the Carthaginians against Rome. On Rome's victory at the Battle of Ilipa in 206, he returned to Africa where Syphax, now reconciled with Carthage, had occupied some of his tribal territory, including Cirta, and his own claims to succession to the chieftainship were disputed. When the Romans landed in Africa in 204, Masinissa rendered them invaluable assistance. Recognized by the Romans as king, he annexed the eastern part of Syphax's kingdom and reigned with success until 148 BCE. The Greek geographer Strabo said that Masinissa "turned the nomads into a nation of farmers." This is exaggerated, since cereal culture had long been established in parts of Numidia, yet there is no doubt that the area of grain production was much enlarged. This was achieved by deliberately encouraging Carthaginian civilization. Along with new techniques, Carthaginian language, religion, and art penetrated rapidly inland, and Masinissa's capital, Cirta, took on the aspects of a Carthaginian city; incipient urbanization of a number of Libyan villages is also possible. Masinissa issued copper, bronze, and lead coinage for local use, as did some of the Carthaginian coastal towns under his rule.

On Masinissa's death in 148, his kingdom was divided among his three sons, possibly on the insistence of the Romans, who did not, however, prevent it from reunifying under Micipsa (148–118 BCE). The progress begun under Masinissa continued as refugees from the destruction of Carthage fled to Numidia. Meanwhile, the Romans had formed a province in the area of Tunisia northeast of a line from Thabraca (Tabarka) to Thaenae but showed little interest in exploiting its wealth. The attempt by the Roman reformer Gaius Gracchus in 122 BCE to found a colony on the site of Carthage failed, though individual colonists who had taken up allotments remained. When Micipsa died, another division of Numidia among three rulers took place, in which Jugurtha (118–105) emerged supreme. He might have been recognized by Rome, but he provoked war when he killed some Italian merchants who were helping a rival defend Cirta. After some successes caused by the incompetence of Roman generals, Jugurtha was surrendered by Bocchus

I, king of Mauretania. The kingdom was again reconstituted under other descendants of Masinissa. The boundaries of the Roman province were slightly enlarged in the area of the upper Majardah valley, where veterans of the army of Gaius Marius received lands. During the next 50 years individual Roman settlers and merchants continued to immigrate to the region, but there was no deliberate attempt to establish a state. The last relatively formidable king of Numidia was Juba I (*c.* 60–46 BCE), who supported the Pompeian side in the Roman civil war between Pompey the Great and Julius Caesar. The kingdom fell in 46 BCE at the Battle of Thapsus. A new province, Africa Nova, was formed from the most developed part of the old Numidian kingdom east of the Ampsaga; it was subsequently (before 27 BCE) amalgamated with the original province of Africa by Augustus. In 33 BCE Bocchus II of Mauretania died, bequeathing his kingdom to Rome, but Augustus was unwilling to accept responsibility for so large and relatively backward an area. In 25 BCE he installed Juba II, son of Juba I, as king; he ruled until his death about 24 CE. He was married to Cleopatra Selene, and under them Iol, renamed Caesarea (Cherchell), and also Volubilis, near Fez (Fès, Mor.), a secondary capital of the rulers of Mauretania, became centres of late Hellenistic culture. Juba himself was a prolific writer in Greek on a number of subjects, including history and geography. His son Ptolemy succeeded as king but, for reasons unknown today, was executed by the Roman emperor Caligula in 40 CE. A brief revolt followed but was easily suppressed, and the kingdom was divided into two provinces, Mauretania Caesariensis, with its capital at Caesarea, and Mauretania Tingitana, with its capital at Tingis (Tangier, Mor.).

CHAPTER 2

Roman North Africa

Over time, the Romans expanded the borders of their African province. Colonization was encouraged, and the region enjoyed four centuries of prosperity.

ADMINISTRATION AND DEFENSE

For more than a century from its acquisition in 146 BCE, the small Roman province of Africa (roughly corresponding to modern Tunisia) was governed from Utica by a minor Roman official, but changes were made by the emperor Augustus, reflecting the growing importance of the area. The governor was thenceforward a proconsul residing at Carthage, after it was refounded by Augustus as a Roman colony, and he was responsible for the whole territory from the Ampsaga River in the west to the border of Cyrenaica. The proconsul also commanded the army of Africa and was one of the few provincial governors in command of an army and yet formally responsible to the Senate rather than to the emperor. This anomaly was removed in 39 CE when Caligula entrusted the army to a *legatus Augusti* of praetorian rank. Although the province was not formally divided until 196, the army commander was de facto in charge of the area later known as the province of Numidia and also of the military area in southern Tunisia and along the Libyan Desert. The proconsulship was normally held for only one year; like the proconsulship of Asia, it was reserved for former consuls and ranked high in the administrative hierarchy. In the 1st century CE it was held by several men who subsequently became emperor—e.g., Galba and Vespasian. The commanders of the army normally held the post for two or three years, and in the 1st and 2nd centuries it was an important stage in the career of a number of successful generals. The two Mauretanian provinces were governed by men of equestrian rank who also commanded the substantial numbers of auxiliary troops in their areas. In times of emergency the two provinces were often united under a single authority.

Tribes on the fringe of the desert and beyond constituted more of a nuisance than a threat as the area of urban and semiurban settlement gradually approached the limit of cultivable land. A number of minor conflicts with nomadic tribes are recorded in the 1st century, the most serious of which was the revolt of Tacfarinas in southern Tunisia, suppressed in 23 CE. As the area of settlement extended westward as well as to the south, so the headquarters of the legion moved also: from Ammaedara (Haïdra, Tun.) to Theveste under Vespasian, thence to Lambaesis (Tazoult-Lambese, Alg.) under Trajan. Tribal lands were reduced and delimited, which compelled the adoption of sedentary life, and the tribes were placed under the supervision of Roman "prefects." A southern frontier was finally achieved under Trajan with the encirclement of the Aurès and Nemencha mountains and the creation of a line of forts from Vescera (Biskra, Alg.) to Ad Majores (Besseriani, Tun.). The mountains were penetrated during the next generation but were never developed or Romanized. During the 2nd century stretches of continuous wall and ditch—the *fossatum Africae*—in some areas provided further control over movement and also marked the division between the settled and nomadic ways of life. To the southwest of the Aurès a fortified zone completed the frontier defensive system, or *limes*, which extended for a while as far as Castellum Dimmidi (Messad), the most southerly fort in Roman Algeria yet identified. South of Leptis Magna in Libya, forts on the trans-Saharan route ultimately reached as far as Cydamus (Ghadāmis).

In the Mauretanias the problem was more difficult because of the rugged nature of the country and the distances involved. The encirclement of mountainous areas, a policy followed in the Aurès, was again pursued in the Kabylia ranges and the Ouarsenis (in what is now northern Algeria). The area round Sitifis (Sétif) was successfully settled and developed in the 2nd century, but farther west the impact of Rome was for long limited to coastal towns and the main military roads. The most important of these roads ran from Zarai (Zraïa) to Auzia (Sour el-Ghozlane) and then to the valley of the Chelif River. Subsequently the frontier ran south of the Ouarsenis as far as Pomaria (Tlemcen). West of this area it is doubtful whether a permanent road connected the two Mauretanias, sea communication being the rule. In Tingitana, Roman control extended as far as a line roughly from Meknès to Rabat, Mor., including Volubilis. Evidence attests to periodic discussions between Roman governors and local chieftains outside Roman control, suggesting peaceful relations. However, the tribes of the Rif Mountains must have lived in virtual independence, and they were probably responsible for a number of wars recorded in Mauretania under Domitian, Trajan, Antonius Pius (which lasted six years), and others in the 3rd century. They did little or no damage to the urbanized areas and never necessitated a permanent increase in the African garrison. The defense of the North African provinces was far less a problem than that of those on the northern periphery of the empire. For Numidia and the military district in the south of Tunisia and Libya, about 13,000 men sufficed; the Mauretanias had auxiliary units only, totaling some 15,000. This may be contrasted with the position in Britain, where three legions and auxiliaries (all told, some 50,000 men) were required. From the mid-2nd century CE the African garrison was largely recruited locally.

THE GROWTH OF URBAN LIFE

The most notable feature of the Roman period in North Africa was the development of a flourishing urban civilization in Tunisia, northern Algeria, and some parts of Morocco. This was possible because nomadic and pastoral movements were controlled, which opened large areas of thinly settled but potentially rich land to consistent exploitation. Also there was the incipient urbanization of some parts, owing to the Carthaginians and the ambitions of Libyan rulers such as Masinissa. In addition, Italian immigrants were settling in Africa; though relatively few in comparison with the population as a whole, they provided the impetus to expand. Julius Caesar settled many veterans in colonies, mostly coastal towns, and, equally important, established a military adventurer named Publius Sittius along with many Italians at Cirta, beginning the Romanization of Numidia. Caesar also planned to refound Carthage, and this was effected by Augustus. The number of his original settlers was 3,000, but the colony grew remarkably quickly because of its geographic position favourable for contact with Rome and Italy. A number of other colonies were founded in the interior of Tunisia and at widely separated places on the Mauretanian coasts. In addition, private individuals from Italy immigrated at that time. Veterans founded colonies in Mauretania under the emperor Claudius, including Tingis, Caesarea, and Tipasa. Cuicul (Djemila, Alg.) and Sitifis were founded by Nerva, and Thamugadi and a number of places nearby, in the area north of the Aurès, were founded by Trajan. The army was a potent vehicle in the spread of Roman civilization and played a major part in urbanizing the frontier regions. On limited evidence it has been suggested that a total of some 80,000 immigrants came to the Maghrib from Rome and Italy in this period.

Though at first inferior to the Roman towns, native communities enjoyed the local autonomy that was the hallmark of Roman administration. Between 400 and 500 such communities were recognized, the majority of them villages or small tribal factions. Many, however, advanced in wealth and standing to rival the Roman colonies, acquiring the grant of Roman citizenship, which put the seal of imperial approval on the prosperity, stability, and cultural evolution of developing communities. Naturally, the earliest to show signs of increasing prosperity were the surviving Carthaginian settlements on the coast and places—particularly in the Majardah valley—where the Libyan population had been much influenced by Carthaginian culture and which now also had Italian immigrants. Leptis Magna and Hadrumetum received Roman citizenship and the status of a colony from Trajan, and Thubursicu Numidarum (Khemissa) and Calama (Guelma) in modern Algeria probably the rank of municipality. But it was under Hadrian, the first emperor to visit Africa, that the flood tide of such grants occurred; Utica, Bulla Regia (near Jendouba, Tun.), Lares (Lorbeus, Tun.), Thaenae, and Zama achieved colonial rank, and the process continued throughout the 2nd century. Finally, Septimius Severus, who originated from a wealthy family of Leptis Magna and was of largely mixed descent, became emperor in 193 CE and greatly favoured his native land.

In the Maghrib, Roman rule was not superimposed on established civic aristocracies, as in the Hellenized provinces of Asia Minor, nor on strongly based tribal aristocracies, as in Celtic Gaul. Roman administration and the development of urban society in general depended, apart from immigrants, on the local leadership of small clan and tribal units and on the activity of individuals. In the 1st century CE there were a few large estates owned by absentee Roman senators, most of which were subsequently absorbed into the extensive imperial estate in Africa. The later pattern was of landowning on a more moderate—though still substantial—scale by residents, both immigrant and indigenous. Many landowners made their homes in the towns and formed a local municipal leadership. Small independent landowners also existed, but the great majority of the inhabitants were tenant farmers (*coloni*). A significant portion of these farmers worked on a sharecropping basis and had labour obligations to their landlords. The number of slave workers was probably smaller than in Italy.

Many of the wealthier Africans entered the imperial administration. The first African consul held office in the reign of Vespasian; at the beginning of the 3rd century, men of African origin held one-sixth of all the posts in the equestrian grade of the administration and also constituted the largest group of provincials in the Senate. It is uncertain what proportion were of native Libyan or mixed origin, but in the 2nd century they were certainly the majority.

During the 2nd and early 3rd centuries the wealthy classes in the towns spent vast sums on their communities in gifts of public buildings such as theatres, baths, and temples, as well as statues, public feasts, and distributions of money. This was a general phenomenon throughout the Roman Empire, as members of local elites competed for fame and prestige among their fellow citizens, but it is particularly well attested in Africa.

ECONOMY

The density of the towns in no way implies that trade or industry were predominant; all but a few were residences of both landowners and peasants, and their prosperity depended on agriculture. By the 1st century CE African exports of grain provided two-thirds of the needs of the city of Rome. Some of this, for distribution by the emperors to the urban proletariat, came from the imperial estates and from taxes, but much went to the open market. Annual grain production in Roman Africa has been estimated at more than a million tons, of which one-fourth was exported. Areas of grain production were the Sharīk Peninsula, the Miliana and Majardah valleys, and tracts of relatively level land north of a line from Sitifis to Madauros (M'Daourouch, Alg.). Cereal crops were the most important in these areas, but fruits, such as figs and grapes, and beans also were produced.

The production of olive oil became almost as important as cereals by the 2nd century CE, particularly in southern Tunisia and along the northern slopes of the Aurès and Bou Taleb mountains in Algeria. By the 4th century Africa exported oil to all parts of the empire. Successful cultivation of olives demanded careful management of available water, and the archaeological evidence indicates that much attention was paid to irrigation in the Roman period.

Livestock was an important part of the economy of Roman Africa, though direct evidence is slight. African horses were used in racing and no doubt also in the Roman cavalry. Cattle, sheep, pigs, goats, and mules were also raised. Africa was the major source of the wild animals for shows in Rome and other major cities of the empire—in particular leopards, lions, elephants, and monkeys. Fishing, which had been developed along the coast as far as the Atlantic in the Carthaginian period, continued to flourish. Timber, from the forests along part of the north coast, and marble, the most important North African source of which was Simitthu (Shimṭū, Tun.), were also exported.

There were no large-scale industries, even by ancient standards, in North Africa, except pottery. By the 4th century production of amphorae, necessitated by the oil trade, was substantial, and these and other locally produced wares were traded throughout the Mediterranean. Mosaic pavements were extremely popular among the wealthy throughout North Africa, and more than 2,000 have been discovered, with enormous variations in quality. The majority were made by local craftsmen, though some of the designs

An olive harvest in Meknes, Mor.—a city famous for its olive groves—c.1955. Evans/Hulton Archive/Getty Images

originated elsewhere. It is also clear that the building trades were major employers of both skilled and unskilled labour.

Prosperity undoubtedly led to a rise in the population of the Maghrib in the first two centuries CE; in the absence of reliable statistics, population estimates have varied from four to eight million (the latter being also the population about the beginning of the 20th century). One study proposed about 6.5 million, of whom about 2.5 million were in present Tunisia. Some two-fifths of the latter (perhaps more) lived in the towns. Of these Carthage was in a class of its own, having at least 250,000 people. The next largest was Leptis Magna (80,000), followed by Hadrumetum, Thysdrus (El-Djem, Tun.), Hippo Regius, and Cirta, with 20,000 to 30,000 each. Many towns in close proximity to each other, especially in the Majardah valley, averaged between 5,000 and 10,000.

The road system in Roman Africa was the most complete of any western province; a total of some 12,500 miles (20,000 km) has been supposed. Most roads were military in origin but were open to commerce, and a number of minor roads linking towns off the main routes were built by the local communities. The main arteries were from Carthage to Theveste, Carthage to Cirta through Sicca Veneria, Theveste to Tacapae through Capsa, Theveste to Lambaesis, Cirta to Sitifis, Cirta to Rusicade, and Cirta to Hippo Regius. Carthage handled by far the greatest volume of overseas official traffic and trade, being the natural port for the wealthiest area of North Africa. Nevertheless, most of the ports originally founded by Phoenicians and Carthaginians expanded during the Roman period; in view of the high costs of land transport, it was natural that agricultural products would go to the nearest port for shipment.

LATER ROMAN EMPIRE

The whole Roman Empire underwent a military and political crisis between the death of Severus Alexander (235 CE) and the accession of Diocletian (284), resulting from serious attacks from outside on the empire's northern and eastern frontiers and from a series of coups d'état and civil wars. Africa suffered less than most parts of the empire, though there was an unsuccessful revolt by landowners in 238 against the fiscal policies of the emperor Maximinus, which ended in widespread pillage. There were tribal revolts in the Mauretanian mountains in 253–254, 260, and 288, and the situation finally brought a visit from the emperor Maximian in 297–298. The revolts had little effect on the urbanized areas, but the towns were injured by economic difficulties and inflation, and building activity almost ceased. Confidence returned at the end of the 3rd century under Diocletian, Constantine, and later emperors. Administrative changes introduced at this time included the division of the province of Africa into three separate provinces: Tripolitania (capital Leptis Magna), covering the western part of Libya; Byzacena, covering

The Arch of Septimius Severus, at the entrance to the Roman citadel of Leptis Magna, Libya. Cris Bouroncle/AFP/Getty Images

southern Tunisia and governed from Hadrumetum; and the northern part of Tunisia, which retained the name Africa and its capital, Carthage. In addition, the eastern part of Mauretania Caesariensis became a separate province (capital Sitifis). In the far west the Romans gave up much of Mauretania Tingitana, including the important town of Volubilis, apparently because of pressure from the tribe of the Baquates. In the general reorganization of the Roman army by Diocletian and Constantine, the field army (*comitatenses*) in Africa, numbering on paper some 21,000 men, was put under a new commander, the *comes Africae*, independent of the provincial governors. Only the governors of Tripolitania and of Mauretania Caesariensis also had troops at their disposal, but these were second-line soldiers, or *limitanei*. The whole frontier region along the desert and mountain fringes was divided into sectors and garrisoned by *limitanei*. These were locally recruited and closely identified with the farming population of their areas. The Tripolitanian plateau, which was increasingly exposed to attacks by the nomadic Austuriani, is notable for having a large number of fortified farms.

Africa, like the rest of the empire, experienced the economic difficulties and governmental pressures that were a feature of the later Roman Empire. The power of the landowners increased at the expense of their tenants and of smaller farmers, both of whom the imperial government sought to bind to the soil in a state of quasi-serfdom. In the cities the tasks of local government that had earlier been eagerly undertaken by the wealthy became burdensome, and again the imperial government sought to make them compulsory and hereditary, while the councillors themselves sought by any means to enter the imperial administration or professions that provided immunity. The process is well attested in Africa. Nevertheless, the view that urban life generally declined throughout the empire during the 4th century must be modified, especially in the case of Africa, where the cities and towns withstood the pressures better than elsewhere and where some towns—Thamugadi, for example—seem to have increased in population. Thamugadi grew doubtlessly because it was relatively immune from damage in civil and external wars and had a solid base of agricultural prosperity.

CHRISTIANITY AND THE DONATIST CONTROVERSY

Christianity grew much more rapidly in Africa than in any other western province. It was firmly established in Carthage and other Tunisian towns by the 3rd century and had produced its own local martyrs and an outstanding apologist in Tertullian (*c.* 160–240). During the next 50 years it expanded remarkably; more than 80 bishops attended a council at Carthage in 256, some from the distant frontier regions of Numidia. Cyprian, the bishop of Carthage from 248 until his martyrdom in 258, was another figure whose writing, like that of Tertullian, was of lasting influence on Latin Christianity. During the next half-century it spread extensively in Numidia (there were at least 70 bishops in 312). The reasons for its exceptionally rapid growth are disputed. In northern Tunisia urban communities provided a social and economic environment similar to that in which Christianity had first spread in Anatolia and Syria, and much the same can be said about smaller communities in which early Christianity can be identified. It has been held that the intermingling of religious currents of Libyan, Carthaginian, and Roman origin tended toward monotheism, but—even if this were true, which is debatable—pagan monotheism was not a necessary stage toward the adoption of Christianity for more than a few. It does, however, appear that African Christianity always included a vigorous and fanatical element that must have had its effect in spreading the new religion, even though there is little evidence of positive missionary efforts.

Christians were still a minority at the end of the 3rd century in all levels of society, but they were in a good position to benefit from Constantine's adoption of the religion and his grants of various privileges to the clergy. At that time (313) a division occurred among the African Christians that lasted more than a century. Some Numidian bishops objected to the choice of Caecilian as the new bishop of Carthage, alleging that his ordination had been performed by a bishop who had weakened during Diocletian's persecution of the church and hence was invalid. They consecrated a rival bishop and, when he died, consecrated another named Donatus, who gave his name to the ensuing schism. The churches in numerous communities, especially in Numidia, followed Donatus from the start and claimed that they alone constituted the true church of the martyrs, who were objects of particularly enthusiastic veneration among African Christians. Among Christians outside Africa, however, Caecilian was universally recognized as the bishop of Carthage, and the emperor Constantine, when the Donatists appealed to him, followed the decisions of non-African church councils, recognizing Caecilian and his followers as the true church and hence as recipients of imperial favour. Some Donatists were killed when their churches were confiscated, the victims being honoured as martyrs, but in 321 Constantine rejected further pressure, and the Donatists continued to increase rapidly in numbers. For the rest of the century, they probably made up half the Christians in North Africa. They were strongest in Numidia and Mauretania Sitifensis, and the antischismatics predominated in the proconsular province of Africa; the position in the Mauretanias was more even, but Christianity did not spread rapidly there until the 5th century. In 347 the emperor Constans exiled a number of Donatist bishops and took repressive measures against the *circumcelliones*, seasonal farm workers who were particularly enthusiastic Donatists. But in 362 Julian the Apostate allowed the exiles to return. These were welcomed with enthusiasm, and the movement proved as strong as ever. Some Donatists appear to have been associated with the revolt of a Mauretanian chieftain, Firmus, and in 377 the first of a series of general laws proscribing Donatism was issued. Nevertheless, these laws were enforced only sporadically, partly because provincial governors and many local magistrates were still pagan and, at a time of growing weakness in the imperial government, were inclined to ignore instructions they found unwelcome. Donatism was further supported by Gildo, brother of Firmus and *comes Africae* (387–397). Then Augustine of Hippo Regius applied his enormous powers of leadership and persuasion to stimulate resolute action, evolving at the same time a theory of the right of orthodox Christian rulers to use force against schismatics and heretics. In 411 an imperial commission summoned a conference at Carthage to establish religious unity. The Donatists had to obey, though the decision against them was a foregone conclusion. The laws that followed their condemnation were more generally enforced and, though there was some resistance (some communities still existed in the 6th century), broke the schism as a powerful movement.

Much controversy surrounds the interpretation of Donatism's significance. An important view considers it in some sense a national or social movement. It is said to have been particularly associated with the rural population of less Romanized areas and with the poorer classes in the towns, whereas orthodox Christianity was the religion of the Romanized upper classes. The imperial government being identified with these Christians would have intensified the strength of the movement, and the *circumcelliones*' violence, moreover, could be considered a form of incipient peasant revolt. Thus the movement is claimed as analogous to Monophysitism in Egypt and Syria, which produced a vernacular literature and a passive rejection of Greco-Roman culture. The hostility of the Donatists to the existing society was typified by Donatus's remark: "What has the emperor to do with the church?" Against this view it may be said that Donatism in the non-Romanized tribal areas was certainly weak, and the relationship of the sect with Firmus and Gildo was of little importance. In Numidia it was at least as strong in the towns as in the rural areas, and in any case the distinction between the two can be exaggerated. The entire controversy was conducted in Latin, and no vernacular literature was produced; in fact, until the time of Augustine, most of the educated class, of the same social background as Augustine himself and fully imbued with Roman tradition, were Donatists if they were not pagan. It was the reluctance of the landowners to have their peasants disturbed, and the negligence of many provincial governors (both attacked by Augustine), that long protected the Donatists. Lastly, in spite of the remark attributed to Donatus, there is no evidence that the movement attacked the imperial system as a whole, as opposed to individual emperors and officials, and it made full use of its many opportunities to defend itself at law both against the other Christians and against divisions in its own ranks.

Nevertheless, although it is difficult to sustain the view that Donatism, especially in Numidia, represented in some way a resurgence of local pre-Roman culture or the speculative, though intriguing, notion that something similar led to the emergence of heretical movements of Islam in the same areas, Donatism certainly appealed to deep-seated traditions of African Christianity. Its fanatical devotion to the memory of martyrs, its doctrinal conservatism, and its total refusal to compromise on its claim to be the true church while its opponents were contaminated by the stain of weakness in the persecutions were fully in line with the heroic days of Tertullian and Cyprian.

EXTENT OF ROMANIZATION

The question of whether Roman civilization in the Maghrib was a superficial phenomenon affecting only a small minority of the population who were economically successful, or whether it had profound effects on the majority, is similarly disputed. A priori the former view may be supported by the fact that, whereas Gaul and Spain emerged from the Dark Ages with a language and religion derived from their Roman past, in the Maghrib both disappeared, arguably because they were superficial. It is not disputed that in the mountainous areas, such as the Aurès, Kabylia, and Atlas, native Libyan language and culture continued little affected by Roman civilization, though the majority appear to have been Christian by the 7th century; nor that Libyan and Carthaginian traditions survived in other areas and affected the modes of acceptance of Roman civilization. As regards language, the late form of Phoenician known as Neo-Punic was still spoken fairly widely in the 4th century—for example, in the hills near Hippo Regius. Inscriptions in the language and script occurred often at the beginning of the Roman period but were very rare after the end of the 1st century CE. An exception may be in Tripolitania, where a form of Neo-Punic was inscribed in Latin script perhaps as late as the 4th century. There was also a Libyan script known solely from funerary stelae and akin to the script of the present Tuareg; it was known in some form over much of the Maghrib but may not have been used later than the 3rd century. On the other hand, there is no evidence that these languages were ever literary languages, and the inscriptions are negligible in number compared with those in Latin. It may also be observed that the areas in which Libyan inscriptions occur do not correspond with the later areas of Berber (Amazigh) dialects. The Latin language unquestionably became general through the whole Maghrib, though to a limited extent in the mountains; it is impossible to define any precise social level at which it was unknown. There is a good deal to be said for the view that Christianity, whether Orthodox or Donatist, furthered the use of Latin among elements which up to that time had perhaps still not used it.

THE VANDAL CONQUEST

The effect of the Donatist controversy on the economy and administration of the African provinces cannot be measured but was certainly profound. At the very moment of the effective victory of the African church, the rest of the Roman Empire was crumbling to ruin. In 406 the Rhine was crossed by Vandals, Alani, Suebi, and others who overran most of Gaul and Spain within the next few years. In 408 Alaric and the Visigoths invaded Italy and in 410 sacked Rome. Although the empire in the west survived for some time longer, the emperors were increasingly at the mercy of their barbarian generals. Meanwhile large tracts of imperial territory were lost as invading tribes settled them. Africa escaped for a while, though only death prevented Alaric from leading the Goths across the Mediterranean. Retaining Africa became ever more vital to the survival of what was left of imperial authority. In this situation the *comites Africae* (Roman military officials) were increasingly tempted to intrigue for their own advantage. One of them, Bonifacius, is said to have invited the Vandals, who at the time were occupying Andalusia, to his aid, but it is more likely that the Vandals were attracted to Africa by its wealth and needed no such formal excuse. Led by their king Gaiseric, the whole people, 80,000 in all, crossed into Africa in 429 and in the next year advanced with little opposition to Hippo Regius, which they took after a siege during which Augustine died. After defeating the imperial forces near Calama, they overran most of the country, though not all the fortified cities. An agreement made in 435 allotted Numidia and Mauretania Sitifensis to the Vandals, but in 439 Gaiseric took and pillaged Carthage and the rest of the province of Africa. A further treaty with the imperial government (442) established the Vandals in Africa Proconsularis, Byzacena, Tripolitania, and Numidia as far west as Cirta.

Although the Vandals were probably no more deliberately destructive than other Germanic invaders (the notion of "vandalism" stems from the 18th century), their establishment had strong adverse effects. The imperial authorities had to reduce the taxes of the Mauretanias by seven-eighths after they were devastated. Over much of northern Tunisia, landowners were expelled and their properties handed over to Vandals. Although the agricultural system remained based on the peasants, the expulsions had a serious effect on the towns with which the landowners had been connected. The Vandals, like other invading tribes except the Franks, were divided from their subjects by their Arianism. Although their persecution of Latin Christians was exaggerated by the latter, Vandal kings certainly exercised more pressure than others. This was no doubt in response to the vigour of African Christianity, which kept the loyalty even of those who had little to lose by the substitution of a Vandal for a Roman landlord.

Gaiseric was perhaps the most perceptive barbarian king of the 5th century in realizing the total weakness of the empire. He rejected the policy of formal alliance with it and from 455 used his large merchant fleet to dominate the western Mediterranean. Rome was sacked, the Balearic Islands, Corsica, Sardinia, and part of Sicily were occupied, and the coasts of Dalmatia and Greece were plundered. Although trade continued, Gaiseric's actions accelerated the breakup of the economic unity of the western Mediterranean, which already was being threatened by the creation of the other barbarian kingdoms. Gaiseric's successors were less formidable: Huneric (477–484) launched a general persecution of the Latin church, apparently from genuine religious fanaticism rather than for political reasons, but his successor adopted a milder policy. Later, under Thrasamund (496–523), there is evidence that many Vandals adopted Roman culture, but the tribe retained its identity until the Byzantine reconquest.

A significant development of the Vandal period was that independent kingdoms, largely of Libyan character, emerged in the mountainous and desert areas. They appeared first in the Mauretanias, where the Roman frontier, already drawn back under Diocletian, receded further under the Vandal kings. By the end of Vandal rule, independent kingdoms existed in the region of Altava (Oulad Mimoun), in the Ouarsenis Mountains, and in the Hodna region (in present-day Algeria). After 480, towns to the north of the Aurès Mountains, such as Thamugadi, Bagai, and Theveste, were sacked by the inhabitants of another kingdom in the Aurès. All the names of the known chieftains are Libyan in character, though the survival of Romanized elements within some of the kingdoms is attested by the fact that epitaphs in Latin continued, Roman names were still used, and a dating system based on the founding date of the Roman province of Mauretania was even maintained. Finally, as a harbinger of a serious threat to settled life, whether Roman or Libyan, tribes that had retained a nomadic way of life on the borders of Cyrenaica and Tripolitania and caused much damage in the 4th century began to push westward and were already a serious threat to the southern parts of Byzacena by the end of Vandal rule.

THE BYZANTINE PERIOD

North Africa held an important place in the emperor Justinian's scheme for reuniting the Roman Empire and destroying the Germanic kingdoms. His invasion of Africa was undertaken against the advice of his experts (an earlier attempt in 468 had failed disastrously), but his general Belisarius succeeded, partly through Vandal incompetence. He landed in 533 with only 16,000 men, and within a year the Vandal kingdom was destroyed. A new administrative structure was introduced, headed by a praetorian prefect with six subordinate governors for civil

Arianism

Arianism is a Christian heresy that affirmed that Christ is not truly divine but a created being. It was first proposed early in the 4th century by the Alexandrian presbyter Arius. His basic premise was the uniqueness of God, who is alone self-existent and immutable; the Son, who is not self-existent, cannot be God. Because the Godhead is unique, it cannot be shared or communicated, so the Son cannot be God. Because the Godhead is immutable, the Son, who is mutable, being represented in the Gospels as subject to growth and change, cannot be God. The Son must, therefore, be deemed a creature who has been called into existence out of nothing and has had a beginning. Moreover, the Son can have no direct knowledge of the Father since the Son is finite and of a different order of existence.

According to its opponents, especially the bishop Athanasius, Arius' teaching reduced the Son to a demigod, reintroduced polytheism (since worship of the Son was not abandoned), and undermined the Christian concept of redemption since only he who was truly God could be deemed to have reconciled man to the Godhead.

matters and a master of soldiers with four subordinate generals.

It required a dozen years, however, to pacify Africa, partly because of tribal resistance in Mauretania to an ordered government being reestablished and partly because support to the army in men and money was poor, leading to frequent mutinies. A remarkable program of fortifications—many of which survive—was rapidly built under Belisarius's successor Solomon. Some were garrison forts in the frontier region, which again seems to have extended, at least for a while, south of the Aurès and then northward from Tubunae to Saldae. But many surviving towns in the interior were also equipped with substantial walls—e.g., Thugga and Vaga (Béja, Tun.). There were further difficulties with the Mauretanian tribes (the Mauri) after Justinian died (565), but the most serious damage was done by the nomadic Louata from the Libyan Desert, who on several occasions penetrated far into Tunisia.

Africa shows a number of examples of the massive help given by Justinian in building—and particularly decorating—churches and in reestablishing Christian orthodoxy, though surviving Donatists were inevitably persecuted. Seriously weakened though it had been under the Vandals, the African church retained some traces of its vigour when it led the opposition of the Western churches to the theological policies of emperors at Constantinople—e.g., those of Justinian himself and also of Heraclius and Constans II immediately before the Arab invasions.

Little is known of the Byzantine period in the Maghrib after the death of Justinian. The power of the military element in the provinces grew, and in the late 6th century a new official, the exarch, was introduced whose powers were almost viceregal. Economic conditions declined because of the increasing insecurity and also the notorious corruption and extortion of the administration, though whether this was worse in Africa than in other parts of the Byzantine Empire is impossible to say. It is certain that the population of the towns was only a small proportion of what it had been in the 4th century. The court of Constantinople tended to neglect Africa because of the more immediate dangers on the eastern and Balkan frontiers. Only once in its latest phase was it the scene of an important historical event; in 610 Heraclius, son of the African exarch at the time, sailed from Carthage to Constantinople in a revolt against the unpopular emperor Phocas and succeeded him the same year. That Africa was still of some importance to the empire was shown in 619; the Persians had overrun much of the east, including Egypt, and only Africa appeared able to provide money and recruits. Heraclius even thought of leaving Constantinople for Carthage but was prevented by popular feeling in the capital.

In view of the lack of evidence for the Byzantine period, and the still greater obscurity surrounding the period of Arab raids and conquest (643–698) and its immediate aftermath, conclusions on the state of the Maghrib at the end of Byzantine rule are speculative. Much of it was in the hands of tribal groups, among which the level of Roman culture was in many cases no doubt negligible. Even before the Arab attacks began, the picture seems to be one of a continual ebb of Latin civilization and the Latin language from all of the Maghrib except along the coastal fringes of Tunisia, and the development and expansion of larger tribal groupings, some, though not all, of which were Christian. Also, the Byzantine administration was, in a sense, foreign to the Latin population. The military forces sent from Constantinople to stem the invasion were ultimately inadequate, though Arab conquest of the region could not be secure until Carthage was captured and destroyed and reinforcements by sea interdicted. The most determined resistance to the Arabs came from nomadic Libyan tribes living in the area around the Aurès Mountains. Destruction in the settled areas in the earlier attacks, which were little more than large-scale raiding expeditions, was certainly immense. It has been held that town life and even an ordered agricultural system almost disappeared at that time, though some scholars believe that a modicum of these survived until the invasions of larger nomadic groups, in particular the Banū Hilāl, in the 11th century. Latin was still in use for Christian epitaphs at El-Ngila in Tripolitania and even at Kairouan (Al-Qayrawān) in the 10th and 11th centuries. However, throughout the Maghrib the conversion of various population groups to Islam rapidly Arabized most of the region in language and culture, though the modalities of these profound changes remain obscure.

Belgian scholar Henri Pirenne formulated a theory, widely discussed, that the essential break between the ancient and medieval European worlds came when the unity of the Mediterranean was destroyed not by the Germanic but by the Arab invasions. The history of the Maghrib is an important element in this debate, for there one can see the complete replacement of a centuries-old political, social, religious, and cultural system by another within a short span of time.

ROMAN CYRENAICA

Much of the Roman period in Cyrenaica was peaceful. Some Roman immigrants resided there at an early date, and some of the Greeks received Roman citizenship. A famous inscription of 4 BCE contains a number of edicts of the emperor Augustus regulating with great fairness the relationship between Roman and non-Roman. The character of its civilization, however, remained entirely Greek. Jews formed a considerable minority group in the province and had their own organizations at Berenice and Cyrene. They took no part in the great revolt of Judaea in 66 CE but in 115 began a formidable rebellion in Cyrene that spread to Egypt. No reason for it is known. It caused great destruction and loss of life, and Hadrian took special measures to reconstruct Cyrene and also sent out some colonists. Peaceful conditions returned, but in 268–269 the Marmaridae, inhabiting the coast between Cyrenaica and Egypt, caused trouble. When Diocletian reorganized the empire, Cyrenaica was separated from Crete and divided into two provinces: Libya Superior, or Pentapolis (capital Ptolemais), and Libya Inferior, or Sicca (capital Paraetonium [Marsā Maṭrūḥ, Egypt]). A regular force was stationed there for the first time under a *dux Libyarum*. At the end of the 4th century, the Austuriani, a nomad tribe that had earlier raided Tripolitania, caused much damage, and Cyrenaica began to suffer from the general decline of security throughout the empire, in this case from desert nomads. A notable phenomenon of the 5th and 6th centuries, as in Tripolitania, was the number of fortified farms, most frequent in the Akhḍar Mountains and south of Boreum (Bū Quraydah) and also apparently in the region of Banghāzī.

Christianity no doubt spread to Cyrenaica from Egypt. In the 3rd century the bishop of Ptolemais was metropolitan, but by the 4th century the powerful bishops of Alexandria consecrated the local bishops. The best-known Cyrenaican is Synesius, a citizen of Cyrene with philosophic tastes who was made bishop of Ptolemais in 410 partly because of his ability to obtain help for his province from the imperial authorities. Under Justinian a number of defensive works were constructed as elsewhere in Africa—e.g., Taucheira, Berenice, Antipyrgos (Tobruk), and Boreum. Recent excavations of a series of churches reveal the expenditure he devoted to their beautification, in what was a province of minor importance. On the eve of the Arab conquest (643), the general condition of Cyrenaica would appear to have been on a par with most of the other eastern provinces of the empire.

CHAPTER 3

From the Arab Conquest to 1830

After the Arabs completed the conquest of Egypt in 642, they started to raid the Berber (Amazigh) territory to its west, which they called Bilād al-Maghrib ("Lands of the West") or simply the Maghrib. In 705 this region became a province of the Muslim empire then ruled from Damascus by the Umayyad caliphs (661–750). The Arab Muslim conquerors had a much more durable impact on the culture of the Maghrib than did the region's conquerors before and after them. By the 11th century the Berbers had become Islamized and in part also Arabized. The region's indigenous Christian communities, which before the Arab conquest had constituted an important part of the Christian world, ceased to exist. The Islamization of the Berbers was a consequence of the Arab conquest, although they were neither forcibly converted to Islam nor systematically missionized by their conquerors. Largely because its teachings became an ideology through which the Berbers justified both their rebellion against the caliphs and their support of rulers who rejected caliphal authority, Islam gained wide appeal and spread rapidly among these fiercely independent peoples.

Arab raids to the west of Egypt concentrated at first on the area of Cyrenaica in present-day Libya. Tunisia was raided several times after 647, but no attempt was made to establish Arab rule there before 670. Conflicts among the Muslim leaders, especially after the assassination of the third

Two Berber women hand-spin fibres in Morocco, c. 1950. Three Lions/Hulton Archive/ Getty Images

caliph, 'Uthmān ibn 'Affān, in 656, hindered Muslim territorial expansion. Only after the Umayyads had consolidated their authority as a caliphal dynasty in the 660s and had come to view the conquest of the Maghrib in the context of their confrontation with the Byzantine Empire did they systematically undertake this conquest. 'Uqbah ibn Nāfi' (Sīdī 'Uqbah) commanded the Arab army that occupied Tunisia in 670. Before his recall in 674, 'Uqbah founded the town of Kairouan, which became the first centre of Arab administration in the Maghrib.

When the conquest of the Maghrib west of Tunisia was initiated by 'Uqbah's successor, Abū al-Muhājir Dīnār al-Anṣārī, the Arabs had to fight semisettled Berber communities that had developed some tradition of centralized political authority. In the course of his campaign, Abū al-Muhājir Dīnār prevailed on the Berber "king" Kusaylah to become Muslim. From his base in Tlemcen, Kusaylah dominated a confederation of the Awrāba tribes living between the western Aurès Mountains and the area of present-day Fès. Since Kusaylah's profession of Islam implied his recognition of caliphal authority, it served as a basis for coexistence between him and the Arabs. However, when 'Uqbah was reinstated as commander of the Arab army in the Maghrib in 681, he insisted on imposing direct Arab rule over the whole region. In 682 he led his troops across Algeria and northern Morocco, reaching the Atlantic Ocean and penetrating south to the areas of the Sūs (Sous) and Drâa rivers in southern Morocco. On his way back to Kairouan, 'Uqbah was attacked near Biskra (in present-day Algeria), on orders from Kusaylah, by Berbers supported by Byzantine contingents. Through his death in this battle and his extended campaign, 'Uqbah became the legendary hero of the Muslim conquest of the Maghrib.

By the 680s the Arabs had gone too far in the conquest of the Maghrib to be willing to accept defeat at the hands of a Berber leader, albeit one professing Islam. Two large armies had to be sent from Egypt, however, before organized Berber resistance could be suppressed. The first, commanded by Zuhayr ibn Qays al-Balawī, reoccupied Kairouan, then pursued Kusaylah westward to Mams, where he was defeated and killed. The dates of these operations are uncertain, but they must have occurred before 688 when Zuhayr ibn Qays himself was killed in an attack on Byzantine positions in Cyrenaica. The second Arab army, commanded by Ḥassān ibn al-Nu'mān, was dispatched from Egypt in 693. It faced stiff resistance in the eastern Aurès Mountains from the Jawāra Berbers, who were commanded by a woman whom the Arabs referred to as Kāhinah (al-Kāhinah, "the Priestess"). After Kāhinah was defeated in 698, Ibn al-Nu'mān occupied Carthage, the centre of Byzantine administration in Tunisia, and began constructing the town of Tunis nearby. These successes and Arab naval supremacy in the Mediterranean forced the Byzantines to evacuate their remaining positions on the Maghribi coast. Under

Ibn al-Nuʿmān's successor, Mūsā ibn Nuṣayr, the Maghrib—at least its eastern portion—was made into a province of the Umayyad Caliphate in 705—the *wilāyah* of Ifrīqiyyah, thus separated from the *wilāyah* of Egypt, to which it had been administratively attached until that time.

KHĀRIJITE BERBER RESISTANCE TO ARAB RULE

Political life of the Maghrib in the 8th century was dominated by the contradiction in the position of the Arab rulers who, while posing as the champions of a religion recognizing the equality of all believers, emphasized their ethnic distinctiveness and exercised authority with little regard for Islamic religious norms. This contradiction surfaced in their relations with the Berbers after the latter became Muslim in large numbers—especially through serving in the Arab army, which is known to have included Berber contingents when it was commanded by Ḥassān ibn al-Nuʿmān and his successor Mūsā ibn Nuṣayr. Many Berber warriors participated in the conquest of Spain in 711. Though professing Islam, they were treated as *mawālī* ("clients") of the Arab tribes and consequently had a status inferior to, and received less pay than, the Arab warriors. Furthermore, the Arab ruling class alone reaped the fruits of conquest, as was clearly the case in Spain. The grievances of the warriors highlighted the resentment of Berbers in general, caused by such practices as levying human tribute on the Berber tribes, through which the Arab ruling class was provided with slaves, especially female slaves. ʿUmar II (717–720) was the only Umayyad caliph who is known to have condemned the levying of human tribute and ordered that it be discontinued. He also sent 10 *tābiʿūn* ("followers"; disciples of the Prophet Muhammad's companions) to teach Islam to the Berbers. The enlightened policy of this pious caliph did not survive his short reign, however. Rather, it contributed toward confirming the conviction of Muslims in the Maghrib that Islam could not be equated with Umayyad caliphal rule.

The Muslim Khārijite sect exploited this revolutionary potential in their struggle against Umayyad rule. Khārijite doctrine apparently appealed to the Berbers because it rejected the Arab monopoly on political leadership of the Muslim community, stressed piety and learning as the main qualifications of the head of the community, and sanctioned rebellion against the head when he acted unjustly. In 740 a major Berber rebellion broke out against Arab rule in the region of Tangier. Its first leader was a Berber called Maysara who had come to Kairouan under the influence of the Ṣufriyyah, the extremist branch of the Khārijite sect. The Berber rebels achieved an astounding military success against the Arab army. By 742 they had taken control of the whole of Algeria and were threatening Kairouan. In the meantime the Ibāḍiyyah, who constituted the moderate branch of the Khārijite sect, had taken control of Tripolitania by converting the

Berber tribes living there, especially the Hawwāra and Nafusa, to their doctrine. Ibāḍī domination in Tripolitania resulted from the activities of *dāʿīs* ("propagandists") sent from the main centre of the group, in Iraq, after the Khārijite rebellion there had been suppressed by the Umayyad army in 697.

Umayyad caliphal rule in the Maghrib came to an end in 747 when the Fihrids, the descendants of ʿUqbah ibn Nāfiʿ—taking advantage of the Umayyads' preoccupation with the ʿAbbāsid rebellion that led to their downfall—seized power in Ifrīqiyyah. The Fihrid dynasty controlled all of Tunisia except for the south, which was dominated at the time by the Warfajūma Berber tribe associated with the Ṣufrī Khārijites. Fihrid rule came to an end in 756 when the Warfajūma conquered the north and captured Kairouan. Immediately thereafter, however, the Ibāḍiyyah in Tripolitania proclaimed one of their religious leaders as imam (the Khārijite equivalent to the Sunni caliph) and in 758 conquered Tunisia from the Ṣufriyyah. An Ibāḍī state comprising Tunisia and Tripolitania thus came into being, which lasted until the ʿAbbāsids, having consolidated their authority as caliphs in the Middle East, sent an army to the region in 761 to restore caliphal rule in the Maghrib.

The ʿAbbāsids could impose their authority only on Tunisia, eastern Algeria, and Tripolitania. The authority of their governors of the reconstituted *wilāyah* of Ifrīqiyyah was hampered because they depended on an army that was recruited predominantly from among the unruly Arabs of the province. After Arab troops mutinied against the ʿAbbāsid governor in 800, Ifrīqiyyah was transformed into an Arab kingdom ruled by the Aghlabid dynasty in the name of the ʿAbbāsid caliphs. The founder of the dynasty, Ibrāhīm ibn al-Aghlab, had commanded until then the Arab army in eastern Algeria. After using his troops to restore order in Tunisia, he established himself as ruler of the province. The acquiescence of the caliph, Hārūn al-Rashīd, to Ibn al-Aghlab's usurpation of authority was linked to the latter's continued recognition of ʿAbbāsid suzerainty and payment of tributes to Baghdad.

THE MAGHRIB UNDER MUSLIM DYNASTIES IN THE 8TH–11TH CENTURIES

Through their rebellion against caliphal rule in the name of Islam, the Berbers forged religious bonds with other Muslim opponents of the caliphs, and Islamic political concepts and religious norms gained favour in Berber society. Their rebellion also led to the rule of caliphs being replaced by four separate Muslim states dominated by dynasties that either nominally recognized caliphal authority, as was the case with the Aghlabids, or totally rejected it, as was the case with the three other states. Only the smallest and most politically insignificant state, the principality of the Banū Midrār in Sijilmāssah (southern Morocco), was ruled by a Berber dynasty. The survival of the four states depended on the balance of political forces within the region itself.

The Rustamid State of Tāhart

The 'Abbāsid conquest of Ifrīqiyyah in 761, which precipitated the collapse of the Ibāḍī state in Tunisia and Tripolitania, also caused important Ibāḍī tribes from Tripolitania and southern Tunisia to migrate to western Algeria. There they were led in attacks on 'Abbāsid positions by 'Abd al-Raḥmān ibn Rustam, an Ibāḍī of Persian origin, born and brought up in Tunisia. Ibn Rustam had acquired prominence among the Ibāḍiyyah as governor of Tunisia between 758 and 761. In 776 or 777 he was proclaimed imam by the Ibāḍī tribes of Algeria, and immediately afterward he started constructing his own capital, Tāhart (modern Tiaret, Alg.), in the area where the most important Ibāḍī tribes of Algeria were settled. Until the 760s the Berber tribes affiliated with the Ṣufrī branch of Khārijīsm were the major forces opposing caliphal rule in Algeria. After the foundation of the Rustamid state, these tribes became subordinate allies of the Ibāḍiyyah.

The imamate of Tāhart was inherited within the family of 'Abd al-Raḥmān ibn Rustam. This breach of Khārijite doctrine led to a split within the Ibāḍī leadership, which, however, had little effect on the position of the Rustamid imams as leaders of Berber opposition to 'Abbāsid authority. The tribes that recognized the religio-political leadership of and paid tribute to the imams of Tāhart lived in western Algeria, southern Tunisia, and Tripolitania. The imams maintained contacts with them by encouraging tribal chiefs to visit Tāhart and by sending emissaries that toured their areas. The Rustamid imams maintained especially close contacts with the Nafusa of Tripolitania—who had been associated with the Ibāḍī movement in the Maghrib since the beginning of the 8th century—and entrusted important state offices to them. Tāhart became prosperous and developed a cosmopolitan character both by serving as a meeting place for numerous trade caravans connecting the various parts of the Maghrib and by playing an important role itself in Maghribi and trans-Saharan trade. The Rustamids' readiness to live in peace with their neighbours, including the Aghlabids, caused discontent among the Ibāḍī tribes of Tripolitania and southern Tunisia but enabled the Rustamids to retain power until Tāhart was conquered by the Fāṭimids in 909.

The Banū Midrār of Sijilmāssah

The principality of the Banū Midrār came into existence after the 740s, when Miknāsah Berbers (a group affiliated with the Ṣufriyyah) migrated from northern Morocco to the oasis of Tafilalt in the south. The principality was named after Abū al-Qāsim ibn Wāsūl, nicknamed Midrār, the Miknāsah chief who founded the town of Sijilmāssah there in 757. Tafilalt had played a role in trans-Saharan trade before the influx and settlement of the Miknāsah. After the establishment of Sijilmāssah, however, it became the foremost centre of trans-Saharan trade in the western Maghrib. At the zenith of its power during the reign of Yasa' ibn Midrār (790–823), the principality controlled the entire region of Drâa in southern Morocco. Nevertheless, the state remained primarily a trading principality, playing almost no role in the political life of the rest of the Maghrib until it, too, was conquered by the Fāṭimids in 909.

The Idrīsids of Fez

The Idrīsid state of Fez (modern Fès, Mor.) originated in the desire of Isḥāq ibn 'Abd al-Ḥamīd, chief of the powerful tribal confederation of the Awrāba, to consolidate his authority in northern Morocco by giving his rule an Islamic religious character. For that purpose he invited Idrīs ibn 'Abd Allāh, a sharif (descendant of the Prophet Muhammad) living in Tangier, to settle at his seat of government in Walīla (Oulili). Idrīs moved to Walīla in 788 and was recognized Imam Idrīs I of the Awrāba the following year, but he was assassinated by agents of the 'Abbāsids in 791. His son, born a few months later and also called Idrīs, was proclaimed imam of the Awrāba in 803, when he was still a young boy. Idrīs II founded the state—called, for himself, Idrīsid—with the help of Arab refugees coming from both Spain and Aghlabid territory. By moving the seat of his authority in 809 to Fez, the capital city he had started to build a year earlier, he made it clear he was establishing a state that was distinct from the Awrāba confederation. The arrival of more Arabs from Spain and Aghlabid territory in the following two decades gave the Idrīsid state a distinctly Arab character.

Although Idrīs I had Shī'ite sympathies, the state founded by his son was Sunni in matters of religious doctrine. Its rulers, however, identified themselves with Berber rejection of caliphal rule and stressed their own descent from the Prophet as a means of legitimizing their authority. During Idrīs II's reign (809–828) the state included the greater part of present-day Morocco. From the 860s, however, the authority of the Idrīsids started to decline, and the tribes of northern Morocco that had previously followed them allied themselves with the Umayyad rulers of Spain. Nevertheless, the Idrīsids continued to rule in Fez until they were deposed by the Fāṭimids in 921. Under the Idrīsids, Islamic urban culture began to appear in Morocco. The foremost urban centre was Fez, which continued to exercise a dominant influence on the religious and cultural as well as the political life of Morocco until the French protectorate was imposed in 1912.

The Aghlabids

After they usurped power in 800, the Aghlabids adapted their government to the requirements of political survival in a land still dominated by an Arab class of large landowners, who also provided the government with its regular troops.

An offering of coins being tossed through an opening in the Mosque of Mullah Idrīs in Fès, Mor., c. 1950. Evans/Hulton Archive/Getty Images

The urban, ethnically mixed communities resented the domination of the state by the old Arab families and the heavy taxes that they and the peasant communities had to pay. Emphasizing Islamic religious norms was the means by which these groups articulated their grievances against the state and the Arab ruling class. By the beginning of the 9th century such grievances could be expressed formally when two of the four Sunni schools of Islamic religious law, the Ḥanafiyyah and the Mālikiyyah, had become established in the Maghrib. The Ḥanafī school developed in Iraq; as it was recognized by the ʿAbbāsid caliphs, it also was adopted by the Aghlabids. Most of the religious scholars in Tunisia, however, adhered to the simpler and stricter teachings of the Mālikī school. By teaching the religious law and admonishing the rulers to adhere to its provisions when administering justice and in such matters as taxation and the prohibition of alcohol, Mālikī scholars have emerged since the 820s as defenders of the rights of the common people against the state.

Political life in the Aghlabid state reflected the rulers' constant fear that their Arab troops would rebel and preoccupation with the need to allay the grievances of the religious scholars. They tried to placate the Mālikī scholars by appointing many of them to the office of *qāḍī* ("judge") and by instituting a program of sacred building construction. The Grand Mosque of Tunis (the Zaytūnah), among others, was built in the Aghlabid period. In order to reduce the threat of Arab troop rebellions, the Aghlabids channeled their energies into conquering Sicily. Initiated in 827, the conquest of Sicily was given a religious character by entrusting the command of the army to the *qāḍī* Asad ibn al-Furāt.

THE FĀṬIMIDS AND ZĪRIDS

The grievances that the inhabitants of Ifrīqiyyah harboured against Aghlabid rule were transformed into a revolutionary movement by the Ismāʿīliyyah, an extremist branch of the Shīʿite sect. From the mid-9th century Ismāʿīlī leadership, operating from Salamyah in northern Syria, sent out *dāʿīs* to organize opposition to the ʿAbbāsid caliphs. One of these, Ḥusayn ibn Zakariyyāʾ, better known as Abū ʿAbd Allāh al-Shīʿī, operated among the Kutāma of the Little Kabylia region in eastern Algeria from 901. The sedentary Kutāma were pious and unsophisticated Muslim Berbers living in small village communities. Aghlabid rule in the region was represented by fortified garrison posts manned by Arab troops, by whom the Kutāma were constantly harassed. Through patient preaching, Abū ʿAbd Allāh molded the Kutāma into a highly motivated and disciplined militant movement. After defeating the Arab troops in the Little Kabylia, he conquered the rest of the Aghlabid territory in Algeria between 904 and 907 and then conquered Tunisia itself. Raqqādah, the fortified residence of the Aghlabids near

Kairouan, was conquered in March 909. The head of the Ismāʿīliyyah in Salamyah, ʿUbayd Allāh Saʿid, entered Raqqādah in January 910.

The state that ʿUbayd Allāh then founded was intended to be completely Shīʿite in character. He styled himself as the imam who, according to Shīʿite doctrine, was the only legitimate head of the Muslim community and the final authority on religious law. The state he founded, known as Fāṭimid (Al-Dawlah al-Fāṭimiyyah) for the Prophet Muhammad's daughter Fāṭimah, was viewed as a stepping-stone to the overthrow of the ʿAbbāsids. Nevertheless, ʿUbayd Allāh was intent on consolidating Shīʿite rule first in the Maghrib itself. He built a fortified capital, Al-Mahdiyyah, on the Tunisian coast and initiated the conquest of the western Maghrib in 917. The Fāṭimids soon ended Idrīsid rule in Fez, but after 40 years of campaigning in western Algeria and Morocco they were unable to impose their authority on the powerful Berber tribes living there. The Umayyads of Spain, moreover, occupied the enclaves of Melilla and Ceuta on the northern coast of Morocco in 927 and 931, respectively, and from there organized tribal resistance to the Fāṭimids. In eastern Algeria, however, the Fāṭimids were loyally supported by Zīrī ibn Manād, chief of the Takalata branch of the Ṣanhājah confederation, to which the Kutāma Berbers belonged. The parts of the Maghrib that the Fāṭimids controlled therefore consisted only of the former province of Ifrīqiyyah, ruled before them by the Aghlabids.

In Ifrīqiyyah itself the Arab aristocratic families, previously affiliated with the Ḥanafī school of law, all converted to Shīʿism and, consequently, preserved under Fāṭimid rule some of their former privileges. The Mālikī scholars, however, opposed the Fāṭimids, who, accordingly, resorted to repression and had several of them tortured. Differences in ritual and religious law, and the exorbitant system of taxation made necessary by the large army that the Fāṭimids had to maintain, were the main causes of Mālikī opposition. Out of desperation, the Mālikī leaders of Kairouan in 944 even supported rebellion by one of their Khārijite rivals, Abū Yazīd, against the Fāṭimids.

Direct Fāṭimid rule in the Maghrib effectively came to an end in 973, when the Fāṭimid imam, al-Muʿizz, whose armies had conquered Egypt four years earlier, took up residence in Cairo. Al-Muʿizz appointed the Berber chief Buluggīn, son of the Fāṭimids' chief ally in Algeria, Zīrī ibn Manād, as his viceroy in the Maghrib. In the 70 years during which the Zīrid dynasty (Banū Zīrī) ruled Ifrīqiyyah in the name of the Fāṭimids, they fell progressively under the influence of the Arab Islamic culture of the region. In this period the Mālikī school of Islamic law reasserted itself in Ifrīqiyyah and produced one of its most prominent scholars, Ibn Abī Zayd al-Qayrawānī (died 996), whose *Risālah* is one of the most widely used and discussed expositions of

Mālikī law. Mālikī riots broke out between October 1016 and March 1017, in which a large number of Shīʿites—estimated at some 20,000—were killed and their property looted. These developments resulted in the renunciation of Fāṭimid authority by the Zīrids in 1044.

The Fāṭimids reacted to this by unleashing two large nomadic Arab tribes on the Maghrib, the Banū Hilāl and the Banū Sulaym (Sulaim), both of which had until then lived in Upper Egypt. This Arab invasion introduced unruly tribal groups who would remain a source of political instability in the eastern Maghrib until well into the 15th century. The Zīrids were overwhelmed by the sheer number of the invaders, who are said to have included 50,000 warriors when they crossed into Cyrenaica in 1050. After the Zīrids suffered defeat at the hands of these nomads in 1052 in southern Tunisia, they vacated Kairouan and retreated to the well-fortified former Fāṭimid capital of Al-Mahdiyyah on the coast. The Banū Hilāl ravaged the Tunisian countryside and then infiltrated eastern Algeria. There they ended the rule of the Banū Hammād, a dynasty related to the Zīrids that had made itself independent of them in 1015.

THE MAGHRIB UNDER THE ALMORAVIDS AND THE ALMOHADS

The fragmentation of political life in the Maghrib, following both the Arab invasion and a general decline in the authority of the Fāṭimids, was arrested by the Almoravids. They were the founders of the first of two empires that unified the Maghrib under Berber Islamic rule.

The Almoravid empire came into being through the success of a militant Islamic movement that was initiated among the Ṣanhājah confederation of tribes in Mauretania by one of its chiefs about 1035. Religious reform was a means of cementing the unity of the Ṣanhājah tribes at a time when the control that they previously had on trans-Saharan trade had become threatened, from the south by the Soninke state of Ghana and from the north by the infiltration of Zanātah Berbers into southern Morocco. The movement's leader, ʿAbd Allāh ibn Yāsīn, was a Ṣanhājah religious scholar from southern Morocco. Before joining the Ṣanhājah tribes, Ibn Yāsīn was attached to a centre of religious learning, Dār al-Murābiṭīn, in Sūs (southern Morocco), then headed by a scholar who had studied previously in Kairouan. Two theories have been proposed to explain the name al-Murābiṭūn (i.e., Almoravids), meaning inmates of a *ribāṭ* (fortified monastery), a term by which Ibn Yāsīn's followers were known. The first is that he founded a *ribāṭ* somewhere in Mauretania to train his followers. The other relates the name to Dār al-Murābiṭīn in Sūs, suggesting that the Almoravid movement was under the direct influence of this centre of learning. Whatever the case, the Almoravids were strict adherents of the Mālikī school of law as it had developed in Ifrīqiyyah since its introduction to the Maghrib in the 9th century.

The Almoravids began the invasion of Morocco after consolidating their control over Sijilmāssah in 1056. When Ibn Yāsīn was killed in 1059 in an attack on the Barghawāṭah tribal confederation on the Moroccan coast, the military and religious leadership of the Almoravids passed to the chief of the Lamtūnah tribe, Abū Bakr ibn ʿUmar. He returned to Mauretania in 1060 to fight against rebels challenging his authority. Command of the Almoravids in southern Morocco was then assumed by Abū Bakr's cousin, Yūsuf ibn Tāshufīn (Tāshfīn), under whose leadership the Almoravids conquered most of the Maghrib and Muslim Spain. By 1082 Almoravid rule extended as far east as Algiers. After the collapse of the Andalusian Umayyads in 1031, Muslim Spain became divided into a number of small Muslim principalities whose rulers were unable to hold out against Christian military advances. At the request of the Spanish Muslims, the Almoravids sent their army into Spain in 1086. By 1110, four years after Ibn Tāshufīn's death, the Almoravids had become masters of the whole of Muslim Spain. The capital of their expanded empire was Marrakech, which Ibn Tāshufīn had started to build in 1070.

In the Almoravid empire the Ṣanhājah tribes of Mauretania constituted a ruling class, distinguished from the rest of the population by the *litham* (face muffler) that their men wore. The Lamtūnah tribe formed the aristocracy of this ruling class and occupied the empire's important administrative and military posts. Strict adherence to the Mālikī version of Islamic law provided the religious legitimization for the authority of this tribal caste. The *fuqahā'* (experts on Islamic law) supervised both the administration of justice by the *qāḍīs* and the work of the provincial governors, and they acted as advisers to the rulers. The empire's simple system of government, in which military commanders acted as administrators, was rendered especially stifling by the narrow legalism of the *fuqahā'*. Mystical tendencies and new religious ideas reaching the Maghrib from Muslim Spain and the Arab east that the *fuqahā'* feared might undermine their authority were fought with the backing of the state.

Out of religious opposition to the Islam of the Almoravid jurists developed the revolutionary movement of the Almohads (al-Muwaḥḥidūn)—i.e., the adherents of *tawḥīd*, the belief in the oneness and uniqueness of God—which caused the downfall of the Almoravids. The founder of the movement was Muḥammad ibn Tūmart, a Berber belonging to the Maṣmūdah tribe of the High Atlas region of Morocco. After returning from a pilgrimage to Mecca in 1117, he preached in public against equating Islam with the provisions of one of the four schools of Islamic law, calling for a return to its original sources—namely, the Qur'ān and the Traditions (Ḥadīth) of the

Prophet. He also condemned the literal interpretation of the Qur'ān endorsed by the Almoravid *fuqahā'*, on grounds that it undermined *tawḥīd* by misleading the faithful to believe that God had human attributes (*tashbīh*). Ibn Tūmart fled from Marrakech in 1122 when he realized that he would be put to death if he did not cease criticizing the state's official religious dogma. After settling with some people of his tribe in the village of Tīnmallal in 1124, he started to organize a religious community of Maṣmūdah tribesmen, who became united not only because of their sense of tribal solidarity but also because of their belief in Ibn Tūmart as the Mahdi (divinely guided redeemer). After Ibn Tūmart's death in 1130, the movement and the conquest of the Almoravid empire continued under his trusted lieutenant, 'Abd al-Mu'min, a Berber from the Qūmiya tribe living in the region of Tlemcen.

'Abd al-Mu'min succeeded in establishing his authority in all the High and Middle Atlas mountains, beginning in 1133. From about 1139 he invaded northern Morocco and then western Algeria. After becoming master of this region in 1145, he advanced into the main centres of Almoravid authority in Morocco, conquering Fez in 1146 and Marrakech in 1147. Muslim Spain passed under Almohad rule between 1148 and 1172. Prior to completing the conquest of Spain, however, the Almohads had advanced into the eastern Maghrib, where the Normans of Sicily, profiting from Zīrid weakness, had occupied several positions on the Tunisian coast. Between 1152 and 1160 the Almohads were able to conquer the whole of the eastern Maghrib, including Tripolitania. For the first and last time in its history, the entire Maghrib was unified under one central indigenous authority.

The Almohad empire, like that of the Almoravids, was a Berber tribal state in which the Maṣmūdah tribes, previously united in the community of Tīnmallal, constituted the ruling class. Unlike the Almoravids, however, the Almohads did not have a clear religious orientation. They rejected the idea of equating Islamic law with any of its established schools, but, for practical reasons, the Almohad judges based their judgments on the provisions of the already established Mālikī school. Moreover, the belief of the common people in Ibn Tūmart as the Mahdi was slowly being superseded by the spread of Sufism (Islamic mysticism) and the veneration of Sufi holy men. Sufism had a prominent representative during the Almohad period in the person of Shu'ayb Abū Madyan al-Ghawth (died 1197). At the Almohad court, however, the sciences and philosophy were cultivated. The philosopher Ibn Rushd (Averroës) wrote his famous commentaries on Aristotle when at the court of the Almohad caliph Abū Ya'qūb Yūsuf (1163–84). These diverse developments meant that Almohad doctrine could not unite even the ruling class, whose coherence was undermined further when 'Abd al-Mu'min appointed his son as heir apparent in 1154, thus making his family, which did not belong to the Maṣmūdah tribe, the ruling dynasty. Through this act 'Abd al-Mu'min bypassed Abū Ḥafṣ 'Umar, the Maṣmūdah chief who gave protection to Ibn Tūmart in the High Atlas during his period of exile and whom the other Maṣmūdah chiefs expected to succeed 'Abd al-Mu'min. Maṣmūdah opposition was dealt with by putting a number of their chiefs to death and by giving the Ḥafṣids (i.e., the family of Abū Ḥafṣ 'Umar) a position in the state hierarchy second only to the ruling dynasty. Nevertheless, the ruling family constantly had to contend with the opposition of the Maṣmūdah chiefs.

Tensions within the ruling class finally led to an open split when the Almohads attempted to reestablish their authority over the eastern Maghrib, after the Banū Ghāniyah—the family that last ruled Muslim Spain in the name of the Almoravids and that after 1148 retained control of the Balearic Islands—had taken control there. The Banū Ghāniyah invaded eastern Algeria in 1184 and, with local Arab tribal support, brought Almohad authority in the region to an end. In 1203 they took control of Tunisia as well. The Almohad caliph al-Nāṣir (Muḥammad ibn Abī Yūsuf Ya'qūb) restored the empire's authority in the region with several large military campaigns from 1205 to 1207. Before returning to Marrakech, he appointed a Ḥafṣid to govern the reconquered eastern Maghrib. The Ḥafṣids were able to squelch the ongoing rebellion of the Banū Ghāniyah in 1227 and to establish control over Ifrīqiyyah, thus emerging as virtual rulers of the region. When the Almohad caliph al-Ma'mun formally renounced the Almohad doctrine in 1229, the Ḥafṣids declared themselves independent of him.

At the time of the Ḥafṣid secession, the control of the Almohads over western Algeria also had weakened, and they were no longer able to restrain the nomadic Zanātah tribes living in the south from moving with their herds to the rich pasturelands of the north. A group of these Zanātah, the Banū Marīn, advanced through northern Algeria into Morocco during the 1240s. Having captured Fez in 1248, they emerged as rulers of northern Morocco. It was only a matter of time before they brought Almohad rule to an end by conquering Marrakech in 1269. In the 1230s another group of Zanātah Berbers, the Banū 'Abd al-Wād ('Abd al-Wādid dynasty), had taken control of the region of Tlemcen in western Algeria. The state they founded there was overrun several times in the 13th and 14th centuries by the Marīnids. Nevertheless, its ruling line, the Banū Zayyān (Zayyānids), was able to maintain its authority in Tlemcen until the beginning of the 16th century.

POLITICAL FRAGMENTATION AND THE TRIUMPH OF ISLAMIC CULTURE (*C.* 1250–*C.* 1500)

After the collapse of Almohad rule, the Maghrib became divided into three Muslim states, each ruled by a Berber (Amazigh) dynasty: the Ḥafṣids, whose territory included Tunisia, eastern Algeria, and Tripolitania; the Marīnids, ruling over Morocco; and the Zayyānids, whose capital was in Tlemcen, ruling over most of western Algeria when this region was not occupied by the Marīnids. Both the rigid legalistic doctrine of the Almoravids and the more enlightened religious orientation of the Almohads had proved to be unsuitable as foundations for durable political authority. Furthermore, the rulers themselves were unsuitable to act as custodians of the faith. Islamic culture came of age in the Maghrib only after the rulers gave up attempting to identify their authority with a single religious doctrine and allowed religious life to develop freely through the interplay of religious ideas and social forces in relative independence from the state. The Maghribi rulers subsequently legitimized their authority by cultivating relations of trust and cooperation with the leading religious scholars of the time. Their capital cities became, consequently, the foremost centres of learning in their realms and were adorned not only with exquisite mosques but also with sumptuous *madrasahs*, residential colleges built and financed by the rulers. The Mālikī school of law was again recognized. Its scholars were held in great esteem and granted various privileges by the rulers, but they were not allowed to determine the conduct of government.

From the 12th century Sufism had spread widely in the Maghrib. Sufi holy men were venerated in both the towns and the countryside. Although in the towns their influence tended to be overshadowed by that of the legal scholars and the organs of the state, in the countryside they were the main custodians of Islamic norms. Often allied with tribal chiefs and sometimes having their own communities, these religious leaders helped establish order and stability by using their moral authority to uphold religious norms and arbitrate conflicts. They could perform these functions and gain influence over the tribal societies because the rulers' administrative authority extended little beyond their capital cities and garrison towns, and the rulers, as well as the urban scholars, considered tribal society to be of marginal importance. Indeed, the tribes exercised direct influence on political life only when they became involved in conflicts for power within the ruling family or when their warriors took part in wars against a foreign enemy.

Relations between the three Maghribi states were greatly influenced by the pressures that the Christian states of the Iberian Peninsula exerted on them from the mid-13th century. The Ḥafṣids claimed to be the heirs of Almohad religious authority, but after the first independent Ḥafṣid ruler, Abū Zakariyyā' (1228–49), they gave up attempting to substantiate this claim, either by pressing forward the conquest of the western Maghrib or by helping the Muslims of Spain militarily. The Marīnids inherited both the heartland of the former Almohad state in Morocco and its confrontation with the Christians in Spain, but, because of political instability, they were never able to take the initiative in the war against the Christians. Through their military outposts in southern Spain, they merely tried to check attacks on Morocco itself and to help the Muslim principality of Granada (Gharnāṭah) survive as a buffer between them and the Christian powers. In March 1344 the Marīnids suffered a serious military defeat when the army of the Christian kingdom of Castile, reinforced by warriors from England, France, and Italy, conquered Algeciras, their last military outpost in Spain. Meanwhile, since the mid-13th century, the Ḥafṣids and Zayyānids had been carrying on commercial relations with Christian Aragon. In return for allowing subjects of the king of Aragon to trade freely in their dominions, they received military help in the form of Catalan mercenaries. Defeat at the hands of the Christians, at a time when the Ḥafṣids and Zayyānids had friendly relations with Aragon, prompted the Marīnid sultan Abū al-Ḥasan ʿAlī (1331–51) to invade their territories. Between 1346 and 1347 his army overran the eastern Maghrib as far east as Tripolitania, but, when the Arab tribes of Tunisia joined in the battle against them, the Marīnids were overwhelmed, and Abū al-Ḥasan himself had to flee by sea from Tunis. His son and successor, Abū ʿInān, also invaded the eastern Maghrib, in 1356–57, but he, too, had to withdraw from Tunisia when faced with Arab tribal resistance.

Political life in the Maghrib from the mid-14th to the end of the 15th century was dominated by the preoccupation of the ruling dynasties with internecine conflicts, which in the case of the Ḥafṣids was complicated by the domination of many parts of their territories by Arab tribes. These conflicts caused the Ḥafṣid state to be divided into two parts between 1348 and 1370, one being ruled from Tunis and the other from Bejaïa, with the ruler of each part supported by a different Arab tribal group. After it was reunified in 1370 by Sultan Abū al-ʿAbbās, the Ḥafṣid state enjoyed periods of relative stability interspersed with strife. Political instability did not, however, prevent learning from developing in the towns. The greatest intellectual figure of the Maghrib before the modern period, the historian and sociologist Ibn Khaldūn, was born and educated at that time in Tunis. Conflicts for power within the Zayyānid state enabled the Marīnids to establish indirect control over Tlemcen in the second half of the 14th century, but, being preoccupied with strife within their own dominions, they were not able to realize their long-held ambition of bringing the whole of the Maghrib under their rule.

THE MAGHRIB FROM ABOUT 1500 TO 1830

Between 1471 and 1510 the line of confrontation between the Muslims of the Maghrib and the Christians of the Iberian Peninsula shifted from Spain to the Maghrib itself. The Portuguese occupied a number of positions on the Moroccan coast between 1471 and 1505, which included Tangier in the north and Agadir in the south. The Spaniards conquered Granada, the last Muslim stronghold on the peninsula, in 1492, and between 1505 and 1510 they began establishing garrison posts along the Maghribi coast. The most important of these were at Oran (Wahrān) and Bejaïa in Algeria and Tripoli in Libya. The strong religious reaction in the Maghrib to Christian colonial intrusion enabled the Saʿdī dynasty of sharifs to capture power in Morocco in 1549 and paved the way for Ottoman rule to be established later in the rest of the Maghrib.

Morocco Under Sharifian Dynasties

As a reaction to the Portuguese presence in Agadir, the tribes in southern Morocco were organized by the sharifian Saʿdī family—with the active support of Sufi leaders—into a militant religious movement directed against both the Portuguese presence and Morocco's own rulers, the Waṭṭāsids. The latter was a branch of the Marīnid dynasty that had usurped power in Fez in 1472 and pursued a policy of coexistence with the Portuguese. After occupying Marrakech in 1525 and consolidating their authority in southern Morocco, the Saʿdīs conquered Agadir in 1541. By 1550 they had forced the Portuguese to evacuate the rest of their positions on the Moroccan coast and conquered the Waṭṭāsid capital of Fez. The Saʿdīs consolidated their rule in Morocco thereafter and, by later defending the territory against Ottoman expansion from Algeria, gave it a national identity distinct from the rest of the Maghrib. Their authority was legitimized by their descent from the Prophet, but the dynasty's mainstay was the support it received from the settled agricultural and commercial communities, as well as the possession and use of firearms by its troops. The dynasty reached the zenith of its power during the reign of Aḥmad al-Manṣūr (1578–1603), who, with the help of Spanish and Turkish mercenaries, built Morocco's first professional army. With this force at his command, al-Manṣūr imposed his will on the whole country, besides defending it against the Ottoman Empire and, in 1591, conquering the West African state of Songhai (present-day Mali). However, conflict for power after his death divided the country into several principalities that lasted until they were reunited through another sharifian family, that of the ʿAlawites.

The ʿAlawites, who rule Morocco to this day, came to power with the help of Arab tribes that had moved into Morocco in large numbers during the Almohad period. The founder of the dynasty, Mawlāy al-Rashīd, mobilized these tribes against the powerful Berber principality of the Dilā'iyyah that had dominated the Middle Atlas and parts of northern Morocco since the 1640s. Mawlāy al-Rashīd's half brother, Mawlāy Ismāʿīl, succeeded in reunifying Morocco with the help of a professional army of slaves (*ʿabīd*) known as ʿAbīd al-Bukhārī, who were drawn from the descendants of the many sub-Saharan Africans who were brought back to Morocco after the conquest of Songhai. After Mawlāy Ismāʿīl's death, however, conflict over succession between his sons, who are said to have numbered about 500, complicated by the intrigues of the ʿAbid officers, ushered in a period of chaos and economic decline that lasted nearly 50 years. Following the dynasty's recovery during the reign of Sultan Muḥammad ibn ʿAbd Allāh (1757–90) and continuing under Sultan Mawlāy Sulaymān (1792–1822), Morocco enjoyed a period of relative stability that was disturbed on a large scale only by conflicts between the ruling dynasty and tribes recognizing the authority of Sufi leaders. The economy of Morocco also started to recover in that period, and the state's external trade expanded. However, the French occupation of Algeria after 1830, together with European political and economic infiltration of Morocco thereafter, created new challenges with which the state's traditional political system could not adequately cope.

Ottoman Rule in the Maghrib

The Ottoman Turks occupied Egypt in 1517. Shortly afterward they became involved in the confrontation between Muslims and Christians in the Maghrib through the exploits of two Muslim privateers, ʿArūj and his brother Khayr al-Dīn Barbarossa, who occupied Algiers in 1516 and made it a base for operations against the Spaniards. After ʿArūj was killed in 1518 in an attack on Tlemcen, Khayr al-Dīn offered submission to the Ottoman sultan in return for military help, which subsequently enabled him to gain control over most of the Maghrib.

Algeria was the first country of the Maghrib to be ruled by the Ottoman Empire. Administered at first by governors sent from Istanbul, the Ottoman regency of Algiers was transformed into a sort of military republic when the troops stationed there rebelled against the Ottoman governor in 1689 and installed one of their officers as ruler, giving him the title of dey (maternal uncle). The Ottoman troops thus emerged as a ruling caste that periodically renewed itself with fresh recruits from various parts of the Mediterranean region. The deys, chosen from within this caste, governed Algeria independently from the Ottoman government. They retained religious ties to the Ottoman sultan, however, by recognizing him as caliph and by making the Ḥanafī school of law—the official school of the Ottoman Empire—the official school of law in Algeria as well. Piracy provided the ruling caste with its main source of revenue. Generated largely from the money received for ransoming Christian captives and from the price of peace levied on obliging Christian countries, such income remained forthcoming until the mid-18th century. Local inhabitants accepted the rule of the deys because the taxes they had to pay them were light and because their own leaders were allowed a large degree of autonomy in managing the affairs of their communities. Furthermore, the deys were

The Ketchaoua Mosque in Algiers, the capital and chief seaport of Algeria. Fayez Nureldine/AFP/Getty Images

careful to cultivate the good will of the influential Sufi personalities in the countryside. From the mid-18th century the balance of power in the Mediterranean started to turn in favour of the European powers. Thereafter the revenue that the deys derived from piracy declined. The heavy taxes that they subsequently had to impose on the Algerians led to conflicts with the tribal communities led by Sufi leaders, which ultimately weakened the regime of the deys on the eve of the French invasion of Algeria in 1830.

The Ottomans occupied Tunis in 1534 but were forced by Spanish troops to evacuate it the following year. Thereafter the Ḥafṣids ruled Tunisia under Spanish protection until the Ottomans reconquered the country in 1574. In 1591 the Ottoman troops stationed in Tunis rebelled against the governor sent from Istanbul and established a regime headed by deys chosen by the troops, which was similar to the dey-ruled regime that appeared in Algeria a little later. In Tunisia the regime of the deys was transformed from within through the importance that the bey, the officer responsible for maintaining order in the countryside and for collecting taxes, came to have in it. In 1705 the bey, Ḥusayn ibn ʿAlī, effectively usurped the power of the dey when, with the help of Tunisian tribal warriors, he repulsed the invasion of Tunisia by the army of Algiers. Thus was established the Ḥusaynid dynasty of beys, which ruled the country until the monarchy was abolished in 1957. While recognizing the religious authority of the Ottoman sultan as caliph, the Ḥusaynids ruled Tunisia independently from the Ottoman government. They officially adopted the Ḥanafī school of law but governed the country through local Mālikī notables and allowed Mālikī religious scholars to manage the religious and legal affairs of their communities, while also bestowing favours on them. In common with other Maghribi states at the time, piracy was an important source of revenue. It was supplemented, however, by trade in the country's products, which the beys controlled through monopolies and sold mostly to Jews at high prices.

The Ottomans conquered Tripoli in 1551, defeating the Knights of Malta. The Ottoman province that they established was governed from Tripoli and included the whole of present-day Libya. In 1711 the province underwent a change similar to the one that Tunisia had experienced in 1705, when the chief of the cavalry, Aḥmad Karamanli, usurped power and established his own dynasty. The Karamanlis ruled Libya until 1835 when, in the wake of a tribal rebellion supported by the British, direct Ottoman rule was reimposed there. From the mid-16th century Libya became active in the lucrative trans-Saharan trade that crossed its territory. In the Karamanli period it also became an important centre of piracy. After Napoleon I occupied Malta in 1798, Libya was opened to European trade, and it consequently became involved in the rivalry between the British and the French for supremacy both in the Mediterranean region and in West Africa.

CHAPTER 4

North Africa After 1830

At the time when Europe began its colonial expansion in the Maghrib—starting with the French occupation of Algiers in 1830—the region was divided into four political entities. Morocco, ruled by the ʿAlawite dynasty, was a sovereign country. Algeria, Tunisia, and Libya were autonomous states that recognized the religious authority of the Ottoman sultan. The French occupation of Algeria had direct and serious consequences for the authority of the rulers of Tunisia and Morocco and, indirectly, for the authority of the rulers of Libya as well.

ADVENT OF EUROPEAN COLONIALISM

The French capture of Algiers in 1830, followed by the Ottoman reoccupation of Tripoli in 1835, rudely interrupted the attempts of North Africa's rulers to follow the example of Muḥammad ʿAlī, the pasha of Egypt, and increase their power along European lines. Of the four powers in North Africa at the beginning of the 19th century, only Tunis and Morocco survived as independent states into the second half of the century to encounter the heavy pressures that Europe then brought to bear on the region for free trade and legal reform, measures originally leveled against the Ottoman Empire and Egypt. Between the death of Tunisia's ambitious reformer, Aḥmad Bey, in 1855, and the dismissal of its talented, reform-minded prime minister, Khayr al-Dīn, in 1877, Tunis responded to these pressures with the Ahd al-Amān, or Fundamental Pact, in 1856 and the short-lived constitution of 1860, the first in the Arab world. The Fundamental Pact guaranteed the equality before the law of all subjects—Muslim, Christian, and Jew—while the constitution provided for a consultative assembly and the administration of justice. The constitution was suspended in 1864, but its chief proponent, Khayr al-Dīn, came to power in 1869 as the president of the International Financial Commission, a group appointed to handle the country's foreign debt, and as prime minister in 1873. At Khayr al-Dīn's departure in 1877, Tunisia was internally strong but internationally weak.

The sultan of Morocco, by contrast, was trapped between the European demands for free trade, conceded in 1856, and an unruly tribal population that resisted the imposition of a central government. Although defeated by France at the Battle of Isly in 1844 and by Spain at Tetuan (Tétouan) in 1860, Morocco was nevertheless able to rely on the support of Great Britain in its dealings with Europe. As a result—although Morocco's immigrant Europeans in this period conducted themselves with impunity under the protection of their consuls—the sultans Muḥammad and Hassan, who ruled Morocco from 1859 to 1894, maintained the country's independence and gradually extended a network of caids (*qāʿids*), or district governors, into the far south of the country. At the beginning of the 20th century—after the fall of Tunisia to French control in 1881—Morocco was the sole exception to colonial rule in North Africa.

In 1835 Libya reverted to the status of a provincial backwater of the Ottoman Empire. The French meanwhile took almost 20 years to complete their conquest of the former Turkish territory of Algiers—from the bey of Constantine in the east and from the Arab hero Abdelkader (ʿAbd al-Qādir) in the west—and another 20 years to replace the army with a civilian administration, following the fall of the French Second Empire in 1870. Algeria's incorporation into metropolitan France was a triumph for the territory's European settlers, achieved at the expense of the native Muslim population, who were denied political rights and were administratively repressed and economically deprived. Immigration from France, Italy, and Spain brought the Europeans in Algeria to about one-sixth of the total population in 1900, a proportion that subsequently fell to about one-tenth at the outbreak of the Algerian revolution in 1954. Most Europeans remained in the cities, of which the two largest, Algiers and Oran, had European majorities. The economy of Algeria came to rest on the large-scale production of wine and wheat for export to France, while the majority of the country's Muslims grew ever more impoverished. The injustices of the system were widely condemned in France, and attempts were made by the

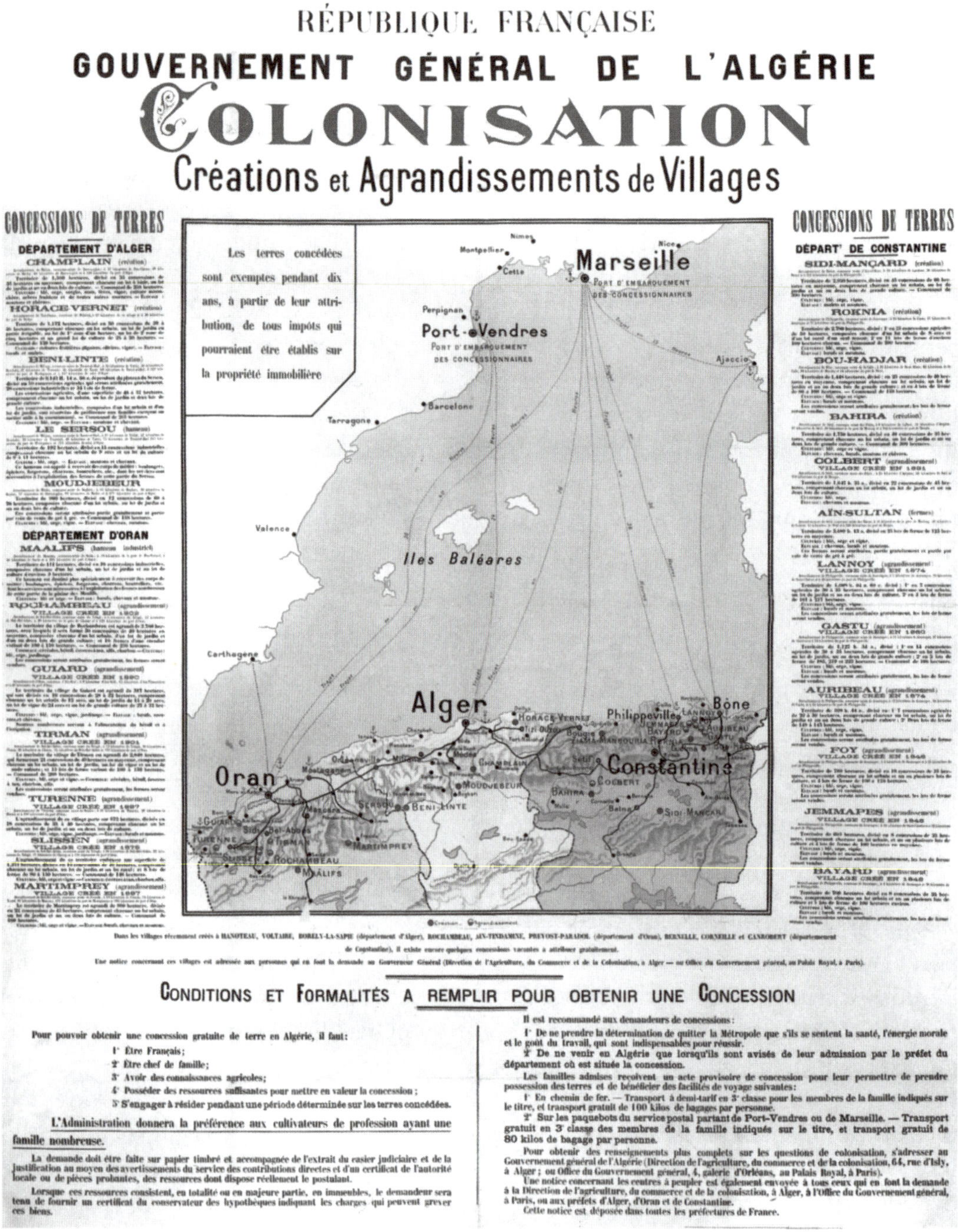

1903 poster encouraging French people to move to Algeria. Apic/Hulton Archive/Getty Images

French to avoid the same mistakes when they colonized Tunisia and Morocco.

A French protectorate was eventually imposed on Tunisia in 1881–83, after the British withdrew their objections to French expansion in North Africa at the Congress of Berlin in 1878. The French preserved the administration of the bey of Tunis, although under French supervision, an indirect form of rule they later applied to Morocco as well. The Moroccan protectorate itself was established only in 1912, after the Entente Cordiale—a treaty concluded between France and Britain in 1904, which settled a number of hostilities between the two countries—and the Cameroons had been ceded to Germany in 1911. Both acts together left France free to divide the country with Spain, which took over the Rif Mountains in the north and the border region with the Spanish Sahara in the south. Pacifying the Moroccan interior was achieved with a minimum of force by French Field Marshal Louis-Hubert-Gonzalve Lyautey until his efforts were interrupted by the Rif War, waged by the Moroccan nationalist Abd el-Krim (Muḥammad ibn ʿAbd al-Karīm al-Khaṭṭabī) and his forces between 1921 and 1926, an event that delayed total pacification of the country until 1934. Libya was similarly invaded by Italy in 1911, but the prolonged resistance of the Sanūsiyyah in Cyrenaica denied the Italian Fascists control of the country until 1931, when they captured and executed the brilliant Sanūsī guerrilla leader ʿUmar al-Mukhtār. By 1939, however, the colonization of Morocco, Tunisia, and Libya by French and Italian settlers was well advanced.

NATIONALIST MOVEMENTS

World War II brought major changes to North Africa, promoting the cause of national independence. A reaction to years of colonialism had set in and was erupting into strong nationalist tendencies in Morocco, Algeria, Tunisia, and Libya. The Sanūsī leader Sīdī Muḥammad Idrīs al-Mahdī al-Sanūsī, exiled in Cairo during the war, was restored to power in Cyrenaica by the British and became King Idris I of a united Libya in 1951. Tunisian nationalism formally emerged with the influential Young Tunisians in 1907. It developed further when the Destour (Constitution) Party was founded in 1920 and the Neo-Destour Party under Habib Bourguiba in 1934. In Morocco the strong nationalist movement of the 1930s culminated in the foundation of the Independence (Istiqlāl) Party in 1943. In Algeria the French refusal of demands by the reform-minded Young Algerians for French citizenship cleared the way for the radical separatist movement of Ahmed Messali Hadj and the Arab Islamic nationalist movement of Sheik ʿAbd al-Hamid Ben Badis. After the war the French were on the defensive, conceding independence to Tunisia and Morocco in 1956 in order to concentrate their efforts on Algeria, where a full-scale rebellion led by the National Liberation Front (FLN) broke out in 1954. This prolonged and costly "savage war of peace" led to Algerian independence in 1962 and,

Sanūsiyyah

The Sanūsiyyah, also spelled Sennusiya, is a Muslim Ṣūfī (mystic) brotherhood established in 1837 by Sīdī Muḥammad ibn 'Alī as-Sanūsī. In modern history, the head of the Sanūsī brotherhood was king of the federal kingdom of Libya from its creation in 1951 until it was superseded by a Socialist republic in 1969.

The Sanūsiyyah brotherhood was a reformist movement aimed at a return to the simple faith and life of early Islam. As a missionary order it sought to reform the lives of the Bedouins and convert the non-Muslim peoples of the Sahara and Central Africa. The vast majority of people called Sanūsī did not practice Sanūsī rites but were personal followers of as-Sanūsī al-Kabīr, the Grand Sanūsī, and his family.

By the turn of the 20th century the order was well-established among most of the Bedouins and the oasis dwellers of Cyrenaica and the Sirtica, the Libyan Desert of Egypt, southern Tripolitania, Fezzan, central Sahara, and the Hejaz. The order was strongest in Cyrenaica, where it integrated its religious lodges (zāwīyahs) with the existing tribal system to such an extent that it was able to marshal its members against the Italians in World War I. After the war the Sanūsīs emerged as political spokesmen for the people of Cyrenaica in the negotiations with the British and the Italians and maintained this role throughout World War II. On Dec. 24, 1951, Idrīs, the head of the Sanūsīyah, was proclaimed king of an independent United Kingdom of Libya. He was overthrown by a military junta led by Col. Muammar al-Qaddafi on Sept. 1, 1969.

afterward, to the mass exodus of Algeria's European population.

The discovery of oil in Libya in the 1950s presaged further transformations there. The Libyan monarchy was overthrown by a military coup in 1969 and replaced by the popular republicanism of Colonel Muammar al-Qaddafi. Oil also came to dominate the economy of Algeria, where agriculture was neglected in favour of a program of industrialization based on the country's huge petroleum and gas reserves. This policy, however, was disappointing, and popular disillusionment led to the end of the one-party presidential regime of the FLN in the 1990s. In Tunisia the pro-Western Bourguiba survived as president until 1987, when he was deposed by his prime minister, Zine el-Abidine Ben Ali. Tunisia's heavy economic reliance on tourism since the mid-1960s, moreover, has been a questionable and precarious substitute for an emphasis on agricultural exports. Like Tunisia, Morocco—dominated by the 'Alawite monarchy since independence—has almost no oil, but it does possess greater reserves of phosphates and a more prosperous agricultural sector. In 1976 Morocco annexed part of the former Spanish territory of Western Sahara, after which it became involved in a protracted guerrilla war with Polisario, a Sahrawi nationalist organization.

CHAPTER 5

ALGERIA

Algeria is located along the Mediterranean coast of northern Africa. The modern-day country gained independence in 1962. The capital is Algiers.

EARLY HISTORY

From a geographic standpoint, Algeria has been a difficult country to rule. The Tell and Saharan Atlas mountain chains impede easy north-south communication, and the few good natural harbours provide only limited access to the hinterlands. This has meant that, before Ottoman rule, the western part of the country was associated more closely with Morocco while the eastern part had closer ties with Tunisia. A further impediment to unifying the country was that a significant minority of the population were native Tamazight speakers and were thus more resistant to Arabization as compared with North African countries to the east. Therefore, Ottoman Algeria, which contained few extensive, original, or long-lived Muslim dynasties, was not nearly as predisposed to developing political nationalism as was Tunisia during the first decades of the 19th century.

FRENCH ALGERIA

Modern Algeria can be understood only by examining the period—nearly a century and a half—that the country was under French colonial rule. The customary beginning date is in April 1827, when Ḥusayn, the last Ottoman provincial ruler, or dey, of Algiers, angrily struck the French consul with a fly whisk. This incident was a manifest sign of the dey's anger toward the French consul, a culmination of what had soured Franco-Algerian relations in the preceding years: France's large and unpaid debt. That same year the French minister of war had written that the conquest of Algeria would be an effective and useful means of providing employment for veterans of the Napoleonic wars. The conquest of Algeria began three years later.

The Conquest of Algeria

The government of the dey proved no match for the French army that landed on July 5, 1830, near Algiers. Ḥusayn accepted the French offer of exile after a brief military encounter. After his departure, and in violation of agreements that had been made, the French seized private and religious buildings, looted possessions mainly in and around Algiers, and seized a vast portion of the country's arable land. The three-century-long period of Algerian history as an autonomous province of the Ottoman Empire had ended.

The French government thought that a quick victory abroad might create enough popularity at home to enable it to win the upcoming elections. Instead, only days after the French victory in Algeria, the July Revolution forced King Charles X from the throne in favour of Louis-Philippe. Although those who led the July Revolution in France had cynically dismissed the campaign in Algeria as foreign adventurism to cover up oppression at home, they were reluctant to simply withdraw. Various alternatives were considered, including an early ill-fated plan to establish Tunisian princes in parts of Algeria as rulers under French patronage. The French general, Bertrand Clauzel, signed two treaties with the bey of Tunis, one of which offered him the right to keep territories conceded to him in exchange for annual payments. Because the treaty was not communicated officially to the government in Paris, however, the bey considered this proof of French duplicity and refused the offer.

The first few years of colonial rule were characterized by numerous changes in the French command, and the military campaign began to prove extremely arduous and costly. The towns of the Mitidja Plain—just outside Algiers—and neighbouring cities fell first to the French. Gen. Camille Trézel captured Bejaïa in the east in 1833 after a naval bombardment. The French took Mers el-Kebir in 1830 and entered Oran in 1831, but they faced stiffer opposition from the Sufi brotherhood leader, Emir Abdelkader ('Abd al-Qādir ibn Muḥyī al-Dīn), in the west. Because towns and cities were plundered and massacres of civilian populations were widespread, the French government sent a royal commission to the colony to examine the situation.

A 1930 illustration of the 1830 Conquest of Algeria by the French army. Apic/Hulton Archive/ Getty Images

During their campaign against Abdelkader, the French agreed to a truce and signed two agreements with him. The treaty signed between Gen. Louis-Alexis Desmichels and Abdelkader in 1834 included two versions, one of which made major concessions to Abdelkader again without the consent or knowledge of the French government. This miscommunication led to a breach of the agreement when the French moved through territory belonging to the emir. Abdelkader responded with a counterattack in 1839 and drove the French back to Algiers and the coast.

France decided at that point to wage an all-out war. Led by Gen. (later Marshal) Thomas-Robert Bugeaud, the campaign of conquest eventually brought one-third of the total French army strength (more than 100,000 troops) to Algeria. The new military campaign and the initial onslaught caused widespread devastation to the Algerians and to their crops and livestock. Abdelkader's hit-and-run tactics failed, and he was forced to surrender in 1847. He was exiled to France but later was permitted to settle with his family in Damascus, Syria, where he and his followers saved the lives of many Christians during the 1860 massacres. Respected even by his opponents as the founder of the modern Algerian state, Abdelkader became, and has remained, the personification of Algerian national resistance to foreign domination.

Abdelkader's defeat marked the end of what might be called resistance on a national scale, but smaller French operations continued, such as the occupation of the Saharan oases (Zaatcha in 1849, Nara in 1850, and Ouargla in 1852). The eastern Kabylia region was subdued only in 1857, while the final major Kabylia uprising of Muḥammad al-Muqrānī was suppressed in 1871. The Saharan regions of Touat and Gourara, which were at that time Moroccan spheres of influence, were occupied in 1900; the Tindouf area, previously regarded as Moroccan rather than Algerian, became part of Algeria only after the French occupation of the Anti-Atlas in 1934.

Colonial Rule

The manner in which French rule was established in Algeria during the years 1830–47 laid the groundwork for a pattern of rule that French Algeria would maintain until independence. It was characterized by a tradition of violence and mutual incomprehension between the rulers and the ruled; the French politician and historian Alexis de Tocqueville wrote that colonization had made Muslim society more barbaric than it was before the French arrived. There was a relative absence of well-established native mediators between the French rulers and the mass population, and an ever-growing French settler population (the colons, also known as *pieds noirs*) demanded the privileges of a ruling minority in the name of French democracy. When Algeria eventually became a part of France juridically, that only added to the power of the colons, who sent delegates to the French parliament. They accounted for roughly one-tenth of the total population from the late 19th century until the end of French rule.

Settler domination of Algeria was not secured, however, until the fall of Napoleon III in 1870 and the rise of the Third Republic in France. Until then Algeria remained largely under military administration, and the governor-general of Algeria was almost invariably a military officer until the 1880s. Most Algerians—excluding the colons—were subject to rule by military officers organized into Arab Bureaus, whose members were officers with an intimate knowledge of local affairs and of the language of the people but with no direct financial interest in the colony. The officers, therefore, often sympathized with the outlook of the people they administered rather than with the demands of the European colonists. The paradox of French Algeria was that despotic and military rule offered the native Algerians a better situation than did civilian and democratic government.

A large-scale program of confiscating cultivable land, after resistance had been crushed, made colonization possible. Settler colonization was of mixed European origin—mainly Spanish in and around Oran and French, Italian, and Maltese in the centre and east. The presence of the non-French settlers was officially regarded with alarm for quite a while, but the influence of French education, the Muslim environment, and the Algerian climate eventually created in the non-French a European-Algerian subnational sentiment. This would probably have resulted, in time, in a movement to create an independent state if Algeria had been situated farther away from Paris and if the settlers had not feared the potential strength of the Muslim majority.

After the overthrow of Louis-Philippe's regime in 1848, the settlers succeeded in having the territory declared French; the former Turkish provinces were converted into departments on the French model, while colonization progressed with renewed energy. With the establishment of the French Second Empire in 1852, responsibility for Algeria was transferred from Algiers to a minister in Paris, but the emperor, Napoleon III, soon reversed this disposition. While expressing the hope that an increased number of settlers would forever keep Algeria French, he also declared that France's first duty was to the three million Arabs. He declared, with considerable accuracy, that Algeria was "not a French province but an Arab country, a European colony, and a French camp." This attitude aroused certain hopes among Algerians, but they were destroyed by the emperor's downfall in 1870. After France's defeat in the Franco-German War, settlers felt they could finally gain more land. Spurred on by this and by years of droughts and famines, Algerians united in 1871 under Muḥammad al-Muqrānī in the last major Kabylia uprising. Its brutal suppression by French forces was followed by the appropriation of another large segment of territory, which provided land for European refugees from Alsace. Much land was also acquired by the French through loopholes in laws originally designed to protect tribal property. Notable among these is the *sénatus-consulte* of 1863, which broke up tribal lands and allowed settlers to acquire vast areas formerly secured under tribal law. Following the loss of this territory, Algerian peasants moved to marginal lands and in the vicinity of forests; their presence in these areas set in motion the widespread environmental degradation that has affected Algeria since then.

It is difficult to gauge in human terms the losses suffered by Algerians during the early years of the French occupation. Estimates of the number of those dead from disease and starvation and as a direct result of warfare during the early years of colonization vary considerably, but the most reliable ones indicate that the native population of Algeria fell by nearly one-third in the years between the French invasion and the end of fighting in the mid-1870s.

Gradually the European population established nearly total political, economic, and social domination over the country and its native inhabitants. At the same time, new lines of communication, hospitals and medical services, and educational facilities became more widely available to Europeans, though they were dispensed to a limited extent—and in the French language—to Algerians. Settlers owned most Western dwellings, Western-style farms, businesses, and workshops. Only primary education was available to Algerians, and only in towns and cities, and there were limited prospects for higher education. Because employment was concentrated mainly in urban settlements, underemployment and chronic unemployment disproportionately affected Muslims, who lived mostly in rural and semirural areas.

For the Algerians service in the French army and in French factories during World War I was an eye-opening experience. Some 200,000 fought for France during the war, and more than one-third of the male Algerians between the ages of 20 and 40 resided in France during that time. When peace returned, some 70,000 Algerians remained in France and, by living frugally, were able to support many thousands of their relatives in Algeria.

Nationalist Movements

Algerian nationalism developed out of the efforts of three different groups. The first consisted of Algerians who had gained access to French education and earned their living in the French sector. Often called assimilationists, they pursued gradualist, reformist tactics, shunned illegal actions, and were prepared to consider permanent union with France if the rights of Frenchmen could be extended to native Algerians. This group, originating from the period before World War I, was loosely organized under the name Young Algerians and included (in the 1920s) Khaled Ben Hachemi

("Emir Khaled"), who was the grandson of Abdelkader, and (in the 1930s) Ferhat Abbas, who later became the first premier of the Provisional Government of the Algerian Republic.

The second group consisted of Muslim reformers who were inspired by the religious Salafī movement founded in the late 19th century in Egypt by Sheikh Muḥammad 'Abduh. The Association of Algerian Muslim 'Ulamā' (Association des Uléma Musulmans Algériens; AUMA) was organized in 1931 under the leadership of Sheikh 'Abd al-Hamid Ben Badis. This group was not a political party, but it fostered a strong sense of Muslim Algerian nationality among the Algerian masses.

The third group was more proletarian and radical. It was organized among Algerian workers in France in the 1920s under the leadership of Ahmed Messali Hadj and later gained wide support in Algeria. Preaching a nationalism without nuance, Messali Hadj was bound to appeal to Algerians, who fully recognized their deprivation. Messali Hadj's strongly nationalistic stance, or even the more muted position of Ben Badis, could have been checked by such gradualist reformers as Ferhat Abbas if only they had been able to show that step-by-step decolonization was possible. Several efforts to liberalize the treatment of native Algerians, promoted by French reformist groups in collaboration with Algerian reformists in the first half of the 20th century, came too late to stem the radical tide.

One such effort, the Blum-Viollette proposal (named for French premier Léon Blum and Maurice Viollette, the former governor-general of Algeria), was introduced during the Popular Front government in France (1936–37). It would have allowed a very small number of Algerians to obtain full French citizenship without forcing them to relinquish their right to be judged by Muslim law on matters of personal status (e.g., marriage, inheritance, divorce, and child custody). The proposal was, therefore, a potential breakthrough because this issue had been shrewdly exploited by the settler population, who understood that most Algerians did not want to abandon this right. The small number of Algerians who would have received full French citizenship—the educated, veterans of French military service, and other narrowly defined groups—could then have been gradually increased in later years. Settler opposition to the measure was so fierce, however, that the project was never even brought to a vote in the French Chamber of Deputies. Many Algerians began to feel that organized violence was the only option, since all peaceful means for resolving the problems of colonial rule for the majority of the population had been denied. The group that inherited this mission, the National Liberation Front (Front de Libération Nationale; FLN), grew out of Messali Hadj's organization, later absorbing many adherents of the other two nationalist groups.

World War II and the Movement for Independence

World War II brought with it the collapse of France and, in 1942, the Anglo-American occupation of North Africa. The occupation forces were to some extent automatically agents of emancipation; both Allied and Axis radio stations began to broadcast in Arabic, promising a new world for formerly subject peoples. The effect was further heightened by the June 1941 promise of emancipation for both Syria and Lebanon, given by the Free French and backed by the British authorities in the Middle East.

Ferhat Abbas drafted an Algerian Manifesto in December 1942 for presentation to Allied as well as French authorities; it sought recognition of political autonomy for Algeria. Gen. Charles de Gaulle declared a year later that France was under an obligation to the Muslims of North Africa because of the loyalty they had shown. French citizenship was extended to certain categories of Muslims three months later, but this did not go far enough to satisfy Algerian opinion. A display of Algerian nationalist flags at Sétif in May 1945 prompted French authorities to fire on demonstrators. An unorganized uprising ensued, in which 84 European settlers were massacred. The violence and suppression that followed resulted in the death of about 8,000 Muslims (according to French sources) or as many as 45,000 (according to Algerian sources). The main outcome of the massacres, however, went far beyond the human losses. They became the foundation for the Algerian War of Independence, which began nearly a decade later. The demonstrations were the last peaceful attempts by Algerians to seek their independence.

The French National Assembly voted for a statute on Algeria on Sept. 20, 1947, in which the country was defined as "a group of departments endowed with a civic personality, financial autonomy, and a special organization." The statute created an Algerian assembly with two separate colleges of 60 members each, one representing some 1.5 million Europeans and the other Algeria's 9 million Muslims. After lengthy debates the statute was passed by a small majority. Muslims were finally considered full French citizens with the right to keep their personal Qur'ānic status and were granted the right to work in France without further formalities. Military territories in the south would be abolished, and Arabic would become the language of educational instruction at all levels.

The law was poorly implemented, however, and the subsequent elections were widely held to have been manipulated to favour the French. Most of the reforms laid down by the statute were never enforced. In spite of this, Algeria remained quiet. The principal change had been the fact that some 350,000 Algerian workers—five times as many as in the post-World War I period—were able to establish themselves in France and remit money to Algeria.

THE ALGERIAN WAR OF INDEPENDENCE

Nationalist parties had existed for many years, but they became increasingly radical as they realized that their goals were not going to be achieved through peaceful means. Prior to World War II the Party of the Algerian People (Parti du Peuple Algérien) had been founded by Messali Hadj. The party was banned in the late 1930s and replaced in the mid-1940s by the Movement for the Triumph of Democratic Liberties (Mouvement pour le Triomphe des Libertés Démocratiques; MTLD). A more radical paramilitary group, the Special Organization (Organization Spéciale; OS), was formed about the same time, but it was discovered by the colonial police in 1950, and many of its leaders were imprisoned. In 1954 a group of former OS members split from the MTLD and formed the Revolutionary Committee of Unity and Action (Comité Révolutionaire d'Unité et d'Action; CRUA). This organization, later to become the FLN, prepared for military action. The leading members of the CRUA became the so-called *chefs historiques* ("historical leaders") of the Algerian War of Independence: Hocine Aït-Ahmed, Larbi Ben M'Hidi, Moustapha Ben Boulaid, Mohamed Boudiaf, Mourad Didouche, Belkacem Krim, Mohamed Khider, Rabah Bitat, and Ahmed Ben Bella. They organized and led several hundred men in the first armed confrontations.

The war began on the night of Oct. 31, 1954. The movement, led by the newly formed FLN, issued a leaflet stating that its aim was to restore a sovereign Algerian state. It advocated social democracy within an Islamic framework and equal citizenship for any resident in Algeria. A preamble recognized that Algeria had fallen behind other Arab states in social and national emancipation but claimed this could be remedied by a difficult and prolonged struggle. Two weapons would be used: guerrilla warfare at home and diplomatic activity abroad, particularly at the United Nations (UN).

Though the first armed assault—which occurred in the region of Batna and the Aurès—was ineffective militarily, it led to the arrest of some 2,000 members of the MTLD who had not been supporters of the rebellion. The armed uprising soon intensified and spread, gradually affecting larger parts of the country, and some regions—notably the northeastern parts of Little Kabylia and parts of the Aurès Mountains—became guerrilla strongholds that were beyond French control. France became more involved in the conflict, drafting some two million conscripts over the course of the war. To counter the spread of the uprising, the French National Assembly declared a state of emergency, first over the affected provinces and later that year over the entire country. Jacques Soustelle arrived in Algiers as the new governor-general in February 1955, but the new plan he announced four months later once again proved to be ineffective.

A decisive turn in the war took place in August 1955 when a widespread armed outbreak in Skikda, north of the Constantine region, led to the killing of nearly 100 Europeans and Muslim officials. Countermeasures by both the French army and settlers claimed the lives of somewhere between 1,200 (according to French sources) and 12,000 (according to Algerian sources) Algerians.

The electoral victory in January 1956 of the Republican Front in France and the premiership of Guy Mollet led to the appointment of the moderate and experienced Gen. Georges Catroux as governor-general. When Mollet personally visited Algiers to prepare the way for the new governor-general, Europeans bombarded him with tomatoes. Yielding to this pressure, he allowed Catroux to withdraw and named in his place the pugnacious socialist Robert Lacoste as resident minister. Lacoste's policy was to rule Algeria through decree, and he gave the military exceptional powers. At the same time, he wanted to give the country a decentralized administrative structure that allowed some autonomy.

A French army of 500,000 troops was sent to Algeria to counter the rebel strongholds in the more distant portions of the country, while the rebels collected money for their cause and took reprisals against fellow Muslims who would not cooperate with them. By the spring of 1956 a majority of previously noncommitted political leaders, such as Ferhat Abbas and Tawfiq al-Madani of the AUMA, had joined FLN leaders in Cairo, where the group had its headquarters.

The first FLN congress took place in August–September 1956 in the Soummam valley between Great and Little Kabylia and brought together the FLN leadership in an appraisal of the war and its objectives. Algeria was divided into six autonomous zones (*wilāyāt*), each led by guerrilla commanders who later played key roles in the affairs of the country. The congress also produced a written platform on the aims and objectives of the war and set up the National Council for the Algerian Revolution (Conseil National de la Révolution Algérienne) and the Committee of Coordination and Enforcement (Comité de Coordination et d'Exécution), the latter acting as the executive branch of the FLN.

Externally, the major event of 1956 was the French decision to grant full independence to Morocco and Tunisia and to concentrate on retaining "French Algeria." The Moroccan sultan and Premier Habib Bourguiba of Tunisia, hoping to find an acceptable solution to the Algerian problem, prepared to hold a meeting in Tunis with some important Algerian leaders (including Ben Bella, Boudiaf, Khider, and Aït-Ahmed) who had been guests of the sultan in Rabat. French intelligence officers, however, forced the plane that had been chartered by the Moroccan government to land in Oran instead of Tunis. The Algerian leaders were then arrested and confined in prison in France for the rest of the war. This act hardened the resolve of the rest of the Algerian leadership to keep fighting and provoked an attack on Meknès,

Mor., that cost the lives of 40 French settlers before the Moroccan government could restore order.

Beginning in 1956 and continuing until the summer of the following year, the FLN attempted to paralyze the administration of Algiers through what has come to be known as the Battle of Algiers. Attacks by the FLN against both military and civilian European targets were countered by paratroopers led by Gen. Jacques Massu. To stem the tide of FLN attacks, the French military resorted to the torture and summary execution of hundreds of suspects. The entire leadership of the FLN was eventually eliminated or forced to flee.

The French also cut Algeria off from independent Tunisia and Morocco by erecting barbed-wire fences that were illuminated at night by searchlights. This separated the Algerian resistance bands within the country from some 30,000 armed Algerians who occupied positions between the fortified fences and the actual frontiers of Tunisia and Morocco, from which they drew supplies. These troops had the advantage, however, of a friendly people and sympathetic government as a base; and, though they could not penetrate into Algeria proper, they could harass the French line.

Provoked by these assaults, in February 1958 the French air force bombed the Tunisian frontier village of Sāqiyat Sīdī Yūsuf; a number of civilians were killed, including children from the local school. This led to an Anglo-American mediation mission, which negotiated the withdrawal of French troops from various districts of Tunisia and their sequestration at a naval base in the Tunisian town of Bizerte.

The Maghrib Unity Congress was held at Tangier in April under the auspices of the Moroccan and Tunisian nationalist parties and the Algerian FLN, and it recommended the establishment of an Algerian government-in-exile and a permanent secretariat to promote Maghrib unity. Five months later the FLN formed the Provisional Government of the Algerian Republic (Gouvernement Provisionel de la République Algérienne; GPRA), initially headed by Ferhat Abbas.

By then, however, conditions had been radically changed by events in May 1958; these began as a typical settler uprising—thousands of them attacked the offices of the governor-general and, with the tacit approval of the army officers, called for the integration of Algeria with France and for the return of de Gaulle to power. The following month de Gaulle, in his capacity as prime minister, visited Algiers amid scenes of great enthusiasm. He granted all Muslims the full rights of French citizenship, and on October 30, while in Constantine, he announced a plan to provide adequate schools and medical services for the Algerian population, to create employment for them, and to introduce them into the higher ranks of the public services.

He went even farther the following September when, in anticipation of the opening of the UN General Assembly, he publicly declared that the Algerians had

Algerians waiting to vote on the passing of the French constitution, 1958. Loomis Dean/Time & Life Pictures/Getty Images

the right to determine their own future. The settler population responded by staging a fresh uprising in January 1960, but it collapsed after nine days from lack of military support. A year later, however, as the prospect of negotiations with the GPRA became more probable, there was another uprising, this time organized by four generals, of whom two—Raoul Salan and Maurice Challe—had previously been commanders in chief in Algeria. De Gaulle remained unshaken, and the rising, lacking support from the army, collapsed after only three days.

Negotiations were opened in France with representatives of the GPRA in May 1961. This body had long been recognized by the Arab and communist states, from which it received aid, though it had never been able to establish itself on Algerian soil. Negotiations were broken off in July, after which Abbas was replaced as premier by the much younger Benyoussef Ben Khedda. Settler opposition was meanwhile coalesced around a body calling itself the Secret Army Organization (Organisation de l'Armée Secrète; OAS), which began to employ random acts of terror in an effort to disrupt peace negotiations.

Negotiations resumed the following March, and an agreement was finally reached. Algeria would become independent, provided only that a referendum, to be held in Algeria by a provisional government, confirmed the desire for it. If approved, French aid would continue, and Europeans could depart, remain as foreigners, or take Algerian citizenship. This announcement produced a violent outburst of terrorism, but in May it subsided as it became obvious that such actions were futile.

INDEPENDENT ALGERIA

A referendum held in Algeria in July 1962 recorded some 6,000,000 votes in favour of independence and only 16,000 against. After three days of continuous Algerian rejoicing, the GPRA entered Algiers in triumph as many Europeans prepared to depart.

The human cost of the war remains unknown, particularly on the Algerian side. Some estimates put French military losses at 27,000 killed and civilian losses at 5,000 to 6,000. French sources suggest that casualties among Algerians totaled between 300,000 and 500,000, while Algerian sources claim as many as 1,500,000.

Scores of villages were destroyed; forests were widely damaged; and some 2,000,000 inhabitants were moved to new settlements. The Europeans who left Algeria at the time of independence constituted the great majority of senior administrators and managerial and technical experts, yet many public services remained functional; only some 10,000 French teachers remained, often in isolated posts. With the loss of management on farms and in factories, however, production fell, while unemployment and underemployment reached extreme levels. The mass exodus of the French left the new government with vast abandoned lands. These and the remaining French estates (all French land had been nationalized by 1963) were turned into state farms run by worker committees, which began to produce export crops, notably wine.

From Ben Bella to Boumedienne

Political life was particularly contentious following independence. The leadership of Ben Khedda, the president of the GPRA, was upset by the release from French custody of five GPRA leaders, including Ben Bella. Soon the heads of the provisional government—and, more decisively, the army commanders—split. Houari Boumedienne and his powerful frontier army sided with Ben Bella, who had formed the Political Bureau to challenge the power of the GPRA. Other dominant figures sided with Ben Khedda, while the commanders of the internal guerrillas, who had led the war, opposed all external factions, both military and civilian. Mounting tension and localized military clashes threatened an all-out civil war. The spontaneous demonstrations of a population weary of nearly eight years of war with France interceded between the military factions and saved the country from sliding into more warfare. Through delicate political maneuvering, Ben Bella and the Political Bureau were able to draw up the list of candidates for the National People's Assembly, which was ratified in September 1962 by an overwhelming majority of the electorate. The new assembly asked Ben Bella to form the nation's first government.

With the military support of Boumedienne, Ben Bella asserted his power, fighting a localized armed rebellion led by fellow rebel leader Aït-Ahmed and Colonel Mohand ou el-Hadj in Great Kabylia. Because Ben Bella's personal style of government and his reckless promises of support for revolutionary movements were not conducive to orderly administration, there were also serious divisions within the ruling group. Following vicious political infighting in April 1963, Political Bureau member and FLN secretary-general Khider left the country, taking a large amount of party funds with him. He was assassinated in Madrid several years later. Other dissident leaders were also gradually eliminated, leaving control securely in the hands of Ben Bella and the army commander Boumedienne. Ben Bella's apparent plan to remove Boumedienne and his supporters was foiled in June 1965 when Boumedienne and the army moved first. Ben Bella's erratic political style and poor administrative record made his removal acceptable to Algerians, but the Boumedienne regime began with little popular support.

In the following years Boumedienne moved undramatically but effectively to consolidate his power, with army loyalty remaining the basic element. Efforts to reorganize the FLN met with some success. Boumedienne's cautious and deliberate approach was apparent in constitutional developments as communal elections were held in 1967 and provincial elections in 1969. Elections for the National People's Assembly, however, did not first take place until 1977.

Socialism was pursued diligently under Boumedienne, who launched an agrarian reform in 1971 aimed at breaking up large privately owned farms and redistributing state-held lands to landless peasants organized in cooperatives. The agrarian reform also aimed at grouping peasants in "socialist villages," where they could benefit from modern amenities. The state also exerted complete control over the economy and the country's resources. French petroleum and natural gas interests were nationalized in 1971, and the vast revenues derived from oil sales abroad, especially after the rise in prices in 1973 and thereafter, financed an ambitious industrialization program. Each branch of industry was placed under the control of a state corporation; Société Nationale de Transport et de Commercialisation des Hydrocarbures (Sonatrach), the oil corporation, was the most powerful. Boumedienne's regime hid serious weaknesses, however, notably a one-party system dominated by the FLN that tolerated no dissent.

Bendjedid's Move Toward Democracy

Following Boumedienne's death in December 1978, there was a short period of indecisiveness about who should succeed him. The army and the FLN both supported Colonel Chadli Bendjedid, another former guerrilla officer, who was confirmed as his replacement in a referendum in February 1979.

Government control of the economy loosened under Bendjedid. State corporations were restructured into smaller companies, and private enterprise was promoted through a series of new regulations and financial incentives. Power was decentralized and gradually passed to elected local assemblies. The press received greater freedom, and restrictions on Algerians traveling abroad were also relaxed. The main foundations of the socialist ideology were increasingly challenged, and by the mid-1980s the state-controlled press was even being encouraged to refute the socialist line.

Bendjedid's rule, however, was marked by serious setbacks. The revolution in Iran in 1979 triggered a continued rise in Islamic militancy, which sometimes broke out as rioting, and the war in Afghanistan spurred greater militant mobilization and direct action. In Algeria the breakdown of the socialist system contributed even further to the rise of Islamists. A sharp fall in petroleum prices in the mid-1980s seriously affected the country's financial capabilities and opened questions regarding the petroleum-based industrialization program conducted under Boumedienne. The regime found itself without the resources it had relied on to pay the wages of its labour force. Basic foods became difficult to find, and social needs—housing in particular—could no longer be fulfilled.

Foreign debt rose tremendously in 1988, and riots continued. Unemployment rates exceeded one-fifth; unofficial figures reported much-higher numbers. Agriculture, already crippled by heavy state interference and bureaucracy, was hit by one of the worst droughts in the country's history. Water shortages were frequent and crippled urban life and industry. This was further compounded by high rates of population growth, which created more demand for social services and food. Public resentment rose, as did awareness of the corruption that existed at all levels in the government.

Late in the year, serious riots broke out in Algiers, Annaba, and Oran. Bendjedid, taking advantage of the discontent, moved to liberalize the system and challenge the FLN political monopoly. A new constitution, approved in February 1989, dropped all references to socialism, removed the one-party state, and initiated political plurality. The emergence of a myriad of parties mainly benefited the Islamic Salvation Front (Front Islamique du Salut; FIS). The FIS built on the population's resentment of the incompetence and corruption of the regime and captured clear majorities in the provincial and municipal councils in 1990. Other less-radical Islamic parties never matched the popularity of the FIS.

Civil War: the Islamists Versus the Army

Relations between the Islamists and the army remained strained. The first round of balloting for the National People's Assembly, held in December 1991, produced a striking victory for the FIS, which won 188 seats, just 28 short of a simple majority and 99 short of the two-thirds majority needed to amend the constitution. There seemed little doubt that the FIS would achieve a majority in the second ballot round, scheduled for January 1992. Instead Bendjedid resigned, and the next day the army intervened to cancel the elections. Mohamed Boudiaf, another former *chef historique*, was sworn in as president of a ruling Supreme State Council. Boudiaf, who was assassinated in June in Annaba, was succeeded by Ali Kafi. He presided over a country descending into civil war, where murder had already claimed some 1,000 lives, generally civilians but also journalists and past figures of the regime.

Retired general Liamine Zeroual succeeded Kafi in January 1994, but few improvements occurred, and countless more civilians were slaughtered. Those initially implicated in the violence included illegal Islamic groups such as the Armed Islamic Group (Groupe Islamique Armé; GIA) and the Islamic Salvation Army (Armée Islamique du Salut; AIS), but subsequent evidence indicated that much of the violence had been at the hands of elements within the state's security services. Zeroual attempted to legitimize his position by holding presidential elections in November 1995. The elections were to include candidates from all legalized parties, but several of them boycotted the proceedings. Because the FIS had been banned, the results gave Zeroual more than three-fifths of the vote, followed by Mahfoud Nahnah, the moderate Islamist leader of Ḥamās (not connected with the Palestinian organization of the same name), with about one-fourth. The new prime minister, Ahmed Ouyahia, soon reaffirmed his government's commitment to further privatization and liberalization of the economy.

A referendum was held in November 1996 to amend the 1989 constitution. The new document was approved by a majority of the voters, although claims of manipulation were made by the opposition parties. The main change, however, took place in early 1997 when a new government party, the National Democratic Rally (Rassemblement National et Démocratique; RND), was formed. Benefiting from unlimited government support, including the use of official buildings and funds, the RND quickly gained power. In the June elections for the National People's Assembly, the RND won 156 out of 380 seats, and it continued its success in regional and municipal elections, where it won more than half the seats. In December elections for seats in the Council of the Nation, the new upper chamber, the RND again won the majority.

Abdelaziz Bouteflika, the former foreign minister under Boumedienne, ran for president unopposed in the elections of April 1999, as opposition candidates withdrew after hearing rumours that the elections were rigged. Bouteflika assured the international community that the elections were legitimate and vowed to work with other political parties. Violence ensued, however, and the number of killed, missing, and injured continued to rise. From the mid-1990s several discussions were held between the government and Ḥamās, the FIS, the GIA, and the AIS, among other parties, in order to clear up differences between the groups. In spite of a 1999 peace initiative, at the outset of the 21st century the situation remained unresolved, and violence continued. By that time the civil war, which had begun in 1992, had claimed the lives of some 100,000 civilians and numerous political figures.

In 2004 Bouteflika was reelected by an overwhelming margin; the election was considered by international observers to be generally free from manipulation. The following year Bouteflika put forth the Charter for Peace and National Reconciliation, which was endorsed by referendum in late September. In February 2006 a presidential decree concerning its implementation was approved by the council of ministers. Among those measures were compensation for the families of the "disappeared," an amnesty for state security forces and militias, and restraints on debate and criticism of those forces' conduct during the armed conflict. Islamist groups that surrendered voluntarily would be pardoned, along with those already held or sought—so long as none were implicated in massacres, rapes, or bombings. The measures were opposed not only by victims' families but also by several

Algerian Pres. Abdelaziz Bouteflika, Dec. 3, 2007. French Pres. Nicolas Sarkozy, seen behind Bouteflika, was in Algeria on a three-day trip. Pascal Parrot/Getty Images

international human rights groups, which jointly stated that the provisions denied justice to victims and their families and violated international law. Although a number of militants took the amnesty as an opportunity to resign their weapons, it was estimated that some 800 militants remained in operation following its expiration in late August. In spite of a general decline in the level of conflict, periodic violence continued.

In November 2008 the Algerian parliament approved a constitutional amendment abolishing presidential term limits. The arrangement permitted Bouteflika the opportunity to run for his third consecutive term, which he easily won in April 2009.

FOREIGN RELATIONS

Since independence Algeria's foreign policy has been revolutionary in word but pragmatic in deed. The country was a haven for Third World guerrilla and revolutionary movements in its early years, and, while some militancy persists, Bendjedid and subsequent leaders have moved away from that stance. Throughout the 1960s and '70s Algeria supported North Vietnam, and from 1975 it supported Vietnam, decolonization in Africa, and the abolition of apartheid in South Africa. The question of Palestine remained a central preoccupation, equal after 1975 with the Western Sahara issue. Yet, while Algeria continued to support the Palestine Liberation Organization, it also took a decisive role in mediating the release of U.S. hostages in Iran in 1981. Throughout the Cold War, Algeria sought to play the leading role in establishing a Third World alternative that was not aligned to the Eastern or Western bloc. The country also tried to obtain high prices for its petroleum within the Organization of Petroleum Exporting Countries, which it joined in 1969, but more often found itself at odds with other members.

Relations with neighbouring Morocco have often been strained. A short border war that broke out in the fall of 1963 (the area in dispute being rich in deposits of iron ore) was resolved through the intervention of the Organization of African Unity. A rapprochement achieved in 1969–70 broke down over Morocco's efforts to absorb Western Sahara (formerly Spanish Sahara), as Algeria supported the Popular Front for the Liberation of Saguia el-Hamra and Río de Oro (Polisario) in resisting Morocco. The strained relations, which kept the two countries on the brink of an all-out war, were connected in part to the somewhat revolutionary leanings of Boumedienne and his antipathy for the Moroccan monarchy. Support for the Polisario continued under Bendjedid, but problems between the two countries gradually eased. Bendjedid and King Hassan II of Morocco met to discuss a possible resolution for the Western Sahara issue in May 1987, and diplomatic relations were restored the following year. Friction reemerged, however, notably in 1993 when Hassan stated that it would have been better if the FIS had been allowed to gain power in Algeria. Tensions over the Western Sahara intensified in the mid-1990s and remained an unresolved issue at the start of the 21st century.

The Arab Maghrib Union (AMU), established in 1989, not only improved relations among the Maghrib states—Algeria, Libya, Mauritania, Morocco, and Tunisia—but also underscored the need for concerted policies. The AMU sought to bring the countries closer together by creating projects of shared interests. Initially there was some sense of enthusiasm regarding a project that included road and railway networks between these states. Tensions between member states, however, have substantially increased, and shared interest in carrying out joint projects has faltered.

Relations with France have frequently been contentious. Disputes developed soon after independence over the Algerian expropriation of abandoned French property (1963) and its nationalization of French petroleum interests (1971). There were also problems with the Algerian migrants living and working in France, who consistently remained at the bottom of the economic scale and were subject to ethnic prejudice. After Algerian independence France banned the importation of Algerian wine, deeming it competitive with its own production. In response Boumedienne uprooted and removed grapevines on large stretches of land. Throughout the 1980s the renegotiation of natural gas prices constituted another source of disagreement between the two countries, although Algeria obtained some concessions. In the 1990s the volatile political situation and violence in Algeria greatly affected the French, who suffered more casualties than any other nationality in the country. This terror reached Paris in the mid-1990s when Algerians set off a number of bombs in the city. Economic ties, however, have remained basically intact and include reciprocal investment agreements. Trade between Algeria and other Western and Southeast Asian countries has grown substantially and has reduced France's importance as a trading partner.

As the role of the European Union (EU) widens, so does the link between Algeria and the member states in that organization. The Barcelona Conference initiative in November 1995 established a Euro-Mediterranean partnership, bringing together the EU and the countries bordering the Mediterranean in North Africa (excluding Libya). The partnership sought to achieve political stability in the region, create a zone of shared prosperity through economic and financial cooperation, and establish a free-trade zone early in the 21st century. There have also been specific European financial efforts directed toward Algeria to fund industrial restructuring and privatization.

Algeria initially was reluctant to accept the intervention of the UN in 1997 to help deal with the civilian massacres. But eventually a high-level UN delegation was sent to Algeria in July 1998 to meet with various parties in an effort to put a halt to the violence, which had declined enough by mid-2000 that Algeria's borders with Tunisia and Morocco could be reopened.

CHAPTER 6

Egypt

Egypt is located in northeastern Africa and has coastlines along both the Mediterranean and Red seas. The modern-day country became independent in 1952. The capital is Cairo.

Egypt is one of the world's oldest continuous civilizations. Its vast and varied history, spanning many millennia, cannot be satisfactorily treated within the context of a regional survey. The coverage of Egypt's history below is primarily focused on the events of the 20th and 21st centuries.

EARLY HISTORY THROUGH THE 19TH CENTURY

Sometime about 2925 BCE, Upper and Lower Egypt were united. This unification ushered in an efflorescence of cultural achievement and began an almost unbroken line of native rulers lasting nearly 3,000 years. Historians divide the ancient history of Egypt into Old, Middle, and New kingdoms, spanning some 30 dynasties and lasting to 332 BCE.

An Assyrian invasion occurred in the 7th century BCE, and the Persian Cambyses II established the Achaemenid dynasty in 525 BCE. The invasion by Alexander the Great in 332 BCE inaugurated the Macedonian and Ptolemaic period, during which the rulers of Egypt remained firmly planted in the Hellenic world. The city of Alexandria, founded by Alexander, developed into a centre not only of Hellenism but of Semitic learning as well, and was soon a focal point of the highest developments of Greek scholarship and science.

The Roman Empire held Egypt from 30 BCE to 395 CE; after the latter date it was administratively placed under the control of the East Roman (later, Byzantine) Empire. The granting of tolerance to the Christians by the emperor Constantine the Great in the early 4th century CE gave impetus to the development of a formal Egyptian church. Alexandria was the scene of the labours of such early Christian figures as Arius, Athanasius, Origen, and Clement.

The Byzantine Empire's control of Egypt came to an end in 642, when Byzantine forces evacuated Egypt after three years' armed conflict with invading Arabs. After hundreds of years, Egypt was transformed into an Arabic-speaking state, with Islam as the dominant religion. Egypt was part of the Umayyad and 'Abbāsid caliphates. It later became the centre of the Fāṭimid caliphate and achieved a significant degree of independence and importance. In 1171 it was returned to the 'Abbāsids. The Mamlūks, who were slaves of non-Arab and non-Muslim origin used to augment the armies of the Arab world, killed the 'Abbāsid sultan in 1250. This and the collapse of the 'Abbāsid caliphate in 1258 brought the Mamlūks into ascendancy. They established a dynasty in Egypt that lasted until 1517 and made Egypt the centre of the eastern Arabic-speaking zone of the Muslim world.

In 1517 Egypt fell to the Ottoman Empire, and the country reverted to the status of a province governed from Constantinople (present-day Istanbul). The economic decline that began under the late Mamlūks continued, and with it came a decline in Egyptian culture.

A French invasion in 1798 lasted only a few years but brought Egypt into the world of European politics. After the departure of the French, the government eventually passed into the hands of Muḥammad 'Alī, possibly an Albanian, who created a dynasty and an empire nominally under Ottoman control. His accumulation of wealth and his expansionist policies and those of his successors left Egypt in debt, and the British occupied the country in 1882 during a period of civil unrest. The next year Britain sent Sir Evelyn Baring (known as Lord Cromer from 1892) to Egypt to serve as the British agent and consul general.

BRITISH OCCUPATION

Initial resistance to Britain's occupation was minimized under the administration of Tawfīq, who was indebted to the British for supporting him in his position as Egypt's khedive (title for one serving as viceroy of the sultan of the Ottoman Empire). This changed in 1892 with the death of Tawfīq and the accession of his 17-year-old son, 'Abbās II (Ḥilmī). The new khedive was not interested in Cromer's tutelage, and Cromer resented the young khedive's attempts to play a serious role in Egyptian politics. In January 1893 ʿAbbās dismissed Prime Minister Muṣṭafā Fahmī, one of Cromer's allies, and tried to appoint his own nominee. With the backing of the British government, Cromer interfered with the young khedive's endeavours, and Fahmī eventually returned to office. ʿAbbās provoked another crisis in January 1894 by publicly criticizing British military officers, especially the sirdar (commander in chief), Horatio Herbert Kitchener. Again, Cromer intervened and forced ʿAbbās to make a public apology.

ʿAbbās's behaviour in the early years of his reign was indicative of the emergence of a new generation who had been children when the British occupation began. Another member of this generation, Muṣṭafā Kāmil, studied in France and had come into contact with a group of writers and politicians opposed to the occupation. When Muṣṭafā Kāmil returned to Egypt in 1894, he reached an understanding with ʿAbbās on the basis of their common opposition to the British occupation. Muṣṭafā Kāmil utilized his speeches and writings in an attempt to create an Egyptian patriotism focused on the khedive. The drive for nationalism was furthered by the campaigns for the reconquest of the Sudan (1896–98) and by the 1899 Anglo-Egyptian Condominium Agreements, which nominally gave Egypt and Britain joint responsibility for the administration of the reconquered territory but in effect made the Sudan a British possession.

During the reconquest of the Sudan, the 1898 confrontation of British and French at Fashoda on the White Nile (section of the Nile between Malakāl and Khartoum) led to the 1904 reconciliation of the two powers with the Entente Cordiale. As a result of the agreement, Britain was allowed a free hand in Egypt. This disappointed Muṣṭafā Kāmil and weakened his alliance with ʿAbbās, who became more willing to cooperate with Cromer. Muṣṭafā Kāmil's attention then shifted to the Ottoman sultan Abdülhamid. When a dispute arose in 1906 between the Ottomans and Britain over the Sinai Peninsula, Muṣṭafā Kāmil attempted to muster Egyptian nationalist opinion in favour of the sultan, but he was accused by some Egyptians of favouring Islamic unity at the expense of Egyptian national interest.

Although British domination in Egypt seemed secure, there were some hidden weaknesses. Cromer was out of touch with the new generation of Egyptians and had little sympathy for them. The occupation had become to all intents and purposes permanent. Educated Egyptians, who sought government posts for themselves and their sons, were frustrated by the growth of the British establishment in Egypt. The British, however, had a different view of their occupation, seeing themselves as the benefactors of the Egyptian peasantry. This view was soon contradicted by what became known as the Dinshawāy Incident; in June 1906 a confrontation between villagers at

Dinshawāy and a party of British officers out pigeon shooting resulted in the death of a British officer. Harsh exemplary punishments dealt to a number of villagers in the wake of the incident sparked an outcry among many Egyptians. Muṣṭafā Kāmil used the incident to help galvanize Egyptian nationalist sentiment against British occupation, and Cromer retired in May 1907.

Cromer was succeeded by Sir Eldon Gorst. Although Gorst had served in Egypt from 1886 to 1904, he brought a new outlook on the role of the British in Egypt. He reached an understanding with ʿAbbās and sought to lessen the burgeoning power of the British establishment while also providing a greater opportunity to Egyptian political institutions for more effective authority. Gorst, however, attained only limited success, hindered by the fact that his policies not only failed to satisfy the Egyptian nationalists but were also resented by many British officials. In 1910 a project to extend the Suez Canal Company's 99-year concession by

Lithograph, by A. H. Zaki depicting ʿAbbās Ḥilmī II, the last khedive (viceroy) of Egypt, visiting Medina, Saudi Arabia, c. 1910. Library of Congress Prints and Photographs Division

40 years was thrown out by the General Assembly (Egypt's quasi-parliamentary body), while Buṭrus Ghālī, the successor to prime minister Muṣṭafā Fahmī and a supporter of extending the concession, was assassinated a few days later by a nationalist. These events spurred Gorst to move away from his previously conciliatory policies towards Egypt's nationalists and pursue those of a harsher nature.

Gorst died in 1911 and was succeeded by Lord Kitchener, signifying the end of what had largely been a harmonious relationship between the positions of the British consul general and khedive. Kitchener was autocratic but not entirely conservative, and although he certainly attempted to limit the power and influence of ʿAbbās, Kitchener's actions also served the interests of the moderate Egyptians who were not aligned with the more extremist faction of nationalists. A new and more powerful Legislative Assembly was created in 1913; it would prove to provide a training ground for the nationalist leaders in the years to come.

In November 1914, shortly after the outbreak of World War I, Britain declared war on the Ottoman Empire. The next month, Britain proclaimed a protectorate over Egypt and deposed ʿAbbās; his uncle, Ḥusayn Kāmil, was given the title of sultan and appointed to take his place. Kitchener was succeeded by Sir Henry McMahon, and he by Sir Reginald Wingate, both with the title of high commissioner. During the war, the declaration of martial law and the suspension of the Legislative Assembly served to temporarily silence the voices of the nationalists. Ḥusayn Kāmil died in October 1917 and was succeeded by his brother, Aḥmad Fu'ād.

In late 1918, shortly after the end of the war, Saʿd Zaghlūl and other Egyptian politicians met with Wingate and demanded autonomy for Egypt. Zaghlūl announced his intention of leading his delegation to state his case in England, but the British government refused to meet with him. The refusal—and Zaghlūl's subsequent arrest—generated widespread revolt in Egypt. To quell the discontent, Sir Edmund Henry Hynman Allenby (later Lord Allenby) was dispatched to Egypt as special high commissioner. In the hopes of reaching a compromise, Allenby insisted on concessions to the nationalists. Zaghlūl was released and later led his delegation to the Paris Peace Conference (1919–20), but the group was denied a hearing there to plead its case for Egypt's independence. Meanwhile, Zaghlūl's delegation, known as the Wafd, had become the basis for a countrywide pro-nationalist organization that was active in Egypt's political scene. Allenby grew alarmed by Zaghlūl's popularity and the agitation he and the Wafd had released in the country. Hoping to establish a group of pro-British politicians in Egypt, Allenby persuaded the British government to promise Egyptian independence without previously securing British interests by a treaty.

Thus, on Feb. 28, 1922, independence was declared. The protectorate was replaced by the Kingdom of Egypt.

There were some caveats to the declaration of independence, however. Pending negotiations, four issues were left to the discretion of the British government: the security of imperial communications, defense, the protection of foreign interests and of minorities, and the Sudan. The next month, Sultan Aḥmad Fu'ād became King Fu'ād I of Egypt.

CONSTITUTIONAL MONARCHY

The new kingdom took the form of a constitutional monarchy, and a constitution, promulgated in April 1923, defined the king's executive powers and established a bicameral legislature. An electoral law provided for universal male suffrage and the indirect election of deputies to the Assembly; the Senate was half elected and half appointed. Despite the declaration of independence, establishment of a constitutional monarchy, and the appearances of constitutionalism, a political struggle was continually waged among the king, the Wafd, and the British.

Fu'ād did not enjoy widespread popularity and thus did not feel secure in his position. He was therefore prepared to negotiate with either the nationalists or with the British in an effort to secure his position and powers. The Wafd, on the other hand, appeared to be quite secure in its position; it was Egypt's only truly national party and had a mass following, an elaborate organization, and a charismatic leader in Zaghlūl. Ideologically, the party advocated against British domination and for true national independence; it also advocated for a constitutional government against royal autocracy. In practice, however, Wafd leaders were prepared to make deals with either the British or the king to obtain or retain power. The British government was intent on guarding imperial interests, especially the control of the Suez Canal. The resulting need for a treaty to guarantee these interests saw Britain appeasing nationalist sentiment by supporting the Wafd against the king on more than one occasion.

In January 1924 the Wafd won a majority in the first general election, and Zaghlūl became prime minister. His brief tenure was marked by unsuccessful treaty discussions with the British, tension with the king, and his inability to control the violent agitation he and the Wafd had set in motion. In November 1924, after a year in which numerous British officials and Egyptian "collaborationists" had been murdered by nationalist extremists, the British sirdar (commander in chief) of the Egyptian army was assassinated. Allenby immediately presented Zaghlūl with an ultimatum that caused him to resign. The shock resulting from the violent British reaction rallied the moderates and discouraged the extremists. The general election of March 1925 left the Wafd still the strongest party, but the parliament no sooner met than it was dissolved, and for more than a year Egypt was governed by decree. In a third general election, held in May 1926, the Wafd still held the allegiance of the country. But Zaghlūl, an old man of nearly 70, was no longer eager for office and the British opposed his return to the premiership. Under pressure from Lord Lloyd, the new British high commissioner, he agreed to the formation of a coalition government. The premiership went instead to ʿAdlī Yakan of the Liberal Constitutionalist party (a splinter group of the Wafd), while Zaghlūl held the presidency of the Chamber of Deputies until his death in 1927. In this capacity he succeeded, by and large, in controlling the actions of his more extreme followers.

Once again, the relationship between the parliament and the king grew strained, and ʿAdlī resigned in April 1927. He was succeeded by another Liberal Constitutionalist, ʿAbd al-Khāliq Tharwat (Sarwat) Pasha. Tharwat managed to negotiate a draft treaty with the British, but it failed to win the approval of the Wafd; he resigned in March 1928. Muṣṭafā al-Naḥḥās Pasha, Zaghlūl's successor as head of the Wafd, then became prime minister, but he did not remain in that position for long, as Fu'ād dismissed him in June. He was succeeded by Muḥammad Maḥmūd Pasha, yet another Liberal Constitutionalist. When Fu'ād dissolved the parliament in July, his actions, in effect, meant that the constitution was suspended, and once again Egypt was governed by decree.

The issue of draft treaty proposals with the British were again in the forefront of the political scene. Although some were agreed upon in June 1929, Maḥmūd could not overcome Wafdist opposition to the proposals. Britain then pressed for a return to constitutional government, hoping that a freely elected parliament would approve them. In December 1929 the fourth general election was held. The Wafd won a majority, and once again, al-Naḥḥās became premier. Treaty negotiations, which by then had resumed, collapsed over the issue of the Sudan, from which the Egyptians had been virtually excluded since 1924. Al-Naḥḥās also clashed with Fu'ād and resigned in June 1930 after differences with the king over limitation of the sovereign's power. Fu'ād appointed Ismāʿīl Ṣidqī Pasha to the premiership, who ruled with an iron hand to curb the Wafd's influence. The 1923 constitution was replaced by one that was promulgated by royal decree. This, with its accompanying electoral law, strengthened the king's power. The 1931 elections, which were boycotted by the Wafd, yielded a cooperative non-Wafdist parliament. Fu'ād dismissed Ṣidqī in September 1933, and for the next two years palace-appointed governments ruled Egypt.

The king's period of domestic political tranquility eventually came to an end as Fu'ād, who was in failing health, could not withstand the internal pressure of the Wafd. Nor could he withstand the pressure of the British, who, over time, had come to see the benefits of negotiating the treaty with Egypt specifically through the popular Wafd and thus desired to do so. In late 1935 the constitution of 1923 was restored. Fu'ād died in April 1936 and was succeeded by his teenaged son Fārūq I.

A general election in May 1936 gave the Wafd a majority once more, and al-Naḥḥās became prime minister for the third time. One of his first duties was to head the Egyptian delegation to London to negotiate the long-awaited treaty between the two countries. Agreement was quickly reached with Britain, and the Anglo-Egyptian Treaty was signed in August 1936. The treaty officially ended the British occupation of Egypt and established a 20-year military alliance between the two countries. The next year Egypt became a member of the League of Nations.

In July 1937 the young king Fārūq came of age and assumed his full royal powers. Fārūq, who was popular and ambitious, soon disagreed with al-Naḥḥās over limitations on the powers of the king and, significantly, over international policies; he dismissed al-Naḥḥās in December 1937. Meanwhile, a split had developed in the Wafd: Maḥmūd Fahmī al-Nuqrāshī Pasha and Aḥmad Māhir Pasha were expelled and formed the Saʿdist Party. Discord was becoming more widespread as the Wafdist youth movement, known as the Blueshirts, fought with the Greenshirts of Young Egypt, an ultranationalist organization. By the time of the next general election, in April 1938, support for the Wafd had diminished, and they won only 12 seats.

World War II (1939–45) brought even more changes to Egypt's political landscape. At the onset of the war, with the declining support for the Wafd, al-Naḥḥās was driven to cooperation with the British, an action that would later bring him to power once again. During the war Egypt provided facilities for the British war effort in accordance with the Anglo-Egyptian Treaty, but few Egyptians truly supported Britain and many expected its defeat. The British were eager for a more cooperative government in Egypt and in 1940 brought pressure on the king to replace his prime minister, ʿAlī Māhir. A second British intervention occurred in February 1942 after German forces threatened to invade Egypt. The British ambassador, armed with an ultimatum and backed by a show of military force, confronted Fārūq with the choice of either abdicating or appointing the now-cooperative al-Naḥḥās prime minister. Fārūq chose the latter; elections in March of that year gave the Wafd an overwhelming victory. With al-Naḥḥās and the Wafd in power, Britain now had the more cooperative Egyptian government it desired. Nevertheless, Britain's February intervention had negative consequences for both Britain and the Wafd; it confirmed Fārūq's hostility to both the British and al-Naḥḥās, and it called into question the Wafd's claim that Egyptian nationalism was its primary focus. The Wafd was further weakened by internal rivalries and allegations of corruption. After the British later withdrew their support of al-Naḥḥās, Fārūq again dismissed him in October 1944. His successor, Aḥmad Māhir of the Saʿdist Party, was acceptable to the British, but he was assassinated in February 1945. He was succeeded by his fellow Saʿdist, al-Nuqrāshī.

Politically, Egypt was in shambles by the end of World War II. The Wafd was in a period of decline and its political opponents, taking advantage of this situation, took up the nationalist demand for a revision of the Anglo-Egyptian Treaty of 1936. Of particular concern were the issues of the complete evacuation of British troops from Egypt and the ending of British control in the Sudan. As the Wafd's political opponents gathered steam, political activity took on a more radical nature—particularly that of the Muslim Brotherhood. Originally a mainstream Islamic reformist movement, it developed into a militant mass organization that held protests in opposition to the Wafd and the government. Demonstrations in Cairo became increasingly frequent and violent. In the face of this domestic pressure, the Egyptian government found itself unable to settle its foreign affairs. Negotiations with Britain regarding Anglo-Egyptian Treaty revisions collapsed over the British refusal to rule out eventual independence for the Sudan. In July 1947, Egypt referred the dispute to the United Nations (UN) but was unsuccessful in winning its case.

In general, neither the Egyptian public nor the politicians had shown much interest in Arab affairs until after World War I. At that point, Egypt became involved in the issue of Palestine, choosing to support the Arab position that opposed the creation of a Jewish state there. In 1943–44 Egypt was one of the lead players in the establishment of the Arab League, a regional organization of Arab states in the Middle East, and Egypt became increasingly committed to the Arab cause in Palestine after World War II. However, when Egypt experienced an unexpected and crushing defeat in the first Arab-Israeli war (1948–49)—launched with fellow Arab League members Syria, Iraq, and Jordan in response to the May 1948 declaration of the State of Israel—many Egyptians were disillusioned. Political instability increased, and the Muslim Brotherhood expanded its violent activities. Al-Nuqrāshī, once again serving as prime minister (and later as military governor of Egypt, following the proclamation of a state of siege after Egypt's unsuccessful incursion into Palestine), tried to outlaw the organization and was assassinated in December 1948. Two months later, Ḥasan al-Bannā', the Muslim Brotherhood's leader, was murdered.

General elections held in January 1950 were won by the Wafd, and once again, al-Naḥḥās was prime minister. Failing to reach agreement with Britain, in October 1951 he unilaterally abrogated both the Anglo-Egyptian Treaty of 1936 and the Condominium Agreement of 1899; he then declared Fārūq king of Egypt and the Sudan. Anti-British demonstrations occurred and were followed by guerrilla warfare against Britain's garrison in the canal zone. British reprisals in Ismailia led to popular protests and the burning of Cairo on Jan. 26, 1952, which became known as Black Saturday. Fārūq dismissed al-Naḥḥās the next day, and there were four prime ministers in the ensuing six months.

By this time, popular opposition to the corruption and policies of both Fārūq and the Wafd had grown. In addition, Egyptian nationalism had suffered from the shattering defeat in the Arab-Israeli war and from the failure to terminate British military occupation of Egypt. The military defeat especially enraged many Egyptian army officers, who saw Fārūq's corruption and incompetence as being largely the cause of it. His activities became intolerable to them, and a group of military conspirators known as the Free Officers, led by Col. Gamal Abdel Nasser, overthrew Fārūq's regime on July 23, 1952, and forced him to abdicate.

The Republic

Egypt was taken over by a Revolutionary Command Council of 11 officers controlled by Nasser, with Maj. Gen. Muḥammad Naguib as the puppet head of state. In June 1953, Egypt became a republic, and Naguib became president. For more than a year Nasser kept his real role so well hidden that astute foreign correspondents were unaware of his existence. It came to light, however, when the relationship between Nasser and Naguib unraveled in February–April 1954. Naguib, who had the support of the small middle class, the former political parties (which had been banned), and the Muslim Brotherhood, wanted to see a speedy return to constitutional government and objected to some of the actions of other Free Officers. In February 1954 he resigned the presidency, but demands by civilian and military groups impelled him to resume the office. Nasser, however, had steadily consolidated his own position; to supplement his power base in the military forces, Nasser drew on the police and on working-class support mobilized by some of the trade unions. In a complicated series of intrigues, Naguib was deposed and placed under house arrest, and Nasser emerged from the shadows and named himself prime minister.

The First Decades

After seizing power, Nasser took a moderate stance towards some of Egypt's key foreign policy challenges of the time. An agreement signed in February 1953 established a transitional period of self-government for the Sudan, which became an independent republic in January 1956. A series of negotiations with the British culminated in the 1954 Anglo-Egyptian Agreement, under which British troops were to be evacuated gradually from the canal zone. A third foreign policy challenge—the question of Israel—was somewhat more complicated. In retrospect, it seems clear that Nasser was a reluctant champion of the Arab struggle against Israel. Egypt found itself drawn into renewed conflict with Israel, however, owing to a dangerous pattern of violent interactions. Small groups of Palestinian raiders, including some operating from Egyptian-controlled Gaza, were infiltrating Israel's borders. In response, the Israeli government began its policy of large-scale retaliation in early 1955. One of the consequences of this action was that it made clear Egypt's need to purchase more arms. After failing in his attempts to buy weapons from Western countries, Nasser announced in September 1955 that an arms agreement had been signed with Czechoslovakia. That country was actually acting for the Soviet Union, which used the deal to establish itself as a force in the region.

Nasser's relationship with Western countries further eroded when the United States and Britain withheld funds they had previously promised Egypt for the construction of the Aswān High Dam. In response, Nasser announced the nationalization of the Suez Canal Company in July 1956, promising that the tolls Egypt collected in five years would build the dam. Nasser's actions angered Britain and France, the major shareholders in the company, and they plotted to regain control of the canal by collaborating with Israel. That country, which continued to suffer raids by Egyptian-supported guerrillas, attacked Egypt in October. Britain and France then reoccupied the canal zone under the pretense of enforcing a UN peace resolution. The United States and the Soviet Union put pressure on the invading powers, however, and the Suez Crisis was soon ended. Although Nasser suffered military losses, he was left holding control of the canal. The situation with Israel remained tense, however, and in 1957 Egypt agreed to the placement of a UN Emergency Force (UNEF) in the Sinai Peninsula to act as a buffer between Egyptian and Israeli forces.

Domestically, Egypt saw many changes and developments during this time. In October 1954, Nasser was the target of an assassination attempt at a mass meeting in Alexandria. When the gunman confessed that he had been given the assignment by the Muslim Brotherhood, Nasser cracked down on the organization. A number of its members were executed and hundreds were imprisoned under brutal conditions.

In January 1956, Nasser announced the promulgation of a constitution under which Egypt became a socialist Arab state with a one-party political system and with Islam as the official religion. In June, 99.948 percent of the five million Egyptians voting marked their ballots for Nasser, the only candidate, for president. The constitution was approved by 99.8 percent.

Perhaps the most dramatic development was the union with Syria, which combined with Egypt in 1958 to form the United Arab Republic (U.A.R.). The new republic proved to be short-lived, however, as Egyptian dominance of the union antagonized many Syrians, and it was dissolved in September 1961 (Egypt retained the name United Arab Republic until 1971). The dissolution of the union left the parties involved with feelings of resentment. Nasser blamed the secession on Syrian reactionaries, and in direct response he moved Egypt's government further to the left. The next year, Egypt embraced a policy of scientific socialism, and most large manufacturing firms, banks, transport services, and insurance companies were nationalized or sequestered.

Under Nasser, Egypt made some dramatic domestic gains. In 1950 manufacturing contributed 10 percent to the total national output; by 1970 that figure had doubled. However, agricultural achievements were lacking and were further undercut by Egypt's rapid population growth.

Egypt was able to enjoy a precarious peace on the Sinai border with Israel, owing to the presence of the UNEF stationed on the Egyptian side. Still, the potential military danger from Israel was constantly on the minds of Nasser and other Egyptian government leaders. They attempted to fortify their ties with the Soviet bloc and tried to promote cooperation among the Arab states, even though such attempts usually failed. In order to preserve his standing in the Arab world, Nasser used a militant rhetoric of confrontation to mask essential Egyptian moderation on the Israeli issue. However, a series of events would influence Nasser to abandon his policy of "militant inaction" toward Israel.

In 1962–67, Egyptian troops supported the Republican Army in Yemen's civil war. Nasser's government soon found itself at odds with Saudi Arabia, which supported the Yemeni royalists, and with the United States, which backed the Saudis. As a result, U.S. aid to Egypt was cut off in 1966. Meanwhile, Palestinian incursions against Israel were launched with greater frequency and intensity from bases in Jordan, Lebanon, and, especially, Syria. When Israel retaliated in late 1966, Arab sentiment was inflamed. Nasser was openly taunted for hiding behind the UNEF, so in June 1967 he requested that the United Nations remove its peacekeeping troops from the Sinai border. When UNEF troops were also removed from Sharm al-Shaykh, at the head of the Gulf of Aqaba, Egyptian troops closed the gulf to Israeli shipping. Israel had made it clear that blockading the gulf would be a cause for war, and on June 5, 1967, it launched what it called a preemptive attack on Egypt, Jordan, and Syria. The ensuing conflict came to be known as the Six-Day (or June) War.

Israel delivered a crushing blow to Egypt and the other countries. The Egyptian air force was destroyed on the ground in the early hours of the war and the Egyptian army was forced to retreat from the Sinai Peninsula across the Suez Canal, leaving the peninsula under Israeli control. An estimated 10,000 Egyptians died during the conflict. In the wake of the humiliating defeat, Nasser attempted to resign, but massive street demonstrations and a vote of confidence by the National Assembly induced him to remain in office. Egypt rearmed rapidly with the help of the Soviet Union, which immediately began replacing all the destroyed war equipment and installed surface-to-air missiles along the Suez Canal as a cover for Egypt's artillery emplacements. A low-level conflict with Israel, which came to be known as the War of Attrition, soon began along the Suez Canal. Nasser had tentatively accepted a U.S. plan leading to peace negotiations with Israel when he died, in 1970, from a heart attack.

The Republic in the 1970s and '80s

Nasser was succeeded by the vice president and fellow Free Officer Anwar el-Sādāt. Although initially perceived as an interim leader, Sādāt quickly displayed a knack for political survival. In May 1971 he outmaneuvered a formidable combination of rivals for power, calling his victory the "Corrective Revolution." Sādāt began to chart a different course for the country, although it continued in the direction Nasser had begun to move towards prior to his death.

Sādāt made dramatic moves in the area of foreign affairs. Feeling that the Soviet Union gave him inadequate support in Egypt's continuing confrontation with Israel, he expelled thousands of Soviet technicians and advisers from the country in 1972. In addition, Egyptian

Anwar el-Sādāt (left), Menachem Begin (right), and Jimmy Carter at Camp David. 1978. Karl Schumacher—AFP/Getty Images

peace overtures toward Israel were initiated early in Sādāt's presidency, when he made known his willingness to reach a peaceful settlement if Israel returned the Sinai Peninsula. Following the failure of this initiative, Egypt launched a military attack in coordination with Syria to retake the territory, sparking the October (Yom Kippur) War of 1973. The Egyptian army achieved a tactical surprise in its attack on the Israeli-held territory, although Israel successfully counterattacked. A cease-fire was secured by the United States.

Sādāt firmly believed that making peace with Israel was in Egypt's best interest. Although Egypt did not win the war in any military sense, the initial successes in October 1973 did allow Sādāt to claim Egyptian victory and seek an honourable peace. In the following years Sādāt—despite the misgivings of his Syrian allies—actively engaged in negotiations with Israel, signing the Sinai I (1974) and Sinai II (1975) disengagement agreements that returned the western Sinai and secured large foreign assistance commitments to Egypt. When additional negotiations were stalled by both Israeli inflexibility and Arab resistance, Sādāt took an unprecedented trip to Jerusalem on Nov. 19, 1977, to address the Israeli Knesset (parliament). This action initiated a series of diplomatic efforts that Sādāt continued despite strong opposition from most of the Arab world and the Soviet Union. U.S. Pres. Jimmy Carter mediated the negotiations between Sādāt and Israeli Prime Minister Menachem Begin that resulted in the Camp David Accords (Sept. 17, 1978), a preliminary peace agreement between Egypt and Israel. Sādāt and Begin were awarded the Nobel Prize for Peace in 1978, and their continued political negotiations resulted in the signing on March 26, 1979, of a treaty of peace between Egypt and Israel—the first between the latter and any Arab country. The treaty called for Israel to withdraw its armed forces and civilians from Sinai Peninsula within three years; it also provided for the establishment of special security arrangements on the peninsula and the creation of a buffer zone along the Sinai-Israel border to be patrolled by UN peacekeeping forces. Treaty provisions also included the normalization of economic and cultural relations between the two countries, including the exchange of ambassadors. Making peace with Israel proved to have negative consequences, though; Egypt lost the financial support of the Arab states and was expelled from the Arab League shortly after signing the peace treaty. Its membership was not reinstated until 1989.

Sādāt linked his peace initiative to the task of economic reconstruction, and proclaimed an open-door policy (Arabic: *infitāḥ*). It was one of his most important domestic initiatives, although in hindsight it proved to largely be a disappointment to the Egyptian population. The *infitāḥ* program called for dramatic economic change that included decentralization and diversification of the economy as well as efforts to attract trade and foreign investment, as Sādāt hoped that a liberalized Egyptian economy would be revitalized by the inflow of both Western and Arab capital. Like his peace initiative, Sādāt's efforts to liberalize the economy also came at some cost, including high inflation and an uneven distribution of wealth, deepening inequality, and eventual discontent. The peace process did, however, bring some economic relief, notably a vast U.S. aid program that began in 1975 and exceeded $1 billion annually by 1981.

Meanwhile, a new constitution promulgated in 1971 had notably improved the ability of individual citizens to participate in the political process, and laws permitting the creation of political parties were instituted by 1976. But the moves towards democratization could not alleviate the dissatisfaction generated by the economic hardships experienced by many in the country, and demonstrations broke out in Egypt's major cities on Jan. 18–19, 1977. Nearly 100 people were killed, and several thousand were either injured or jailed.

The 1970s also saw signs of increasing Muslim extremism in Egypt. Under Nasser, the Muslim Brotherhood had been firmly suppressed. Under Sādāt, however, groups of Muslim activists were allowed to proselytize, and members of the Muslim Brotherhood were released from prison and allowed to operate with few restrictions. There was a growing rise in religious violence during this time, particularly directed against the country's Coptic community but also against the government. The group al-Takfīr wa al-Hijrah (roughly, "Identification of Unbelief and Flight from Evil") engaged in several terrorist attacks during the decade, and other groups, such as the Islamic Jihad (al-Jihād al-Islāmī) and the Islamic Group (al-Jamāʿah al-Islāmiyah), were formed with the goal of overthrowing Egypt's secular government.

By the early 1980s, Sādāt's popularity had fallen dramatically in Egypt because of internal opposition to the treaty, the worsening economic crisis, and Sādāt's suppression of the resulting public dissent. In September 1981 he ordered a massive police strike against his opponents, jailing more than 1,500 people from across the political spectrum. The following month, Sādāt was assassinated by militant soldiers associated with Islamic Jihad during the Armed Forces Day military parade commemorating the Yom Kippur War.

THE REPUBLIC SINCE THE 1980S

Reaction in Egypt to Sādāt's assassination included uprisings in some areas but mostly consisted of a deafening calm. He was succeeded by Hosnī (Ḥusnī) Mubārak, an air force general and hero of the Yom Kippur War who had worked closely with Sādāt since 1973.

Mubārak struck a moderate tone during his first year as president. On the foreign policy front, he continued to cultivate good relations with the United States, which remained Egypt's principal aid donor. Mubārak also did not back

Hosnī Mubārak, 1982. Barry Iverson/Gamma

away from the peace with Israel, and the Sinai Peninsula was returned to Egyptian sovereignty in April 1982 per the terms of the 1979 treaty. Relations with Israel soon cooled, however, after that country invaded Lebanon in June 1982 and did not improve until Israel initiated its partial withdrawal from Lebanon in 1985.

Mubārak's policies were cautious and enabled Egypt to repair its relationships with most of the moderate Arab states, and an Arab League summit in 1987 authorized each country's government to restore diplomatic relations with Egypt as it saw fit. Two years later, Egypt's membership in the league was reinstated.

Domestically, Mubārak tried to address the problems that had surfaced in the last year of Sādāt's era. Mubārak declared that the reign of the privileged minority that had profited from the invigorated private sector during Sādāt's years would come to an end. He also released Sādāt's political prisoners and vigorously prosecuted the Islamic militants who had plotted the late president's assassination. Still, opposition to a variety of political, economic, and social policies remained—primarily among discontented labour and religious groups—and the government faced labour strikes, food riots, and other incidents of unrest. It also undertook several measures designed to counter a determined campaign by Islamic extremists to destabilize the regime.

In the late 1980s Egypt's worsening economy was further undermined by a reduction in the number of remittances sent from the many Egyptians working abroad. The government continued to rely heavily on foreign economic aid despite its rising debt burden, which led to the increasing involvement of the International Monetary Fund (IMF) in Egypt's economic policies. In 1991 the Egyptian government signed the Economic Reform and Structural Adjustment Program with the IMF and the World Bank. As part of the program, the country's currency underwent several devaluations, interest rates rose, and subsidies on food and fuel were lowered. These policies especially harmed the poorest Egyptians. A growing disparity in income and access to resources became more evident, straining relations between its rich and poor citizens.

Egyptian politics during this time continued along an authoritarian route, as Mubārak was reelected to the presidency without opposition in 1987, 1993, and 1999. Opposition candidates did contest the 2005 election, but Mubārak won reelection that year as well. Meanwhile, his National Democratic Party consistently performed well in legislative elections and continued to increase its majority of delegates in the People's Assembly. It was widely believed, however, that the electoral process was tampered with to ensure that Mubārak's supporters would win.

Egypt continued to experience acts of Islamist terrorism in the 1990s and 2000s; several government ministers were assassinated—one such attempt nearly killed Mubārak himself in Addis Ababa, Eth., in 1995—and terrorists attacked tourists near Egypt's most famous monuments and popular tourist sites, including an especially violent attack at Luxor in 1997. In response, the government used such tactics as preventive detention and, allegedly, torture. Despite government initiatives to curb domestic terrorism, it continued to be a threat to Egypt's stability.

Another source of tension that the Egyptian government has had to deal with was the precarious relationship between the country's Muslim and Coptic Christian populations. While some Muslims accused the Copts of serving as agents for foreign powers and of controlling Egypt's economy, some Copts accused Muslims of destroying churches and compelling Egyptian Christians to convert to Islam. Both Muslim and Christian Egyptians have, for the most part, made an effort to minimize their differences publicly in order to maintain national unity. Tensions erupted periodically, however, and such was the case in 2009 when Coptic Christian pig farmers clashed with the predominantly Muslim authorities over the slaughter of their animals. The slaughter was ordered ostensibly as a measure to prevent the spread of the H1N1 influenza virus, even though international health authorities said there was no evidence of the virus being transmitted to humans from Egypt's pigs. The slaughter order was later deemed to be an action taken for general public heath, but the Coptic farmers claimed the order was a way to punish them by economic means and that it was rooted in Muslim resentment of the Christian Copts. Sectarian clashes flared again in early 2010 after an incident in which gunmen killed seven people outside of a Coptic church following the Coptic Christmas Eve Mass; three Muslim men were charged with the attack.

CHAPTER 7

LIBYA

Libya is located along the Mediterranean coast of northern Africa. The modern-day country became independent in 1951. The capital is Tripoli.

EARLY HISTORY

Largely desert with some limited potential for urban and sedentary (non-migratory) life in the northwest and northeast, Libya has historically never been heavily populated nor has it been a power centre. Like that of its neighbour Algeria, Libya's very name is a neologism, created by the conquering Italians early in the 20th century. Also like that of Algeria, much of Libya's earlier history—not only in the Islamic period but even before—reveals that both Tripolitania and Cyrenaica were more closely linked with neighbouring territories Tunisia and Egypt, respectively, than with each other. Even during the Ottoman era, the country was divided into two parts, one linked to Tripoli in the west and the other to Banghāzī in the east.

Libya thus owes its present unity as a state less to earlier history or geographic characteristics than to several recent factors: the unifying effect of the Sanūsiyyah movement since the 19th century; Italian colonialism from 1911 until after World War II; an early independence by default, since the great powers could agree on no other solution; and the discovery of oil in commercial quantities in the late 1950s.

Downtown Tripoli, Libya, 2004. John MacDougall/AFP/Getty Images

Yet the Sanūsiyyah is based largely in the eastern region of Cyrenaica and has never really penetrated the more populous northwestern region of Tripolitania. Italian colonization was brief and brutal. Moreover, most of the hard-earned gains in infrastructure implanted during the colonial period were destroyed by contending armies during World War II. Sudden oil wealth has been both a boon and a curse as changes to the political and social fabric—as well as to the economy—have accelerated. This difficult legacy of disparate elements and forces helps to explain the unique character of present-day Libya.

OTTOMAN RULE

Part of the Ottoman Empire from the early 16th century, Libya experienced autonomous rule (analogous to that in Ottoman Algeria and Tunisia) under the Karamanli dynasty from 1711 to 1835. In the latter year the Ottomans took advantage of a succession dispute and local disorder to reestablish direct administration. For the next 77 years the area was administered by officials from the Ottoman capital of Constantinople (present-day Istanbul) and shared in the limited modernization common to the rest of the empire. In Libya the most significant event of the period was the foundation in 1837 of the Sanūsiyyah, an Islamic order, or fraternity, that preached a puritanical form of Islam, giving the people instruction and material assistance and so creating among them a sense of unity. The first Sanūsī *zāwiyah* (monastic complex) in Libya was established in 1843 near the ruins of Cyrene in eastern Cyrenaica. The order spread principally in that province but also found adherents in the south. The Grand al-Sanūsī, as the founder came to be called, moved his headquarters to the oasis of Al-Jaghbūb near the Egyptian frontier, and in 1895 his son and successor, Sīdī Muḥammad Idrīs al-Mahdī, transferred it farther south into the Sahara to the oasis group of Al-Kufrah. Though the Ottomans welcomed the order's opposition to the spread of French influence northward from Chad and Tibesti, they regarded with suspicion the political influence it exerted within Cyrenaica. In 1908 the Young Turk revolution gave a new impulse to reform; in 1911, however, the Italians, who had banking and other interests in the country, launched an invasion.

The Ottomans sued for peace in 1912, but Italy found it more difficult to subdue the local population. Resistance to the Italian occupation continued throughout World War I. After the war Italy considered coming to terms with nationalist forces in Tripolitania and with the Sanūsiyyah, which was strong in Cyrenaica. These negotiations foundered, however, and the arrival of a strong governor, Giuseppe Volpi, in Libya and a Fascist government in Italy (1922) inaugurated an Italian policy of thorough colonization. The coastal areas of Tripolitania were subdued by 1923, but in Cyrenaica Sanūsī resistance, led by 'Umar al-Mukhtār, continued until his capture and execution in 1931.

ITALIAN COLONIZATION

In the 1920s and '30s the Italian government expended large sums on developing towns, roads, and agricultural colonies for Italian settlers. The most ambitious effort was the program of Italian immigration called "demographic colonization," launched by the Fascist leader Benito Mussolini in 1935. As a result of these efforts, by the outbreak of World War II, some 150,000 Italians had settled in Libya and constituted roughly one-fifth of that country's total population.

These colonizing efforts and the resulting economic development of Libya were largely destroyed during the North Africa campaigns of 1941–43. Cyrenaica changed hands three times, and by the end of 1942 all of the Italian settlers had left. Cyrenaica largely reverted to pastoralism. Economic and administrative development fostered by Italy survived in Tripolitania; however, Libya by 1945 was impoverished, underpopulated, and also divided into regions—Tripolitania, Cyrenaica, and Fezzan—of differing political, economic, and religious traditions.

INDEPENDENCE

The future of Libya gave rise to long discussions after the war. In view of the contribution to the fighting made by a volunteer Sanūsī force, the British foreign minister pledged in 1942 that the Sanūsīs would not again be subjected to Italian rule. During the discussions, which lasted four years, suggestions included an Italian trusteeship, a UN trusteeship, a Soviet mandate for Tripolitania, and various compromises. Finally, in November 1949, the UN General Assembly voted that Libya should become a united and independent kingdom no later than Jan. 1, 1952.

A constitution creating a federal state with a separate parliament for each province was drawn up, and the pro-British head of the Sanūsiyyah, Sīdī Muḥammad Idrīs al-Mahdī al-Sanūsī, was chosen king by a national assembly in 1950. On Dec. 24, 1951, King Idris I declared the country independent. Political parties were prohibited, and the king's authority was sovereign. Though not themselves Sanūsīs, the Tripolitanians accepted the monarchy largely in order to profit from the British promise that the Sanūsīs would not again be subjected to Italian rule. King Idris, however, showed a marked preference for living in Cyrenaica, where he built a new capital on the site of the Sanūsī *zāwiyah* at Al-Bayḍāʾ. Though Libya joined the Arab League in 1953 and in 1956 refused British troops permission to land during the Suez Crisis, the government in general adopted a pro-Western position in international affairs.

THE DISCOVERY OF OIL

With the discovery of significant oil reserves in 1959, Libya changed abruptly from being dependent on international aid and the rent from U.S. and British air bases to being an oil-rich monarchy. Major petroleum deposits in both

This photograph, c. 1960, shows the Esso Standard Libya Inc. storage facility at the Zalṭan and Al-Rāqūbah (Raguba) refinery and pipeline terminal. Zalṭan, part of an "oasis" of regional oil fields, was the site of the first exploited oil field in Libya. Three Lions/Hulton Archive/ Getty Images

Tripolitania and Cyrenaica ensured the country income on a vast scale. The discovery was followed by an enormous expansion in all government services, massive construction projects, and a corresponding rise in the economic standard and the cost of living.

Precipitated by the king's failure to speak out against Israel during the Arab-Israeli Six-Day War (June War) in 1967, a coup was carried out on Sept. 1, 1969, by a group of young army officers led by Col. Muammar al-Qaddafi, who deposed the king and proclaimed Libya a republic.

Muammar al-Qaddafi

(b. 1942, near Surt, Libya)

Muammar al-Qaddafi (also spelled Muammar Khadafy, Moammar Gadhafi, or Mu'ammar al-Qadhdhāfī) has been the de facto leader of Libya from 1969. He has been active in both Arab and African intergovernmental affairs.

The son of an itinerant Bedouin farmer, Qaddafi was born in a tent in the Libyan desert. He proved a talented student and graduated from the University of Libya in 1963. A devout Muslim and ardent Arab nationalist, Qaddafi early began plotting to overthrow the Libyan monarchy of King Idris I. He graduated from the Libyan military academy in 1965 and thereafter rose steadily through the ranks, all the while continuing to plan a coup with the help of his fellow army officers. On Sept. 1, 1969, Qaddafi seized control of the government in a military coup that deposed King Idris. Qaddafi was named commander in chief of the armed forces and chairman of Libya's new governing body, the Revolutionary Command Council.

Qaddafi removed the U.S. and British military bases from Libya in 1970. He expelled most members of the native Italian and Jewish communities from Libya that same year, and in 1973 he nationalized all foreign-owned petroleum assets in the country. He also outlawed alcoholic beverages and gambling, in accordance with his own strict Islamic principles. Qaddafi also began a series of persistent but unsuccessful attempts to unify Libya with other Arab countries. He was adamantly opposed to negotiations with Israel and became a leader of the so-called rejectionist front of Arab nations in this regard. He also earned a reputation for military adventurism; his government was implicated in several abortive coup attempts in Egypt and Sudan, and Libyan forces persistently intervened in the long-running civil war in neighbouring Chad.

From 1974 onward Qaddafi espoused a form of Islamic socialism as expressed in his The Green Book. *This combined the nationalization of many economic sectors with a brand of populist government ostensibly operating through people's congresses, labour unions, and other mass organizations. Meanwhile, Qaddafi was becoming known for his erratic and unpredictable behaviour on the international scene. His government financed a broad spectrum of revolutionary or terrorist groups worldwide, including the Black Panthers and the Nation of Islam in the United States and the Irish Republican Army in Northern Ireland. Squads of Libyan agents assassinated émigré opponents abroad, and his government was allegedly involved in several bloody terrorist incidents in Europe perpetrated by Palestinian or other Arab extremists. These activities brought him into growing conflict with the U.S. government, and in April 1986 a force of British-based U.S. warplanes bombed several sites in Libya, killing or wounding several of his children and narrowly missing Qaddafi himself.*

Libya's purported involvement in the destruction of a civilian airliner over Lockerbie, Scot., in 1988, led to United Nations and U.S. sanctions that further isolated Qaddafi from the international community. In the late 1990s, however, Qaddafi turned over the alleged perpetrators of the bombing to international authorities. UN sanctions against Libya were subsequently lifted in 2003, and, following Qaddafi's announcement that Libya would cease its unconventional-weapons program, the United States dropped most of its sanctions as well. Although some observers remained critical—particularly when, in 2009, Qaddafi warmly welcomed convicted Lockerbie bomber 'Abd al-Basit al-Magrahi back home to Libya (Megrahi had been released on compassionate grounds owing to his terminal cancer)—the lifting of sanctions nevertheless provided an opportunity for the rehabilitation of Qaddafi's image abroad, facilitating his country's gradual return to the global community.

In February 2009 Qaddafi was elected chairman of the African Union (AU), and later that year he gave his first speech before the UN General Assembly. The lengthy critical speech, in which he threw a copy of the UN charter, generated a significant measure of controversy within the international community. In early 2010 Qaddafi's attempt to remain as chairman of the AU beyond the customary one-year term was met with resistance from several other African countries and ultimately was denied.

The new regime, passionately Pan-Arab, broke the monarchy's close ties to Britain and the United States and also began an assertive policy that led to higher oil prices along with 51 percent Libyan participation in oil company activities and, in some cases, outright nationalization.

The Qaddafi Regime

Equally assertive in plans for Arab unity, Libya obtained at least the formal beginnings of unity with Egypt, Sudan, and Tunisia, but these and other such plans failed as differences arose between the governments concerned. Qaddafi's Libya supported the Palestinian cause and intervened to support it, as well as other guerrilla and revolutionary organizations in Africa and the Middle East. Such moves alienated the Western countries and some Arab states. In July–August 1977 hostilities broke out between Libya and Egypt, and, as a result, many Egyptians working in Libya were expelled. Indeed, despite expressed concern for Arab unity, the regime's relations with most Arab countries deteriorated. Qaddafi signed a treaty of union with Morocco's King Hassan II in August 1984, but Hassan abrogated the treaty two years later.

The regime, under Qaddafi's ideological guidance, continued to introduce innovations. On March 2, 1977, the General People's Congress declared that Libya was to be known as the People's Socialist Libyan Arab Jamāhīriyyah (the latter term is a neologism meaning "government through the masses"). By the early 1980s, however, a drop in the demand and price for oil on the world market was beginning to hamper Qaddafi's efforts to play a strong regional role. Ambitious efforts to radically change Libya's economy and society slowed, and there were signs of domestic discontent.

Col. Muammar al-Qaddafi, 1999. Marwan Naamani—AFP/Getty Images

Libyan opposition movements launched sporadic attacks against Qaddafi and his military supporters but met with arrest and execution.

Libya's relationship with the United States, which had been an important trading partner, deteriorated in the early 1980s as the U.S. government increasingly protested Qaddafi's support of Palestinian Arab militants. An escalating series of retaliatory trade restrictions and military skirmishes culminated in a U.S. bombing raid of Tripoli and Banghāzī in 1986, in which Qaddafi's adopted daughter was among the casualties. U.S. claims that Libya was producing chemical warfare materials contributed to the tension between the two countries in the late 1980s and '90s. Within the region, Libya sought throughout the 1970s and '80s to control the mineral-rich Aozou strip along the disputed border with neighbouring Chad. These efforts produced intermittent warfare in Chad and confrontation with both France and the United States. In 1987 Libyan forces were bested by Chad's more mobile troops, and diplomatic ties with that country were restored late the following year. Libya denied involvement in Chad's December 1990 coup led by Idrīss Déby.

In 1996 the United States and the UN implemented a series of economic sanctions against Libya for its purported involvement in destroying a civilian airliner over Lockerbie, Scot., in 1988. In the late 1990s, in an effort to placate the international community, Libya turned over the alleged perpetrators of the bombing to international authorities and accepted a ruling by the international court in The Hague stating that the contested Aozou territory along the border with Chad belonged to that country and not to Libya. The United Kingdom restored diplomatic relations with Libya at the end of the decade, and UN sanctions were lifted in 2003; later that year Libya announced that it would stop producing chemical weapons. The United States responded by dropping most of its sanctions, and the restoration of full diplomatic ties between the two countries was completed in 2006. In 2007 five Bulgarian nurses and a Palestinian doctor who had been sentenced to death in Libya after being tried on charges of having deliberately infected children there with HIV were extradited to Bulgaria and quickly pardoned by its president, defusing widespread outcry over the case and preventing the situation from posing an obstacle to Libya's return to the international community.

In the years that followed the lifting of sanctions, one of Qaddafi's sons, Sayf al-Islam al-Qaddafi, emerged as a proponent of reform and helped lead Libya toward adjustments in its domestic and foreign policy. Measures including efforts to attract Western business and plans to foster tourism promised to gradually draw Libya more substantially into the global community.

CHAPTER 8

Morocco

Morocco is a country on the Atlantic coast of northwestern Africa. The modern-day country became independent in 1956. The capital is Rabat.

EARLY HISTORY

Situated in the northwest corner of Africa and, on a clear day, visible from the Spanish coast, Morocco has resisted outside invasion while serving as a meeting point for European, Eastern, and African civilizations throughout history. Its early inhabitants were Tamazight-speaking nomads; many of these became followers of Christianity and Judaism, which were introduced during a brief period of Roman rule. In the late 7th century, Arab invaders from the East brought Islam, which local Imazighen gradually assimilated. Sunni Islam triumphed over various sectarian tendencies in the 12th and 13th centuries under the doctrinally rigorous Almohad dynasty. The Christian reconquest of Spain in the later Middle Ages brought waves of Muslim and Jewish exiles from Spain to Morocco, injecting a Hispanic flavour into Moroccan urban life. Apart from some isolated coastal enclaves, however, Europeans failed to establish a permanent foothold in the area. In the 16th century, Ottoman invaders from Algeria attempted to add Morocco to their empire, thus threatening the country's independence. They, too, were thwarted, leaving Morocco virtually the only Arab country never to experience Ottoman rule. In 1578, three kings fought and died near Ksar

Sabbath services at a Moroccan synagogue, c. 1955. Evans/Hulton Archive/Getty Images

el-Kebir (Alcazarquivir), including the Portuguese monarch Sebastian. This decisive battle, known as the Battle of the Three Kings, was claimed as a Moroccan victory and put an end to European incursions onto Moroccan soil for three centuries. The 17th century saw the rise of the ʿAlawite dynasty of sharifs, who still rule Morocco today. This dynasty fostered trade and cultural relations with sub-Saharan Africa, Europe, and the Arab lands, though religious tensions between Islam and Christendom often threatened the peace.

By the late 17th century, Morocco's cultural and political identity as an Islamic monarchy was firmly established. The figure of the strong sultan was personified by Mawlāy Ismāʿīl (1672–1727), who used a slave army, known as the ʿAbīd al-Bukhārī, to subdue all parts of the country and establish centralized rule. Subsequent monarchs often used their prestige as religious leaders to contain internal conflicts caused by competition among tribes. In the late 18th and early 19th centuries, when Europe was preoccupied with revolution and

'Abīd al-Bukhārī

The 'Abīd al-Bukhārī, also known as the Buākhar, was an army of Saharan blacks organized in Morocco by the 'Alawī ruler Ismā'īl (reigned 1672–1727). Earlier rulers had recruited black slaves (Arabic: 'abīd*) into their armies, and these men or their descendants eventually formed the core of Ismā'īl's guard.*

The 'abīd *were sent to a special camp at Mechra' er-Remel to beget children. The communal children, male and female, were presented to the ruler when they were about 10 years old and proceeded to a prescribed course of training. The boys acquired such skills as masonry, horsemanship, archery, and musketry, whereas the girls were prepared for domestic life or for entertainment. At the age of 15 they were divided among the various army corps and married, and eventually the cycle would repeat itself with their children.*

Ismā'īl's army, numbering 150,000 men at its peak, consisted mainly of the "graduates" of the Mechra' er-Remel camp and supplementary slaves pirated from black Saharan tribes, all foreigners whose sole allegiance was to the ruler. The 'abīd *were highly favoured by Ismā'īl, well paid, and often politically powerful; in 1697–98 they were even given the right to own property.*

After Ismā'īl's death the quality of the corps could not be sustained. Discipline slackened, and, as preferential pay was no longer forthcoming, the 'abīd *took to brigandage. Many left their outposts and shifted into the cities, and others became farmers or peasants. Those who remained in the army were an unstable element, ready for intrigue. Under strong rulers, the 'Abīd al-Bukhārī were periodically reorganized, though never regaining their former military and numerical strength. The* 'abīd *were finally dissolved late in the 19th century, with only a nominal number retained as the king's personal bodyguard.*

continental war, Morocco withdrew into a period of isolation. On the eve of the modern era, despite their geographic proximity, Moroccans and Europeans knew little about each other.

DECLINE OF TRADITIONAL GOVERNMENT

During the French invasion of Algeria in 1830, the sultan of Morocco, Mawlāy 'Abd al-Raḥmān (1822–59), briefly sent troops to occupy Tlemcen but withdrew them after French protests. The Algerian leader Abdelkader in 1844 took refuge from the French in Morocco. A Moroccan army was sent to the Algerian frontier; the French bombarded Tangier on Aug. 4, 1844, and Essaouira (Mogador) on August 15. Meanwhile, on August 14, the Moroccan army had been totally defeated at Isly, near the frontier town of Oujda. The sultan then promised to intern or expel Abdelkader if he should again enter Moroccan territory. Two years later, when he was again driven into Morocco, the Algerian leader was attacked by Moroccan troops and was forced to surrender to the French.

Immediately after ʿAbd al-Raḥmān's death in 1859, a dispute with Spain over the boundaries of the Spanish enclave at Ceuta led Madrid to declare war. Spain captured Tétouan in the following year. Peace had to be bought with an indemnity of $20 million, the enlargement of Ceuta's frontiers, and the promise to cede to Spain another enclave—Ifni.

The new sultan, Sīdī Muḥammad, attempted with little success to modernize the Moroccan army. Upon his death in 1873, his son Mawlāy Hassan I struggled to preserve independence. Hassan I died in 1894, and his chamberlain, Bā Aḥmad (Aḥmad ibn Mūsā), ruled in the name of the young sultan ʿAbd al-ʿAzīz until 1901, when the latter began his direct rule.

ʿAbd al-ʿAzīz surrounded himself with European companions and adopted their customs, while scandalizing his own subjects, particularly the religious leaders. His attempt to introduce a modern system of land taxation resulted in complete confusion because of a lack of qualified officials. Popular discontent and tribal rebellion became even more common, while a pretender, Bū Ḥmāra (Abū Ḥamārah), established a rival court near Melilla. European powers seized the occasion to extend their own influence. In 1904 Britain gave France a free hand in Morocco in exchange for French noninterference with British plans in Egypt. Spanish agreement was secured by a French promise that northern Morocco should be treated as a sphere of Spanish influence. Italian interests were satisfied by France's decision not to hinder Italian designs on Libya. Once these various interests were settled, the Western powers met with Moroccan representatives at Algeciras, Spain, in 1906, to discuss the country's future.

The Algeciras Conference confirmed the integrity of the sultan's domains but sanctioned French and Spanish policing Moroccan ports and collecting the customs dues. In 1907–08 the sultan's brother, Mawlāy ʿAbd al-Ḥāfiẓ, led a rebellion against him from Marrakech, denouncing ʿAbd al-ʿAzīz for his collaboration with the Europeans. ʿAbd al-ʿAzīz subsequently fled to distant Tangier. ʿAbd al-Ḥāfiẓ then made an abortive attack on French troops, which had occupied Casablanca in 1907, before proceeding to Fès, where he was duly proclaimed sultan and recognized by the European powers (1909).

The new sultan proved unable to control the country. Disorder increased until, besieged by tribesmen in Fès, he was forced to ask the French to rescue him. When they had done so, he had no choice but to sign the Treaty of Fez (March 30, 1912), by which Morocco became a French protectorate. In return, the French guaranteed that the status of the sultan and his successors would be maintained. Provision was also made to meet the Spanish claim for a special position in the north of the country; Tangier, long the seat of the diplomatic missions, retained a separate administration.

THE FRENCH PROTECTORATE

In establishing their protectorate over much of Morocco, the French had behind them the experience of the conquest of Algeria and of their protectorate over Tunisia; they took the latter as the model for their Moroccan policy. There were, however, important differences. First, the protectorate was established only two years before the outbreak of World War I, which brought with it a new attitude toward colonial rule. Second, Morocco had a thousand-year tradition of independence; though it had been strongly influenced by the civilization of Muslim Spain, it had never been subject to Ottoman rule. These circumstances and the proximity of Morocco to Spain created a special relationship between the two countries.

Morocco was also unique among the North African countries in possessing a coast on the Atlantic, in the rights that various nations derived from the Act of Algeciras, and in the privileges that their diplomatic missions had acquired in Tangier. Thus, the northern tenth of the country, with both Atlantic and Mediterranean coasts, together with the desert province of Tarfaya in the southwest adjoining the Spanish Sahara, were excluded from the French-controlled area and treated as a Spanish protectorate. In the French zone, the fiction of the sultan's sovereignty was maintained, but the French-appointed resident general held the real authority and was subject only to the approval of the government in Paris. The sultan worked through newly created departments staffed by French officials. The negligible role that the Moroccan government (*makhzan*) actually played can be seen by the fact that Muḥammad al-Muqrī, the grand vizier when the protectorate was installed, held the same post when Morocco recovered its independence 44 years later; he was by then more than 100 years old. As in Tunisia, country districts were administered by *contrôleurs civils*, except in certain areas such as Fès, where it was felt that officers of the rank of general should supervise the administration. In the south certain Amazigh chiefs (*qāʾid*s), of whom the best known was Thami al-Glaoui, were given a great deal of independence.

The first resident general, Gen. (later Marshal) Louis-Hubert-Gonzalve Lyautey, was a soldier of wide experience in Indochina, Madagascar, and Algeria. He was of aristocratic outlook and possessed a deep appreciation of Moroccan civilization. The character he gave to the administration exerted an influence throughout the period of the protectorate.

Lyautey's idea was to leave the Moroccan elite intact and rule through a policy of cooptation. He placed ʿAbd al-Ḥāfiẓ's more amenable brother, Mawlāy Yūsuf, on the throne. This sultan succeeded in cooperating with the French without losing the respect of the Moroccan people. A new administrative capital was created on the Atlantic coast at Rabat, and a commercial port subsequently was developed at Casablanca. By the end of the protectorate in 1956, Casablanca was a flourishing city, with nearly a million inhabitants and a substantial industrial establishment. Lyautey's plan to build new European cities separate from the old Moroccan towns left the traditional medinas intact. Remarkably, World War I did little to interrupt this rhythm of innovation. Though the French government had proposed retiring to the coast, Lyautey managed to retain control of all the French-occupied territory.

After the war Morocco faced two major problems. The first was pacifying the outlying areas in the Atlas Mountains, over which the sultan's government often had had no real control; this was finally completed in 1934. The second problem was the spread of the uprising of Abd el-Krim from the Spanish to the French zone, which was quelled by French and Spanish troops in 1926. That same year, Marshal Lyautey was succeeded by a civilian resident general. This marked a change to a more conventional colonial-style administration, accompanied by official colonization, the growth of the European population, and the increasing impact of European thought on the younger generation of Moroccans, some of whom had by then received a French education.

As early as 1920 Lyautey had submitted a report saying that "a young generation is growing up which is full of life and needs activity.... Lacking the outlets which our administration offers only sparingly and in subordinate positions they will find an alternative way out." Only six years after Lyautey's report, young Moroccans both in Rabat, the new administrative capital, and in Fès, the centre of traditional Arab-Islamic learning and culture, were meeting independently of one another to discuss demands for reforms within the terms of the protectorate treaty. They asked for more schools, a new judicial system, and the abolition of the regime of the Amazigh *qā'ids* in the south; for study missions in France and the Middle East; and for the cessation of official colonization—objectives that would be fully secured only when the protectorate ended in 1956.

On the death of Mawlāy Yūsuf (1927) the French chose as his successor his younger son, Sīdī Muḥammad (Muḥammad V). Selected in part for his retiring disposition, this sultan eventually revealed considerable diplomatic skill and determination. Also significant was the French attempt to use the purported differences between Arabs and Imazighen to undercut any growing sense of national unity. This led the French to issue the Berber Decree in 1930, which was a crude effort to divide Imazighen and Arabs. The result was just the opposite of French intentions; it provoked a Moroccan nationalist reaction and forced the administration to modify its proposals. In 1933 the nationalists initiated a new national day called the Fête du Trône (Throne Day) to mark the anniversary of the sultan's accession. When he visited Fès the following year, the sultan received a tumultuous welcome, accompanied by anti-French demonstrations that caused the authorities to terminate his visit abruptly. Shortly after this episode political parties were organized that sought greater Moroccan self-rule. These events coincided with the completion of the French occupation of southern Morocco, which paved the way for the Spanish occupation of Ifni. In 1937 rioting occurred in Meknès, where French settlers were suspected of diverting part of the town water supply to irrigate their own lands at the expense of the Muslim cultivators. In the ensuing repression, Muḥammad ʿAllāl al-Fāsī, a prominent nationalist leader, was banished to Gabon in French Equatorial Africa, where he spent the following nine years.

WORLD WAR II AND INDEPENDENCE

As previously noted, parts of Morocco were under Spanish rule, while others were part of the French protectorate. It is helpful to examine the events of mid-20th century Moroccan history through these divisions.

The French Zone

At the outbreak of World War II in 1939, the sultan issued a call for cooperation with the French, and a large Moroccan contingent (mainly Amazigh) served with distinction in France. The collapse of the French in 1940 followed by the installation of the German collaborationist Vichy regime produced an entirely new situation. The sultan signified his independence by refusing to approve anti-Jewish legislation. When Anglo-American troop landings took place in 1942, he refused to comply with the suggestion of the resident general, Auguste Noguès, that he retire to the interior. In 1943 the sultan was influenced by his meeting with U.S. Pres. Franklin D. Roosevelt, who had come to Morocco for the Casablanca Conference and was unsympathetic to continued French presence there. The majority of the people were equally affected by the arrival of U.S. and British troops, who exposed Moroccans to the outside world to an unprecedented degree. In addition, Allied and Axis radio propaganda, both of which were supportive of Moroccan independence, strongly attracted Arab listeners. Amid these circumstances, the nationalist movement took the new title of Ḥizb al-Istiqlāl (Independence Party). In January 1944 the party submitted to the sultan and the Allied (including the French) authorities a memorandum asking for independence under a constitutional regime. The nationalist leaders, including Aḥmad Balafrej, secretary general of the Istiqlāl, were unjustly accused and arrested for collaborating with the Nazis. This caused rioting in Fès and elsewhere in which some 30 or more demonstrators were killed. As a result, the sultan, who in 1947 persuaded a new and reform-minded resident general, Eirik Labonne, to ask the French government to grant him permission to make an official state visit to Tangier, passing through the Spanish Zone on the way. The journey became a triumphal procession. When the sultan made his speech in Tangier, after his stirring reception in northern Morocco, he emphasized his country's links with the Arab world of the East, omitting the expected flattering reference to the French protectorate.

Labonne was subsequently replaced by Gen. (later Marshal) Alphonse Juin, who was of Algerian settler origin. Juin, long experienced in North African affairs, expressed sympathy for the patriotic nationalist sentiments of young Moroccans and promised to comply with their wish for the creation of elected municipalities in the large cities. At the same time, he roused opposition by proposing to introduce French citizens as members of these bodies. The sultan used his one remaining prerogative and refused to countersign the resident general's decrees, without which they had no legal validity. A state visit to France in October 1950 and a flattering reception there did nothing to modify the sultan's views, and on his return to Morocco he received a wildly enthusiastic welcome.

In December General Juin dismissed a nationalist member from a budget proposal meeting of the Council of Government; consequently, the 10 remaining nationalist members walked out in protest. Juin then contemplated the possibility of using the Amazigh feudal notables, such as Thami al-Glaoui, to counter the nationalists. At a palace reception later in the month al-Glaoui in fact confronted the sultan, calling him not the sultan of the Moroccans but of the Istiqlāl and blaming him for leading the country to catastrophe.

With Sīdī Muḥammad still refusing to cooperate, Juin surrounded the palace, under the guard of French troops supposedly placed there to protect the sultan from his own people, with local tribesmen. Faced with this threat, Sīdī Muḥammad was forced to disown "a certain political party," without specifically naming it, though he still withheld his signature from many decrees, including one that admitted French citizens to become municipal councillors. Juin's action was widely criticized in France, which led to his replacement by Gen. Augustin Guillaume in August 1951. On the anniversary of his accession (November 18), the sultan declared his hopes for an agreement "guaranteeing full sovereignty to Morocco" but (as he added in a subsequent letter addressed to the president of the French Republic) "with the continuation of Franco-Moroccan cooperation." This troubled situation continued until December 1952, when trade unions in Casablanca organized a protest meeting in response to the alleged French terrorist assassination of the Tunisian union leader Ferhat Hached. Subsequently, a clash with the police resulted in the arrest of hundreds of nationalists, who were held for two years without trial.

In April 1953 ʿAbd al-Ḥayy al-Kattānī, a noted religious scholar and the head of the Kattāniyyah religious brotherhood, together with a number of Amazigh notables led by al-Glaoui (along with the connivance of several French officials and settlers) began to work for the deposition of the sultan. The government in Paris, preoccupied with internal affairs, finally demanded that the sultan transfer his legislative powers to a council, consisting of Moroccan ministers and French directors, and append his signature to all blocked legislation. Although the sultan yielded, it was insufficient for his enemies. In August al-Glaoui delivered the equivalent of an ultimatum to the French government, who deported the sultan and his family and appointed in his place the more subservient Mawlāy Ben ʿArafa. These actions failed to remedy the situation, as Sīdī Muḥammad immediately became a national hero. The authorities in the Spanish Zone, who had not been consulted about the measure, did nothing to conceal their disapproval. The Spanish Zone thus became a refuge for Moroccan nationalists.

In November 1954 the French position was further complicated by the outbreak of the Algerian war for independence, and the following June the Paris government decided on a complete change of policy and appointed Gilbert Grandval as resident general. His efforts at conciliation, obstructed by tacit opposition among many officials and the outspoken hostility of the majority of French settlers, failed. A conference of Moroccan representatives was then summoned to meet in France, where it was agreed that the substitute sultan be replaced with a crown council. Sīdī Muḥammad approved this proposal, but it took weeks to persuade Mawlāy Ben ʿArafa to withdraw to Tangier. Meanwhile, a guerrilla liberation army began to operate against French posts near the Spanish Zone.

In October al-Glaoui declared publicly that only the reinstatement of Muḥammad V could restore harmony. The French government agreed to allow the sultan to form a constitutional government for Morocco, and Sīdī Muḥammad returned to Rabat in November; on March 2, 1956, independence was proclaimed. The sultan formed a government that included representation from various elements of the indigenous population, while the governmental departments formerly headed by French officials became ministries headed by Moroccans.

The Spanish Zone

The Spanish protectorate over northern Morocco extended from Larache (El-Araish) on the Atlantic to 30 miles (48 km) beyond Melilla (already a Spanish possession) on the Mediterranean. The mountainous Tamazight-speaking area had often escaped the sultan's control. Spain also received a strip of desert land in the southwest, known as Tarfaya, adjoining Spanish Sahara. In 1934, when the French occupied southern Morocco, the Spanish took Ifni.

Spain appointed a *khalīfah*, or viceroy, chosen from the Moroccan royal family as nominal head of state and provided him with a puppet Moroccan government. This enabled Spain to conduct affairs independently of the French Zone while nominally preserving Moroccan unity. Tangier, though it had a Spanish-speaking population of 40,000, received a special international administration under a *mandūb*, or a representative of the sultan. Although the *mandūb* was, in theory, appointed by the sultan, in reality he was chosen by the French. In 1940, after the defeat of France, Spanish troops occupied Tangier, but they withdrew in 1945 after the Allied victory.

The Spanish Zone surrounded the ports of Ceuta and Melilla, which Spain had held for centuries, and included the iron mines of the Rif Mountains. The Spanish selected Tétouan for their capital. As in the French Zone, European-staffed departments were created, while the rural districts were administered by *interventores*, corresponding to the French *contrôleurs civils*. The first area to be occupied was on the plain, facing the Atlantic, which included the towns of Larache, Ksar el-Kebir, and Asilah. That area was the stronghold of the former Moroccan governor Aḥmad al-Raisūnī (Raisūlī), who was half patriot and half brigand. The Spanish government found it difficult to tolerate his independence; in March 1913 al-Raisūnī retired into a refuge in the mountains, where he remained until his capture 12 years later by another Moroccan leader, Abd el-Krim.

Abd el-Krim was an Amazigh and a good Arabic scholar who had a knowledge of both the Arabic and Spanish languages and ways of life. Imprisoned after World War I for his subversive activities, he later went to Ajdir in the Rif Mountains to plan an uprising. In July 1921 Abd el-Krim destroyed a Spanish force sent against him and subsequently established the Republic of the Rif. It took a combined French and Spanish force numbering more than 250,000 troops before he was defeated. In May 1926 he surrendered to the French and was exiled.

The remainder of the period of the Spanish protectorate was relatively calm. Thus, in 1936, Gen. Francisco Franco was able to launch his attack on the Spanish Republic from Morocco and to enroll a large number of Moroccan volunteers, who served him loyally in the Spanish Civil War. Though the Spanish had fewer resources than the French, their subsequent regime was in some respects more liberal and less subject to ethnic discrimination. The language of instruction in the schools was Arabic rather than Spanish, and Moroccan students were encouraged to go to Egypt for a Muslim education. There was no attempt to set Amazigh against Arab as in the French Zone, but this might have been the result of the introduction of Muslim law by Abd el-Krim himself. After the Republic of the Rif was suppressed, there was little cooperation between the two protecting powers. Their disagreement reached a new intensity in 1953 when the French deposed and deported the sultan. The Spanish high commissioner, who had not been consulted, refused to recognize this action and continued

Abd el-Krim in Cairo 1947. AFP/Getty Images

to regard Muḥammad V as the sovereign in the Spanish Zone. Nationalists forced to leave the French area used the Spanish Zone as a refuge.

In 1956, however, the Spanish authorities were taken by surprise when the French decided to grant independence to Morocco. A corresponding agreement with the Spanish was nevertheless reached on April 7, 1956, and was marked by a visit of the sultan to Spain. The Spanish protectorate was thus brought to an end without the troubles that marked the termination of French control. With the end of the Spanish protectorate and the withdrawal of the Spanish high commissioner, the Moroccan *khalīfah,* and other officials from Tétouan, the city again became a quiet, provincial capital. The introduction of the Moroccan franc to replace the *peseta* as currency, however, caused a great rise in the cost of living in the former Spanish area, along with difficulties brought on by the introduction of French-speaking Moroccan officials. In 1958–59 these changes generated disorders in the Rif region. Tangier, too, lost much of the superficial brilliance it had developed as a separate zone. As in the former French Zone, many European and Jewish inhabitants left. The southern protectorate area of Tarfaya was handed back to Morocco in 1958, while the Spanish unconditionally gave up Ifni in 1970, hoping to gain recognition of their rights to Melilla and Ceuta.

Ceuta, on the Strait of Gibraltar, and Melilla, farther east on the Mediterranean coast, continue to be Spanish presidios on Moroccan soil, both with overwhelmingly Spanish populations. In October 1978 the United States turned over to Morocco a military base, its last in Africa, at Kenitra.

INDEPENDENT MOROCCO

The French protectorate had successfully developed communications, added modern quarters to the cities, and created a flourishing agriculture and a modern industry based on a colonial model. Most of these activities, however, were managed by Europeans. In the constitutional field there had been virtually no development. Though the government was in practice under French supervision, in theory the powers of the sultan were unrestrained. By French insistence, the first cabinet was composed of ministers representing the various groups of Moroccan society, including one from Morocco's Jewish minority. Mubarak Bekkai, an army officer who was not affiliated with any party, was selected as prime minister. The sultan (who officially adopted the title of king in August 1957) selected the ministers personally and retained control of the army and the police; he did, however, nominate a Consultative Assembly of 60 members. His eldest son, Mawlāy Hassan, became chief of staff, and by degrees successfully integrated the irregular liberation forces into the military even after they had supported an uprising against the Spanish in Ifni and against the French in Mauritania.

In general, the changeover to Moroccan control, assisted by French advisers, took place smoothly. Because of the continuing war in Algeria, which Morocco tacitly supported, relations with France were strained; close ties were maintained, however, because Morocco still depended on French technology and financial aid.

A major political change occurred in 1959 when the Istiqlāl split into two sections. The main portion remained under the leadership of Muḥammad ʿAllāl al-Fāsī, while a smaller section, headed by Mehdi Ben Barka, ʿAbd Allāh Ibrāhīm, ʿAbd al-Raḥīm Bouabid, and others, formed the National Union of Popular Forces (Union Nationale des Forces Populaires, or UNFP). Of these groupings the original Istiqlāl represented the more traditional elements, while the UNFP, formed from the younger intelligentsia, favoured socialism with republican leanings. Muḥammad V made use of these dissensions to assume the position of an arbiter above party strife. He nevertheless continued preparations for the creation of a parliament until his unexpected death in 1961, when his son succeeded him as Hassan II.

In 1963, when parliamentary elections were finally held, the two halves of the former Istiqlāl formed an opposition, while a party supporting the king was created out of miscellaneous elements and came to be known as the Front for the Defense of Constitutional Institutions. This included a new, predominantly Amazigh, rural group opposed to the Istiqlāl. The ensuing near deadlock caused the king to dissolve Parliament after only one year, and, with himself or his nominee as prime minister, a form of personal government was resumed. In 1970 a new constitution was promulgated that provided for a one-house legislature; yet this document did not survive an abortive coup by army elements against the monarchy in July 1971. The following year Hassan announced another constitution, but its implementation was largely suspended following another attempted military coup in August. The second coup was apparently led by Minister of Defense Gen. Muḥammad Oufkir; he had earlier been implicated in the kidnapping (1965) and disappearance in Paris of the exiled Moroccan UNFP leader Mehdi Ben Barka, who had been regarded as a likely candidate for the presidency of a Moroccan republic. Oufkir subsequently died at the royal palace, supposedly by his own hand, while hundreds of suspects, including members of his family, were imprisoned. Elections held in 1977, which were widely regarded as fraudulent, brought a landslide victory to the king's supporters. King Hassan's forceful policies to absorb Spanish (Western) Sahara gave him increased popularity in the mid-1970s. This, in addition to his method of mixing efforts to co-opt the political opposition with periods of political repression, served to maintain royal control.

By the early 1980s, however, several bad harvests, a sluggish economy, and the continued financial drain of the war in Western Sahara increased domestic strains, of which violent riots in Casablanca in June 1981 were symptomatic. The need for political reform became even more pressing when international lending agencies and human rights organizations turned their attention to Morocco's troubled internal state of affairs.

The threat of an Algerian-style insurrection fueled by a radical Islamic opposition worried the political leadership throughout the 1990s and into the early 21st century. The government has continued to closely watch the most militant groups. Along with the disaffected urban youth who occasionally took to the streets, the Islamist sympathizers have tested the limits of a new political tolerance. Thus, the 1990s were marked by greater liberalization and a sense of personal freedom, although direct criticism of the king and the royal family were still prohibited. Amnesties for political prisoners long held in remote regions of the country signaled a new attention to human rights, while much publicized curbs on the power of the police and security forces suggested closer adherence to the rule of law.

Foreign Policy

The foreign policy of independent Morocco has often differed from that of its Arab neighbours. Throughout the Cold War, Morocco generally sided with the western European powers and the United States rather than with the Eastern bloc, whereas other Arab states usually chose neutral or even pro-Soviet positions. King Hassan helped to prepare the way for the Camp David Accords (1978) between Israel and Egypt by opening up a political dialogue with Israel in the 1970s, well in advance of other Arab leaders, and by continually pressing both Palestinians and Israelis to seek a compromise solution. Morocco closely supported the United States in the Gulf War (1991) and its pursuit of peace in the Middle East. Unlike other Arab states, Morocco has maintained ties with its former Jewish citizens who now reside in Israel, Europe, and North and South America.

Morocco's relations with neighbouring North African states have not always been smooth, especially those with Libya and its leader Col. Muammar al-Qaddafi. Shunning the Libyan leader's volatile political style, Hassan nevertheless tried, in the 1990s, to reintegrate Libya into the Maghribī fold. Events in Western Sahara disrupted relations with Algeria beginning in the early 1970s, because Algeria generally opposed Morocco's policies there.

Western Sahara

From the mid-1970s King Hassan actively campaigned to assert Morocco's claim to Spanish Sahara, initially using this nationalist issue also to rally much-needed domestic support. In November 1975, after a UN mission had reported that the majority of Saharans wanted independence and had recommended self-determination for the region, Hassan responded with the "Green March," in which some 200,000 volunteers were sent unarmed across the border to claim Spanish Sahara. To avoid a confrontation, Spain signed an agreement relinquishing its claim to the territory. The region, renamed Western Sahara, was to be administered jointly by Morocco and Mauritania. By early 1976 the last Spanish troops had departed, leaving Morocco to struggle with a growing Saharan guerrilla group named the Popular Front for the Liberation of Saguia el Hamra and Río de Oro (Polisario), actively supported by Algeria and later by Libya.

Hassan offered to hold a referendum in the area in 1981, but it was rejected by the Polisario leadership as being too much on Moroccan terms. Fighting continued, and Morocco was able to secure some two-thirds of the territory within defensive walls by 1986. In the meantime, the territory's government-in-exile, the Saharan Arab Democratic Republic, won recognition from an increasing number of foreign governments. Improving ties between Morocco and Algeria beginning in 1987–88, along with a UN-sponsored peace proposal accepted by Morocco in 1988, augured a solution to the problem, but military action by the Polisario the following year prompted King Hassan to cancel further talks.

In 1991 a UN Security Council resolution promised the most definitive solution to Morocco's claim to Western Sahara in 15 years. The resolution called for a referendum on the future of the territory to decide whether it should be annexed to Morocco or become an independent state. However, both Morocco and the Polisario front were unable to agree on the makeup of the voter lists for the referendum, fearful of entering into an electoral process they might lose. Although agreement on other issues such as political detainees and prisoners of war was reached through UN mediation, stalemate over the code of conduct of the referendum has continued, leaving the issue unresolved.

Hassan's Last Years

By the end of the 1990s, King Hassan II had the distinction of being the Arab world's longest-surviving monarch. Actively promoting a program of liberalization in Morocco, he managed to recast an image of an old-style autocrat, reshaping himself and his country to reflect more progressive values. New political freedoms and constitutional reforms enacted in the 1990s culminated in the election of the first opposition government in Morocco in more than 30 years. In 1997 opposition parties won the largest bloc of seats in the lower house, and in March 1998 Abderrahmane Youssoufi ('Abd al-Raḥmān Yūsufī), a leader of the Socialist Union of Popular Forces, was appointed as prime minister. Under pressure from human rights organizations, Hassan also directed a vigorous cleanup campaign that led to the ousting and even execution of corrupt officials as well as the release of more than a thousand political detainees, some of whom had been

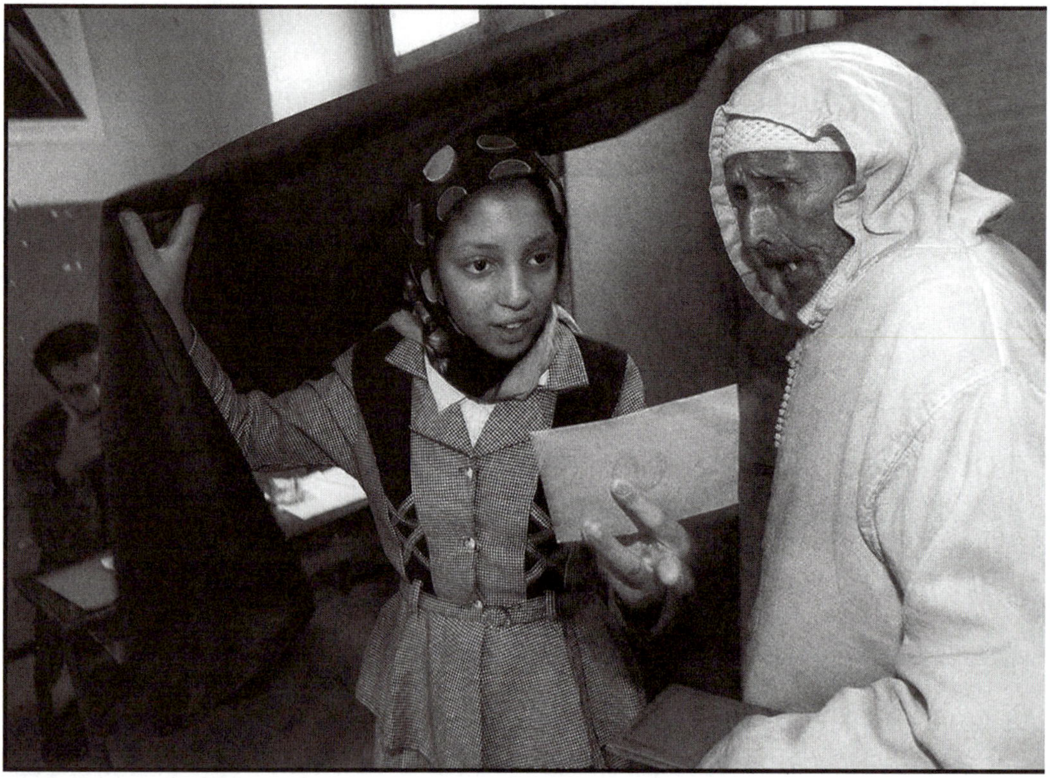

A Moroccan girl helps her illiterate father cast his vote outside Rabat, Nov. 14, 1997. The parliamentary elections marked the first time since independence that voters elected all the country's deputies by universal suffrage. Abdelhak Senna/AFP/Getty Images

held for nearly 25 years. Despite these major political reforms, the king retained ultimate political authority, including the right to dismiss the government, veto laws, and rule by emergency decree.

Hassan also guarded his status as religious head of state and carefully nurtured those aspects of his public image that garnered widespread support in the countryside and among the urban poor. Using public donations, he oversaw the completion in August 1993 of a huge $600 million mosque built on the shoreline at Casablanca, which features a retractable roof and a powerful green laser beam aimed at Mecca from atop its towering minaret. Paradoxically, his main political foes were also found in the religious arena, among the Islamic militants, whom he tried to hold within strict limits. But even at this point of contention, he showed some flexibility: In 1994 a number of political prisoners with ties to religious groups critical of the monarchy were pardoned by Hassan, and in December 1995 Abdessalam Yassine (ʿAbd al-Salām Yāsīn), the leader of the outlawed Islamic organization The Justice and Charity Group (Jamāʿat al-ʿAdl wa al-Iḥsān), was released after spending six years under house arrest.

Into the 21st Century

When Hassan died in July 1999, his son, Muḥammad VI, took up the reins of government and immediately faced a political maelstrom. Controversy raged in Morocco over government proposals to afford women broader access to public life—including greater access to education and more thorough representation within the government and civil service—and to provide them with more equity within society, such as greater rights in marriage, inheritance, and divorce. A liberal program of this type, in Morocco's conservative and religious society, fueled dissent among Islamic groups, and a number of organizations—ranging from Muslim fundamentalist groups to members of international human rights organizations—gathered in large demonstrations in Casablanca and Rabat to support or oppose the government's program. The country saw an increase in violence, including suicide bombings in 2003 and 2007, which led the government to impose more stringent security measures.

CHAPTER 9

SUDAN

Sudan is located in northeastern Africa. Its long history is closely intertwined with that of neighbouring Egypt, and the two are often examined separately from the other countries that also fall under the northern Africa designation. The capital of Sudan is Khartoum.

ANCIENT NUBIA

The earliest inhabitants of what is now Sudan can be traced to African peoples who lived in the vicinity of Khartoum in Mesolithic times (Middle Stone Age; 30,000–20,000 BCE). They were hunters and gatherers who made pottery and (later) objects of ground sandstone. Toward the end of the Neolithic Period (New Stone Age; 10,000–3,000 BCE) they had domesticated animals. These Africans were clearly in contact with predynastic civilizations (before *c.* 2925 BCE) to the north in Egypt, but the arid uplands separating Egypt from Nubia appear to have discouraged the predynastic Egyptians from settling there.

EGYPTIAN INFLUENCE

At the end of the 4th millennium BCE, kings of Egypt's 1st dynasty conquered Upper Nubia south of Aswān, introducing Egyptian cultural influence to the African peoples who were scattered along the riverbanks. In subsequent centuries, Nubia was subjected to successive military expeditions from Egypt in search of slaves or building materials for royal tombs, destroying much of the Egyptian-Nubian culture that had sprung from the initial conquests of the 1st dynasty. Throughout these few centuries (*c.* 2925–*c.* 2575 BCE), the descendants of the Nubians continued to eke out an existence along the Nile River, an easy prey for Egyptian military expeditions. Although the Nubians were no match for the armies of Egypt's Old Kingdom, the interactions arising from their enslavement and colonization led to ever-increasing African influence upon the art, culture, and religion of dynastic Egypt.

Sometime after about 2181 BCE, in the period known to Egyptologists as the First Intermediate Period (*c.* 2130–1938), a new wave of immigrants entered Nubia from Libya, in the west, where the increasing desiccation of the Sahara drove them to settle along the Nile as cattle farmers. Other branches of these people seem to have gone beyond the Nile to the Red Sea Hills, while still others pushed south and west to Wadai and Darfur. These newcomers were able to settle on the Nile and assimilate the existing Nubians without opposition from Egypt. After the fall of the 6th dynasty (*c.* 2150), Egypt experienced more than a century of weakness and internal strife, giving the immigrants in Nubia time to develop their own distinct civilization with unique crafts, architecture, and social structure, virtually unhindered by the potentially more dynamic civilization to the north. With the advent of the 11th dynasty (2081), however, Egypt recovered its strength and pressed southward into Nubia, at first sending only sporadic expeditions to exact tribute but by the 12th dynasty (1938–1756) effectively occupying Nubia as far south as Semna. The Nubians resisted the Egyptian occupation, which was maintained only by a chain of forts erected along the Nile. Egyptian military and trading expeditions, of course, penetrated beyond Semna, and Egyptian fortified trading posts were actually established to the south at Karmah in order to protect against frequent attacks upon Egyptian trading vessels by Nubian tribesmen beyond the southern frontier.

THE KINGDOM OF KUSH

Despite the Egyptian presence in Upper Nubia, the indigenous culture of the region continued to flourish. This culture was deeply influenced by African peoples in the south and was little changed by the proximity of Egyptian garrisons or the imports of luxury articles by Egyptian traders. Indeed, the Egyptianization of Nubia appears to actually have been enhanced during the decline in Egypt's political control over Nubia in the Second Intermediate Period (*c.* 1630–1540 BCE), when Nubians were employed in large numbers as mercenaries against the Asian Hyksos invaders of Egypt. This experience did more to introduce Egyptian culture, which the mercenaries absorbed while fighting

Darfur

Darfur is the name used for both a historical region and a former province in western Sudan. It was an independent kingdom from c. 2500 BCE. Its first traditional rulers, the Daju, probably traded with ancient Egypt; they were succeeded by the Tunjur. Darfur's Christian period (c. 900–1200) was ended by the advance of Islam with the empire of Kanem-Bornu. In the 1870s Darfur came under Egyptian rule, and in 1916 it became a province of Sudan. Long-standing ethnic tensions between Arab nomads and sedentary Fur and other agriculturalists erupted in the late 1980s, and sporadic violence ensued. The conflict escalated in 2003, when rebels among the agriculturalist population began attacking government installations in protest of perceived neglect of non-Arabs and of the country's western region. The government responded with the creation of the Janjaweed (also spelled Jingaweit or Janjawid) militia, which attacked sedentary groups in Darfur. Despite a 2004 cease-fire and the subsequent presence of international peacekeeping troops, by 2007 hundreds of thousands of people had been killed and more than two million displaced.

in Egyptian armies, than did the preceding centuries of Egyptian military occupation. Conversely, the presence of these mercenaries in Egypt contributed to the growing African influence within Egyptian culture.

The defeat of the Hyksos was the result of a national rising of the Egyptians who, once they had expelled the Hyksos from the Nile valley, turned their energies southward to reestablish the military occupation of Nubia that the Hyksos invasion had disrupted. Under Thutmose I (reigned 1493–c. 1482 BCE) the Egyptian conquest of the northern Sudan was completed as far as Kurqus, 50 miles south of Abū Ḥamad, and subsequent Egyptian military expeditions penetrated even farther up the Nile. This third Egyptian occupation was the most complete and the most enduring, for despite sporadic rebellions against Egyptian control, Nubia was divided into two administrative units: Wawat in the north, with its provincial capital at Aswān, and Kush (also spelled Cush) in the south, with its headquarters at Napata (Marawī). Nubia as a whole was governed by a viceroy, usually a member of the royal entourage, who was responsible to the Egyptian pharaoh. Under him were two deputies, one for Wawat and one for Kush, and a hierarchy of lesser officials. The bureaucracy was staffed chiefly by Egyptians, but Egyptianized Nubians were not uncommon. Colonies of Egyptian officials, traders, and priests surrounded the administrative centres, but beyond these outposts the Nubians continued to preserve their own distinct traditions, customs, and crafts. A syncretistic culture thus arose in Kush, fashioned by that of Egypt to the north and those of African peoples to the south.

Kush's position athwart the trade routes from Egypt to the Red Sea, and from the Nile to the south and west, brought considerable wealth from far-off places. Moreover, its cultivated areas along the Nile were rich, and in the hills the gold and emerald mines produced bullion and jewels for Egypt. The Nubians were also highly valued as soldiers.

As Egypt slipped once again into decline at the close of the New Kingdom (11th century BCE), the viceroys of Kush, supported by their Nubian armies, became virtually independent kings, free of Egyptian control. By the 8th century BCE the kings of Kush came from hereditary ruling families of Egyptianized Nubian chiefs who possessed neither political nor family ties with Egypt. Under one such king, Kashta, Kush acquired control of Upper (i.e., southern) Egypt, and under his son Piye (formerly known as Piankhi; reigned *c.* 750–*c.* 719 BCE) the whole of Egypt to the shores of the Mediterranean was brought under the administration of Kush. As a world power, however, Kush was not to last. Just when the kings of Kush had established their rule from Abū Ḥamad to the Nile delta, the Assyrians invaded Egypt (671 BCE) and with their superior iron-forged weapons defeated the armies of Kush under the redoubtable Taharqa; by 654 the Kushites had been driven back to Nubia and the safety of their capital, Napata.

Although reduced from a great power to an isolated kingdom behind the barren hills that blocked the southward advance from Aswān, Kush continued to rule over the middle Nile for another thousand years. Its unique Egyptian-Nubian culture with its strong African accretions was preserved, while that of Egypt came under Persian, Greek, and Roman influences. Although Egyptianized in many ways, the culture of Kush was not simply Egyptian civilization in a Nubian environment. The Kushites developed their own language, expressed first by Egyptian hieroglyphs, then by their own, and finally by a cursive script. They worshipped Egyptian gods but did not abandon their own. They buried their kings in pyramids but not in the Egyptian fashion. Their wealth continued to flow from the mines and to grow with their control of the trade routes. Soon after the retreat from Egypt, the capital was moved from Napata southward to Meroe near Shandī, where the kingdom was increasingly exposed to the long-established African cultures farther south at the very time when its ties with Egypt were rapidly disappearing. The subsequent history of Kush is one of gradual decay, ending with inglorious extinction in 350 CE by the king of Aksum, who marched down from the Ethiopian highlands, destroyed Meroe, and sacked the decrepit towns along the river.

CHRISTIAN AND ISLAMIC INFLUENCE

After the fall of Kush, the Sudan gradually increased interaction with the outside

Kushite pyramids in the Meroe desert north of Khartoum, Sudan, Feb. 2010. AFP/Getty Images

world. New religions were introduced to the region—first Christianity, then Islam.

Medieval Christian Kingdoms

The 200 years from the fall of Kush to the middle of the 6th century is an unknown age in the Sudan. Nubia was inhabited by a people called the Nobatae by the ancient geographers and the X-Group by modern archaeologists, who are still at a loss to explain the origins of these people. The X-Group were clearly, however, the heirs of Kush, for their whole cultural life was dominated by crafts and customs of the Kushan city of Meroe. They occasionally even felt themselves sufficiently strong, in alliance with the nomadic Blemmyes (the Beja of the eastern Sudan), to attack the Romans in Upper Egypt. When this happened, the Romans retaliated, defeating the Nobatae and Blemmyes and driving them into obscurity once again.

When the Sudan was once more brought into the orbit of the Mediterranean world by the arrival of Christian missionaries in the 6th century CE, the middle course of the Nile was divided into three kingdoms: Nobatia, with its capital at Pachoras (modern Faras); Maqurrah, with its capital at Dunqulah (Old Dongola); and the kingdom of ʿAlwah in the south, with its capital at Sūbah (Soba) near what is now Khartoum. Between 543 and 575 these three kingdoms were converted to Christianity by the work of Julian, a missionary who proselytized in Nobatia (543–545), and his successor Longinus, who between 569 and 575 consolidated the work of Julian in Nobatia and even carried Christianity to ʿAlwah in the south. The new religion appears to have been adopted with considerable enthusiasm. Christian churches sprang up along the Nile, and ancient temples were refurbished to accommodate Christian worshippers. After the retirement of Longinus, however, the Sudan once again receded into a period about which little is known, and it did not reemerge into the stream of recorded history until the coming of the Arabs in the middle of the 7th century.

After the death of the Prophet Muhammad in 632 CE, the Arabs erupted from the desert steppes of Arabia and overran the lands to the east and west. Egypt was invaded in 639, and small groups of Arab raiders penetrated up the Nile and pillaged along the frontier of the kingdom of Maqurrah, which by the 7th century had absorbed the state of Nobatia. Raid and counterraid between the Arabs and the Nubians followed until a well-equipped Arab expedition under ʿAbd Allāh ibn Saʿd ibn Abī Sarḥ was sent south to punish the Nubians. The Arabs marched as far as Dunqulah, laid siege to the town, and destroyed the Christian cathedral. They suffered heavy casualties, however, so that, when the king of Maqurrah sought an armistice, ʿAbd Allāh ibn Saʿd agreed to peace, happy to extricate his battered forces from a precarious position. Arab-Nubian relations were subsequently regularized by an annual exchange of gifts, by trade relations, and by the mutual understanding that no Muslims were to settle in Nubia and no Nubians were to take up residence in Egypt. With but few interruptions, this peaceful, commercial relationship lasted nearly six centuries, its very success undoubtedly the result of the mutual advantage that both the Arabs and the Nubians derived from it. The Arabs had a stable frontier; they appear to have had no designs to occupy the Sudan and were probably discouraged from doing so by the arid plains south of Aswān. Peace on the frontier was their object, and this the treaty guaranteed. In return, the kingdom of Maqurrah gained another 600 years of life.

Islamic Encroachments

When non-Arab Muslims acquired control of the Nile delta, friction arose in Upper Egypt. In the 9th century the Turkish Ṭūlūnid rulers of Egypt, wishing to rid themselves of the unruly nomadic Arab tribes in their domain, encouraged them to migrate southward. Lured by the prospect of gold in the Nubian Desert, the nomads pressed into Nubia, raiding and pillaging along the borders, but the heartland of Maqurrah remained free from direct hostilities until the Mamlūks established their control over Egypt (1250). In the late 13th and early 14th centuries, the Mamlūk sultans sent regular military expeditions against Maqurrah, as much to rid Egypt of uncontrollable Arab Bedouin as to capture Nubia. The Mamlūks never succeeded in actually occupying Maqurrah, but they devastated the country, draining its political and economic vitality and plunging it into chaos and depression. By the 15th century Dunqulah was no longer strong enough to withstand Arab encroachment, and the country was open to Arab immigration. Once the Arab nomads, particularly the Juhaynah people, learned that the land beyond the Aswān reach could support their herds and that no political authority had the power to turn them back, they began to migrate southward, intermarrying with the Nubians and introducing Arab Muslim culture to the Christian inhabitants. The Arabs, who inherited through the male line, soon acquired control from the Nubians, who inherited through the female line, intermarriage resulting in Nubian inheritances passing from Nubian women to their half-Arab sons, but the Arabs replaced political authority in Maqurrah only with their own nomadic institutions. From Dunqulah the Juhaynah and others wandered east and west of the Nile with their herds; in the south the kingdom of ʿAlwah stood as the last indigenous Christian barrier to Arab occupation of the Sudan.

ʿAlwah extended from Kabūshiyyah as far south as Sennar (Sannār). Beyond, from the Ethiopian escarpment to the White Nile, lived peoples about which little is known. ʿAlwah appears to have been much more prosperous and stronger than Maqurrah. It preserved the ironworking techniques of Kush, and its capital at Sūbah possessed many impressive buildings, churches, and gardens. Christianity remained the state religion, but 'Alwah's long isolation from the Christian world had probably resulted in bizarre and syncretistic accretions to liturgy and ritual. 'Alwah was able to maintain its integrity so long as the Arabs failed to combine against it, but the continuous and corrosive raids of the Bedouin throughout the 15th century clearly weakened its power to resist. Thus, when an Arab confederation led by 'Abd Allāh Jammā' was at last brought together to assault the Christian kingdom, 'Alwah collapsed (*c.* 1500). Sūbah and the Blue Nile region were abandoned, left to the Funj, who suddenly appeared, seemingly from nowhere, to establish their authority from Sennar to the main Nile.

THE FUNJ

The Funj were a strange and mysterious people. Neither Arabs nor Muslims, their homeland was probably on the upper Blue Nile in the borderlands between Ethiopia and the Sudan. Under their leader 'Amārah Dūnqas, the Funj founded their capital at Sennar and throughout the 16th century struggled for control of the Al-Jazīrah (Gezira) region against the Arab tribes who had settled around the confluence of the Blue and the White Niles. The Funj appear to have firmly established their supremacy by 1607–08.

By the mid-17th century the Funj dynasty had reached its golden age under one of its greatest kings, Bādī II Abū Daqn (reigned 1644/45–80), who extended Funj authority across the White Nile into Kordofan and reduced the tribal chieftaincies scattered northward along the main Nile to tribute-paying feudatories. But as Bādī II expanded Funj power, he also planted the seeds of its decline. During his conquests, slaves were captured and taken to Sennar, where, as they grew in numbers and influence, they formed a military caste. Loyal to the monarch alone, the slaves soon came to compete with the Funj aristocracy for control of the offices of state. Intrigue and hostility between these two rival groups soon led to open rebellion that undermined the position of the traditional ruling class.

Under Bādī IV Abū Shulūkh (reigned 1724–62), the ruling aristocracy was finally broken, and the king assumed arbitrary power, supported by his slave troops. So long as Bādī IV could command the loyalty of his army, his position was secure and the kingdom enjoyed respite from internal strife, but at the end of his long reign he could no longer control the army. Under the leadership of his viceroy in Kordofan, Abū Likaylik, the military turned against the king and exiled him to Sūbah. Abū Likaylik probably represented a resurgence of older indigenous elements who had been Arabized and Islamized but were neither Arab nor Funj. Thereafter the Funj kings were but puppets of their viziers (chief ministers), whose struggles to win and to keep control precipitated the kingdom's steady decline, interrupted by only infrequent periods of peace and stability established by a strong vizier who was able to overcome his rivals. During its last half century the Funj kingdom was a spent state, kept intact only through want of a rival but gradually disintegrating through wars, intrigue, and conspiracy, until the Egyptians advanced on Sennar in 1821 and pushed the Funj dynasty into oblivion.

The Spread of Islam

The Funj were originally non-Muslims, but the aristocracy soon adopted Islam and, although they retained many traditional African customs, remained nominal Muslims. The conversion was largely the work of a handful of Islamic missionaries who came to the Sudan from the larger Muslim world. The great success of these missionaries, however, was not among the Funj themselves but among the Arabized Nubian population settled along the Nile. Among these villagers the missionaries instilled a deep devotion to Islam that appears to have been conspicuously absent among the nomadic Arabs who had first reached the Sudan after the collapse of the kingdom of Maqurrah. One early missionary was Ghulām Allāh ibn ʿĀ'id from Yemen, who settled at Dunqulah in the 14th century. He was followed in the 15th century by Ḥamad Abū Danana, who appears to have emphasized the way to God through mystical exercises rather than through the more orthodox interpretations of the Qur'ān taught by Ghulām Allāh.

The spread of Islam was advanced in the 16th century when the hegemony of the Funj enhanced security. In the 16th and 17th centuries, numerous schools of religious learning were founded along the White Nile, and the Shāyqiyyah confederacy was converted. Many of the more famous Sudanese missionaries who followed them were Sufi holy men, members of influential religious brotherhoods who sought the way to God through mystical contemplation. The Sufi brotherhoods played a vital role in linking the Sudan to the larger world of Islam beyond the Nile valley. Although the fervour of Sudanese Islam waned after 1700, the great reform movements that shook the Muslim world in the late 18th and early 19th centuries produced a revivalist spirit among the Sufi brotherhoods, giving rise to a new order, the Mīrghāniyyah or Khatmiyyah, later one of the strongest in the modern Sudan.

The "missionaries" were *faqīhs* (Islamic jurists) who attracted a following through their teachings and piety and laid the foundations for a long line of indigenous Sudanese holy men. They passed on the way to God taught them by their masters or founded their own religious schools or, if extraordinarily successful, gathered their own following into a religious order. The *faqīhs* played a vital role in educating their followers and helped place them in the highest positions of government, which allowed them to spread Islam and the influence of their respective brotherhoods. The *faqīhs* held a religious monopoly until the introduction, under Egyptian-Ottoman rule, of an official hierarchy of jurists and scholars—the *'ulamā'*, whose orthodox legalistic conception of Islam was as alien to the Sudanese as were their origins. This disparity between the mystical, traditional *faqīhs* (close to the Sudanese, if not of them) and the orthodox *'ulamā'* (aloof, if not actually part of the government bureaucracy) created a rivalry that produced open hostility in times of trouble and sullen suspicion in times of peace. This schism has since diminished; the *faqīhs* continue their customary practices unmolested, while the Sudanese have acknowledged the position of the *'ulamā'* in society.

EGYPTIAN-OTTOMAN RULE

In July 1820, Muḥammad 'Alī, viceroy of Egypt under the Ottoman Empire, sent an army under his son Ismā'īl to conquer the Sudan. Muḥammad 'Ali was interested in the gold and slaves that the Sudan could provide and wished to control the vast hinterland south of Egypt. By 1821 the Funj and the sultan of Darfur had surrendered, and the Nilotic Sudan from Nubia to the Ethiopian foothills and from the 'Aṭbarah River to Darfur became part of Muḥammad 'Alī's expanding empire.

MUḤAMMAD 'ALĪ AND HIS SUCCESSORS

The collection of taxes under Muḥammad 'Alī's regime amounted to virtual confiscation of gold, livestock, and slaves, and opposition to his rule became intense, eventually erupting into rebellion and the murder of Ismā'īl and his bodyguard. But the rebels lacked leadership and coordination, and their revolt was brutally suppressed. A resentful hostility in the Sudanese was met by continued repression until the appointment of 'Alī Khūrshīd Āghā as governor-general in 1826. His administration marked a new era in Egyptian-Sudanese relations. He reduced taxes and consulted the Sudanese through the respected Sudanese leader 'Abd al-Qādir wad al-Zayn. Letters of amnesty were granted to fugitives. A more equitable system of taxation was implemented, and the support of the powerful class of holy men and sheikhs (tribal chiefs) for the administration was obtained by exempting them from taxation. But 'Alī Khūrshīd was not content merely to restore the Sudan to its previous condition. Under his initiative, trade routes were protected and expanded, Khartoum was developed as the administrative capital, and a host of agricultural and technical improvements were undertaken. When he retired to Cairo in 1838, he left a prosperous and contented country behind him.

His successor, Aḥmad Pasha Abū Widān, continued his policies with but few exceptions and made it his primary concern to root out official corruption. Abū Widān dealt ruthlessly with offenders or those who sought to thwart his schemes to reorganize taxation. He was particularly fond of the army, which reaped the benefits of regular pay and tolerable conditions in return for bearing the brunt of the expansion and consolidation of

Egyptian administration in Kassalā and among the Baqqārah Arabs of southern Kordofan. Muḥammad ʿAlī, suspecting Abū Widān of disloyalty, recalled him to Cairo in the autumn of 1843, but he died mysteriously, many believed of poison, before he left the Sudan.

During the next two decades the country stagnated because of ineffective government at Khartoum and vacillation by the viceroys at Cairo. If the successors of Abū Widān possessed administrative talent, they were seldom able to demonstrate it. No governor-general held office long enough to introduce his own plans, let alone carry on those of his predecessor. New schemes were never begun, and old projects were allowed to languish. Without direction the army and the bureaucracy became demoralized and indifferent, while the Sudanese became disgruntled with the government. In 1856 the viceroy Saʿīd Pasha visited the Sudan and, shocked by what he saw, contemplated abandoning it altogether. Instead, he abolished the office of governor-general and had each Sudanese province report directly to the viceregal authority in Cairo. This state of affairs persisted until Saʿīd's death in 1863.

During these quiescent decades, however, two ominous developments began that presaged future problems. Reacting to pressure from the Western powers, particularly Great Britain, the governor-general of the Sudan was ordered to halt the slave trade. But not even the viceroy himself could overcome established custom with the stroke of a pen and the erection of a few police posts. If the restriction of the slave trade precipitated resistance among the Sudanese, the appointment of Christian officials to the administration and the expansion of the European Christian community in the Sudan caused open resentment. European merchants, mostly of Mediterranean origin, were either ignored or tolerated by the Sudanese and confined their contacts to compatriots within their own community and to the Turko-Egyptian officials whose manners and dress they frequently adopted. The merchants became a powerful and influential group, whose lasting contribution to the Sudan was to take the lead in opening the White Nile and the southern Sudan to navigation and commerce after Muḥammad ʿAlī had abolished state trading monopolies in the Sudan in 1838 under pressure from the European powers.

Ismāʿīl Pasha and the Growth of European Influence

After Saʿīd's death in 1863, Ismāʿīl Pasha became viceroy of Egypt. Educated in Egypt, Vienna, and Paris, Ismāʿīl had absorbed the European interest in overseas adventures as well as Muḥammad ʿAlī's desire for imperial expansion and had imaginative schemes for transforming Egypt and the Sudan into a modern state by employing Western technology. First Ismāʿīl hoped to acquire the rest of the Nile basin, including the southern Sudan and the Bantu states by the Great

Lakes of east-central Africa. To finance this vast undertaking and his projects for the modernization of Egypt itself, Ismāʿīl turned to the capital-rich nations of western Europe, where investors were willing to risk their savings at high rates of interest in the cause of Egyptian and African development. But such funds would be attracted only as long as Ismāʿīl demonstrated his interest in reform by intensifying the campaign against the slave trade in the Sudan. Ismāʿīl needed no encouragement, for he required the diplomatic and financial support of the European powers in his efforts to modernize Egypt and expand his empire. Thus, these two major themes of Ismāʿīl's rule of the Nilotic Sudan—imperial expansion and the suppression of the slave trade—became intertwined, culminating in a third major development, the introduction of an ever-increasing number of European Christians to carry out the task of modernization.

In 1869 Ismāʿīl commissioned English explorer Samuel White Baker to lead an expedition up the White Nile to establish Egyptian hegemony over the equatorial regions of central Africa and to curtail the slave trade on the upper Nile. Baker remained in equatorial Africa until 1873, where he established the Equatoria province as part of the Egyptian Sudan. He had extended Egyptian power and curbed the slave traders on the Nile, but he had also alienated certain African tribes and, being rather tactless in matters of religion, Ismāʿīl's Muslim administrators as well. Moreover, Baker had struck only at the Nilotic slave trade. To the west, on the vast plains of the Baḥr al-Ghazāl, slave merchants had established enormous empires with stations garrisoned by slave soldiers. From these stations the long lines of human chattels were sent overland through Darfur and Kordofan to the slave markets of the northern Sudan, Egypt, and Arabia. Not only did the firearms of the Khartoumers (as the traders were called) establish their supremacy over the peoples of the interior but also those merchants with the strongest resources gradually swallowed up lesser traders until virtually the whole of the Baḥr al-Ghazāl was controlled by the greatest slaver of them all, al-Zubayr Raḥmah Manṣūr, more commonly known as Zubayr (or Zobeir) Pasha. So powerful had he become that in 1873, the year Baker retired from the Sudan, the Egyptian viceroy (now called the khedive) appointed Zubayr governor of the Baḥr al-Ghazāl. Ismāʿīl's officials had failed to destroy Zubayr as Baker had crushed the slavers east of the Nile, and to elevate Zubayr to the governorship appeared the only way to establish at least the nominal sovereignty of Cairo over that enormous province. Thus, the agents of Zubayr continued to pillage the Baḥr al-Ghazāl under the Egyptian flag, while officially Egypt extended its dominion to the tropical rainforests of the Congo region. Zubayr remained in detention in Cairo after going there in 1876 to press his claims for a new title.

Ismāʿīl next offered the governorship of the Equatoria province to another

Englishman, Charles George Gordon, who in China had won fame and the sobriquet Chinese Gordon. Gordon arrived in Equatoria in 1874. His object was the same as Baker's—to consolidate Egyptian authority in Equatoria and to establish Egyptian sovereignty over the kingdoms of the great East African lakes. He achieved some success in Equatoria but none in the lakes region. When Gordon retired from Equatoria, the lake kingdoms remained stubbornly independent.

In 1877 Ismāʿīl appointed Gordon governor-general of the Sudan. Gordon returned to the Sudan to lead a crusade against the slave trade and, to assist him in this humanitarian enterprise, surrounded himself with a cadre of European and American Christian officials. In 1877 Ismāʿīl had signed the Anglo-Egyptian Slave Trade Convention, which provided for the termination of the sale and purchase of slaves in the Sudan by 1880. Gordon set out to fulfill the terms of this treaty, and, in whirlwind tours through the country, he broke up the markets and imprisoned the traders. His European subordinates did the same in the provinces.

Gordon's crusading zeal blinded him to his invidious position as a Christian in a Muslim land and obscured from him the social and economic effects of arbitrary repression. Not only did his campaign create a crisis in the Sudan's economy but the Sudanese soon came to believe that the crusade, led by European Christians, violated the principles and traditions of Islam. By 1879 a strong current of reaction against Gordon's reforms was running through the country. The powerful slave-trading interests had, of course, turned against the administration, while the ordinary villagers and nomads, who habitually blamed the government for any difficulties, were quick to associate economic depression with Gordon's Christianity. And then suddenly, in the middle of rising discontent in the Sudan, Ismāʿīl's financial position collapsed. In difficulties for years, he could now no longer pay the interest on the Egyptian debt, and an international commission was appointed by the European powers to oversee Egyptian finances. After 16 years of glorious spending, Ismāʿīl sailed away into exile. Gordon resigned.

Gordon left a perilous situation in the Sudan. The Sudanese were confused and dissatisfied. Many of the ablest senior officials—both European and Egyptian—had been dismissed by Gordon, departed with him, or died in his service. Castigated and ignored by Gordon, the bureaucracy had lapsed into apathy. Moreover, the office of governor-general, on which the administration was so dependent, devolved upon Muḥammad Ra'ūf Pasha, a mild man ill-suited to stem the current of discontent or to shore up the structure of Egyptian rule, particularly when he could no longer count on Egyptian resources. Such then was the Sudan in June of 1881 when Muḥammad Aḥmad declared himself to be the Mahdī (the "Divinely Guided").

THE MAHDIYYAH

Muḥammad Aḥmad ibn ʿAbd Allāh, was the son of a Dunqulahwi boatbuilder who claimed descent from the Prophet Muhammad. Deeply religious from his youth, Muḥammad Aḥmad was educated in one of the Sufi orders, the Sammāniyyah, but he later secluded himself on Ābā Island in the White Nile to practice religious asceticism. In 1880 he toured Kordofan, where he learned of the discontent of the people and observed those actions of the government that he could not reconcile with his own religious beliefs. Upon his return to Ābā Island, he clearly viewed himself as a *mujaddid,* a "renewer" of the Muslim faith, his mission to reform Islam and return it to the pristine form practiced by the Prophet. To Muḥammad Aḥmad the orthodox *ʿulamāʾ* who supported the administration were no less infidels than Christians, and, when he later lashed out against misgovernment, he was referring as much to the theological heresy as to secular maladministration. Once he had proclaimed himself Mahdī, Muḥammad Aḥmad was regarded by the Sudanese as an eschatological figure who foreshadowed the end of an age of darkness (his arrival coincided with the end of a century—in this case, the 13th—of the Islamic calendar, a period traditionally associated with religious renewal) and heralded the beginnings of a new era of light and righteousness. Thus, as a divinely guided reformer and symbol, Muḥammad Aḥmad fulfilled the requirements of *mahdī* in the eyes of his supporters.

Surrounding the Mahdī were his followers, the *anṣar* ("helpers," a Qurʾānic term referring to one group of Muhammad's early followers). Foremost among them was ʿAbd Allāh ibn Muḥammad, who came from the Taʿāʾishah tribe of the Baqqārah Arabs and, as caliph (*khalīfah,* "successor"), assumed the leadership of the Mahdist state upon the death of Muḥammad Aḥmad. The holy men, the *faqīh*s who had long lamented the sorry state of religion in the Sudan brought on by the legalistic and unappealing orthodoxy of the Egyptians, looked to the Mahdī to purge the Sudan of the faithless ones. Also in his following, more numerous and powerful than the holy men, were the merchants formerly connected with the slave trade. All had suffered from Gordon's campaign against the trade, and all now hoped to reassert their economic position under the banner of religious war. Neither of these groups, however, could have carried out a revolution by themselves. The third and vital participants were the Baqqārah Arabs, the cattle nomads of Kordofan and Darfur who hated taxes and despised government. They formed the shock troops of the Mahdist revolutionary army, whose enthusiasm and numbers made up for its primitive technology. Moreover, the government itself managed only to enhance the prestige of the Mahdī by its fumbling attempts to arrest him and proscribe his movement.

By September 1882 the Mahdists controlled all of Kordofan, and at Shaykān on Nov. 5, 1883, they destroyed an Egyptian army of 10,000 men under the command of a British colonel. After Shaykān, the Sudan was lost, and not even the heroic leadership of Gordon, who was hastily sent to Khartoum, could save the Sudan for Egypt. On Jan. 26, 1885, the Mahdists captured Khartoum and massacred Gordon and the defenders.

The Reign of the Khalīfah

Five months after the fall of Khartoum, the Mahdī died suddenly on June 22, 1885. He was succeeded by the Khalīfah ʿAbd Allāh. The Khalīfah's first task was to secure his own precarious position among the competing factions in the Mahdist state. He frustrated a conspiracy by the Mahdī's relatives and disarmed the personal retinues of his leading rivals in Omdurman, the Mahdist capital of the Sudan.

Having curtailed the threats to his rule, the Khalīfah sought to accomplish the Mahdī's dream of a universal jihad (holy war) to reform Islam throughout the Muslim world. With a zeal compounded from a genuine wish to carry out religious reform, a desire for military victory and personal power, and utter ignorance of the world beyond the Sudan, the Khalīfah sent his forces to the four points of the compass to spread Mahdism and extend the domains of the Mahdist state. By 1889 this expansionist drive was spent. In the west the Mahdist armies had achieved only an unstable occupation of Darfur. In the east they had defeated the Ethiopians, but the victory produced no permanent gain. In the southern Sudan the Mahdists had scored some initial successes but were driven from the upper Nile in 1897 by the forces of the Congo Free State of Leopold II of Belgium. On the Egyptian frontier in the north the jihad met its worst defeat, at Tūshkī in August 1889, when an Anglo-Egyptian army under Gen. F.W. (later Baron) Grenfell destroyed a Mahdist army led by ʿAbd al-Raḥmān al-Nujūmī.

The Mahdist state had squandered its resources on the jihad, and a period of consolidation and contraction followed, necessitated by a sequence of bad harvests resulting in famine, epidemic, and death. Between 1889 and 1892 the Sudan suffered its most devastating and terrible years, as the Sudanese sought to survive on their shriveled crops and emaciated herds. After 1892 the harvests improved, and food was no longer in short supply. Moreover, the autocracy of the Khalīfah had become increasingly acceptable to most Sudanese, and, having tempered his own despotism and eliminated the gross defects of his administration, he, too, received the widespread acceptance, if not devotion, that the Sudanese had accorded the Mahdī.

In spite of its many defects, the Khalīfah's administration served the Sudan better than its many detractors would admit. Certainly the Khalīfah's government was autocratic, but, while autocracy might be repugnant to

The tomb of al-Mahdī in Omdurman, Sudan. Charles Beery/Shostal Associates

European democrats, it not only was understandable to the Sudanese but appealed to their deepest feelings and attitudes formed by tribe, religion, and past experience with the centralized authoritarianism of the Ottomans. For them the Khalīfah was equal to the task of governing bequeathed him by the Mahdī. Only when confronted by new forces from the outside world, of which he was ignorant, did ʿAbd Allāh's abilities fail him. His belief in Mahdism, his reliance on the superb courage and military skill of the *anṣar*, and his own ability to rally them against an alien invader were simply insufficient to preserve his independent Islamic state against the overwhelming technological superiority of Britain. And, as the 19th century drew to a close, the rival imperialisms of the European powers brought the full force of this technological supremacy against the Mahdist state.

The British Conquest

British forces invaded and occupied Egypt in 1882 to put down a nationalist revolution hostile to foreign interests and remained there to prevent any further threat to the khedive's government or the possible intervention of another European power. The consequences of this were far-reaching. A permanent British occupation of Egypt required the inviolability of the Nile waters—without which Egypt could not survive—not from any African state, which did not possess the technical resources to interfere with it, but from rival European powers, which could. Consequently, the British government, by diplomacy and military maneuvers, negotiated agreements with the Italians and the Germans to keep them out of the Nile valley. They were less successful with the French, who wanted the British to withdraw from Egypt.

Once it became apparent that the British were determined to remain, the French cast about for means to force them from the Nile valley. In 1893 an elaborate plan was concocted by which a French expedition would march across Africa from the west coast to Fashoda (Kodok) on the upper Nile, where it was believed a dam could be constructed to obstruct the flow of the Nile waters. After inordinate delays, the French Nile expedition set out for Africa in June 1896, under the command of Capt. Jean-Baptiste Marchand.

As reports reached London during 1896 and 1897 of Marchand's march to Fashoda, Britain's inability to insulate the Nile valley became embarrassingly exposed. British officials desperately tried one scheme after another to beat the French to Fashoda. They all failed, and by the autumn of 1897 British authorities had come to the reluctant conclusion that the conquest of the Sudan was necessary to protect the Nile waters from French encroachment. In October an Anglo-Egyptian army under the command of Gen. Sir (later Lord) Horatio Herbert Kitchener was ordered to invade the Sudan. Kitchener pushed steadily but cautiously up the Nile. His Anglo-Egyptian forces defeated a large Mahdist army at the ʿAṭbarah River on April 8, 1898. Then, after spending four months preparing for the final advance to Omdurman, Kitchener's army of about 25,000 troops met the massed 60,000-man army of the Khalīfah outside the city on Sept. 2, 1898. By midday the Battle of Omdurman was over. The Mahdists were decisively defeated with heavy losses, and the Khalīfah fled, to be killed nearly a year later.

Kitchener did not long remain at Omdurman but pressed up the Nile to Fashoda with a small flotilla. There, on Sept. 18, 1898, he met Capt. Marchand, who declined to withdraw: the long-expected Fashoda crisis had begun. Both the French and British governments prepared for war. Neither the French army nor the navy was in any condition to fight, however, and the French were forced to give way. An Anglo-French agreement of March 1899 stipulated that French expansion eastward in Africa would stop at the Nile watershed.

THE ANGLO-EGYPTIAN CONDOMINIUM

Having conquered the Sudan, the British now had to govern it. But the administration of this vast land was complicated by the legal and diplomatic problems that had accompanied the conquest. The Sudan campaigns had been undertaken by the British to protect their imperial position as well as the Nile waters, yet the Egyptian treasury had borne the greater part of the expense, with Egyptian troops far outnumbering those of Britain in the Anglo-Egyptian army. The British, however, did not simply want to hand the Sudan over to Egyptian rule; most Englishmen were convinced that the Mahdiyyah was the result of 60 years of Egyptian oppression. To resolve this dilemma, the Anglo-Egyptian Condominium was declared in 1899, whereby the Sudan was given separate political status under which sovereignty was jointly shared by the khedive and the British crown, and the Egyptian and the British flags were flown side by side. The military and civil government of the Sudan was invested in a governor-general appointed by the khedive of Egypt but nominated by the British government. In reality, however, there was no equal partnership between Britain and Egypt in the Sudan.

THE EARLY YEARS OF BRITISH RULE

From the very beginning, the British dominated the condominium and set about pacifying the countryside and suppressing local religious uprisings, which created insecurity among British officials but never posed a major threat to their rule. The north was quickly pacified and modern improvements were introduced under the aegis of civilian administrators, who began to replace the military as early as 1900. In the south, resistance to British rule was more prolonged; administration there was confined to keeping the peace rather than making any serious attempts at modernization.

The first governor-general was Lord Kitchener himself, but in 1899 his former aide, Sir Reginald Wingate, was appointed to succeed him. Wingate knew the Sudan well and, during his long tenure as governor-general (1899–1916), became devoted to its people and their prosperity. His tolerance and trust in the Sudanese resulted in policies that did much to establish confidence in Christian British rule by a devoutly Muslim, Arab-oriented people.

Modernization was slow at first. Taxes were purposely kept light, and the government consequently had few funds available for development. In fact, the Sudan remained dependent on Egyptian subsidies for many years. Nevertheless, railway, telegraph, and steamer services were expanded, particularly in Al-Jazīrah, in order to launch the great cotton-growing scheme that remains today the backbone of Sudan's economy. In addition, technical and primary schools were established, including the Gordon Memorial College. Opening in 1902, the college soon began to produce a Western-educated elite that was gradually drawn away from the traditional political and social framework. Scorned by the British officials (who preferred the illiterate but contented fathers to the ill-educated, rebellious sons) and adrift from their own customary tribal and religious affiliations, these Sudanese turned for encouragement to Egyptian nationalists; from that association 20th-century Sudanese nationalism was born.

This nationalism first manifested itself in 1921, when ʿAlī ʿAbd al-Laṭīf founded the United Tribes Society and was arrested for nationalist agitation. In 1924 he formed the White Flag League, dedicated to driving the British from the Sudan. Demonstrations followed in Khartoum in June and August and were suppressed. When the governor-general (also known as the sidar), Sir Lee Stack, was assassinated in Cairo on Nov. 19, 1924, the British forced the Egyptians to withdraw from the Sudan and annihilated a Sudanese battalion that mutinied in support of the Egyptians. The Sudanese revolt was ended, and British rule remained unchallenged until after World War II.

The Growth of National Consciousness

In 1936 Britain and Egypt had reached a partial accord in the Anglo-Egyptian Treaty that enabled Egyptian officials to return to the Sudan. Although the traditional Sudanese sheikhs and chiefs remained indifferent to the fact that they had not been consulted in the negotiations over this treaty, the educated Sudanese elite were resentful that neither Britain nor Egypt had bothered to solicit their opinions. Thus, they began to express their grievances through the Graduates' General Congress, which

Ismā'īl al-Azharī. Encyclopædia Britannica, Inc.

had been established as an alumni association of Gordon Memorial College and soon embraced all educated Sudanese.

At first the Graduates' General Congress confined its interests to social and educational activities, but, with Egyptian support, the organization demanded recognition by the British to act as the spokesman for Sudanese nationalism. The Sudanese government refused, and the Congress split into two groups: a moderate majority, prepared to accept the good faith of the government, and a radical minority, led by Ismā'īl al-Azharī, which turned to Egypt. By 1943 Azharī and his supporters had won control of the Congress and organized the Ashiqqā' (Brothers), the first genuine political party in the Sudan. Seeing the initiative pass to the militants, the moderates formed the Ummah (Nation) Party under the patronage of Sayyid 'Abd al-Raḥmān al-Mahdī, the posthumous son of the Mahdī, with the intention of cooperating with the British toward independence.

Sayyid 'Abd al-Raḥmān had inherited the allegiance of the thousands of Sudanese who had followed his father. He now sought to combine to his own advantage this power and influence with the ideology of the Ummah. His principal rival was Sayyid 'Alī al-Mīrghānī, the leader of the Khatmiyyah brotherhood. Although personally remaining aloof from politics, Sayyid 'Alī threw his support to Azharī. The competition between the Azharī-Khatmiyyah faction—remodeled in 1951 as the National Unionist Party (NUP)—and the Ummah-Mahdist group quickly rekindled old suspicions and deep-seated hatreds that soured Sudanese politics for years, eventually strangling parliamentary government. These sectarian religious elites virtually controlled Sudan's political parties until the last decade of the 20th century, stultifying any attempt to democratize the country or to include the millions of Sudanese remote from Khartoum in the political process.

Although the Sudanese government had crushed the initial hopes of the Congress, the British officials were well aware of the pervasive power of nationalism among the elite and sought to introduce new institutions to associate the Sudanese more closely with the task of governing. An advisory council was established for the northern Sudan consisting of the governor-general and 28 Sudanese, but Sudanese nationalists soon began to agitate to transform the advisory council into a legislative one that would include the southern Sudan. The British had facilitated their control of the Sudan by segregating the animist or Christian Africans who predominated in the south from the Muslim Arabs who were predominant in the north. The decision to establish a legislative council forced the British to abandon this policy; in 1947 they instituted southern participation in the legislative council.

The creation of this council produced a strong reaction on the part of the Egyptian government, which in October 1951 unilaterally abrogated the Anglo-Egyptian Treaty of 1936 and proclaimed Egyptian rule over the Sudan. These hasty and ill-considered actions only managed to alienate the Sudanese from Egypt until the revolution in July 1952 led by Col. Gamal Abdel Nasser and Maj. Gen. Muḥammad Naguib placed men with more understanding of Sudanese aspirations in power in Cairo. On Feb. 12, 1953, the Egyptian government signed an agreement with Britain granting self-government for the Sudan and self-determination within three years for the Sudanese. Elections for a representative parliament to rule the Sudan followed in November and December 1953. The Egyptians threw their support behind Ismāʿīl al-Azharī, the leader of the NUP, who campaigned on the slogan "Unity of the Nile Valley." This position was opposed by the Ummah Party, which had the less-vocal but pervasive support of British officials. To the shock of many British officials and to the chagrin of the Ummah, which had enjoyed power in the legislative council for nearly six years, Azharī's NUP won an overwhelming victory. Although Azharī had campaigned to unite the Sudan with Egypt, the realities of disturbances in the southern Sudan and the responsibilities of political power and authority ultimately led him to disown his own campaign promises and to declare Sudan an independent republic with an elected representative parliament on Jan. 1, 1956.

THE REPUBLIC OF THE SUDAN

The triumph of liberal democracy in Sudan was short-lived. Compared with the strength of tradition, which still shaped the life of the Sudanese, the liberalism imported from the West was a weak force, disseminated through British education and adopted by the Sudanese intelligentsia. At first parliamentary government had been held in high esteem as the symbol of nationalism and independence. But, at best, the parliament was a superficial instrument. It had been introduced into Sudan at precisely the time parliamentary forms were rapidly disappearing from other countries in the Middle East.

Political parties were not well-organized groups with distinct objectives but loose alliances motivated primarily by personal interests and loyalty to the various religious factions. When the tactics of party management were exhausted, parliament became debased, benefiting only those politicians who reaped the rewards of power and patronage. Disillusioned with their experiment in liberal democracy, the Sudanese turned once again to authoritarianism.

The ʿAbbūd Government

On the night of Nov. 16–17, 1958, the commander in chief of the Sudanese army, Gen. Ibrāhīm ʿAbbūd, carried out a bloodless coup d'état, dissolving all political parties, prohibiting assemblies, and temporarily suspending newspapers. A Supreme Council of the Armed Forces, consisting of 12 senior officers, was set up, and army rule brought rapid economic improvements. The ʿAbbūd government at once abolished the fixed price on cotton and sold all the Sudanese cotton, rebuilding the nation's foreign reserves. On Nov. 8, 1959, the government concluded an agreement with Egypt on the Nile waters, by which Egypt not only recognized but also appeared to be reconciled to an independent Sudan. In the southern Sudan, ʿAbbūd's policies were less successful. In the name of national unity, the army officers introduced many measures designed to facilitate the spread of Islam and the Arabic language. Important positions in the administration and police were staffed by northern Sudanese. Education was shifted from the English curriculum of the Christian missionaries, who had long been solely responsible for education in the south, to an Arabic, Islamic orientation. Foreign Christian missionaries were expelled between 1962 and 1964.

In southern Sudan itself, the measures of the central government met ever-increasing resistance. In October 1962 a widespread strike in southern schools resulted in antigovernment demonstrations followed by a general flight of students and others over the border. In September 1963 rebellion erupted in eastern Al-Istiwāʾiyyah (Equatoria) and in the Aʿālī al-Nīl (Upper Nile) province, led by the Anya Nya, a southern Sudanese guerrilla organization that believed that only violent resistance would make the government of General ʿAbbūd seek a solution acceptable to the southerners. In return the generals in Khartoum increased repression.

Although the northern Sudanese had little sympathy for their countrymen in the south, the intelligentsia was able to use the government's failure there to assail authoritarian rule in the north and to revive demands for democratic government. By 1962, numerous urban elements, including the intelligentsia, the trade unions, and the civil service, as well as the powerful religious brotherhoods, had become alienated from the military regime. Moreover, the tribal masses and growing proletariat had become increasingly apathetic toward the government. In the end the regime was overwhelmed by boredom and overthrown by the reaction to its lassitude. The means of its overthrow was the southern problem.

In October 1964, in defiance of a government prohibition, students at the University of Khartoum held a meeting in order to condemn government action in the southern Sudan and to denounce the regime. Demonstrations followed, and, with most of its forces committed in the southern Sudan, the military regime was unable to maintain control. The disorders soon spread, and General ʿAbbūd resigned as head of state; a transitional government was appointed to serve under the provisional constitution of 1956.

SUDAN SINCE 1964

Under the leadership of Sirr al-Khātim al-Khalīfah, the transitional government held elections in April and May 1965 to form a representative government. A coalition government headed by a leading Ummah politician, Muḥammad Aḥmad Maḥjūb, was formed in June 1965. As before, parliamentary government was characterized by factional disputes. On the one hand Mahjūb enjoyed the support of the traditionalists within the Ummah Party, represented by the Imām al-Hādī, the spiritual successor to the Mahdī, while on the other hand he was challenged by Sayyid Ṣādiq al-Mahdī, the young great-grandson of the Mahdī, who led the more progressive forces within the Ummah. Unable to find common objectives, parliament failed to deal with the economic, social, and constitutional problems in Sudan. Moreover, the earlier hopes expressed by the transitional government of cooperation with the southerners soon vanished. Conflict continued in the south, with little hope of resolution. A group of young officers led by Col. Gaafar Mohamed el-Nimeiri (Jaʿfar Muḥammad Numayrī)—tired of having no workable constitution, a stagnant economy, a political system torn by sectarian interests, and a continuing civil conflict in the south—seized the government on May 25, 1969.

THE EARLY NIMEIRI REGIME

When Nimeiri and his young officers assumed power, they were confronted by threats from communists on the left and the Ummah on the right. Nimeiri disbanded the Sudanese Communist Party, which went underground; its leader, Imām al-Hādī, was killed and his supporters dispersed. An abortive coup by the resilient communists in July 1971 collapsed after popular and foreign support held steadfast for the reinstallation of Nimeiri. The abortive coup had a profound effect on Nimeiri. He promised a permanent constitution and National Assembly, established himself as president of the state, and instituted the Sudanese Socialist Union (SSU) as the country's only party. The affair also produced the incentive to press for a resolution to the southern rebellion.

THE ADDIS ABABA AGREEMENT

In 1971 the southern Sudanese rebels, who had theretofore consisted of several independent commands, were united under Gen. Joseph Lagu, who combined under his authority both the fighting units of the Anya Nya and its political wing, the Southern Sudan Liberation Movement (SSLM). Thereafter throughout 1971 the SSLM, representing General Lagu, maintained a dialogue with the Sudanese government over proposals for regional autonomy and the ending of hostilities. These talks culminated in the signing of the Addis Ababa Agreement on Feb. 27, 1972. The agreement ended the 17-year conflict between the Anya Nya and the Sudanese army, ushering in autonomy for the southern region, which would no longer be divided into the three provinces of Al-Istiwāʾiyyah (Equatoria), Baḥr al-Ghazāl, and Aʿālī al-Nīl (Upper Nile). The region's affairs would be controlled by a separate legislature and executive body, and the soldiers of the Anya Nya would be integrated into the Sudanese army and police. The Addis Ababa Agreement brought Nimeiri both prestige abroad and popularity at home.

ECONOMIC DEVELOPMENT

The signing of the Addis Ababa Agreement enabled economic development in Sudan to proceed using funds that had previously been allocated for the civil war. This redirection of government resources to peaceful projects coincided with the dramatic growth of petroleum revenues in the Persian Gulf, and the Arab states there began investing large sums in Sudan in order to transform it into the "breadbasket" of the Arab world. The resulting spate of development projects in the 1970s was followed by investments from private multinational corporations and generous loans from the International Monetary Fund. The highest priority was placed on expanding Sudan's production of sugar, wheat, and cotton in order to provide foreign exchange. The new projects were accompanied by efforts to expand the national infrastructure and to construct the Junqalī (Jonglei) Canal through the great swamps of Al-Sudd.

Though these projects were laudable in conception, their flawed implementation plunged Sudan into a severe economic crisis by 1980. Few projects were completed on time, and those that were never met their production targets. The steady decline of Sudan's gross domestic output from 1977 left the country in a cycle of increasing debt, severe inflation, and an ever-diminishing standard of living.

There were two fundamental causes for the failure of Sudan's economic development. First, planning was deficient, and decisions were increasingly precipitous and mercurial. There was no overall control, so individual ministries negotiated external loans for projects without the approval of the central planning authority. The result was not only incompetent management but also innumerable opportunities for corruption. The second cause of economic failure lay in external events over which Sudan had no control. Rising oil prices dramatically increased Sudan's bill for petroleum products, while the concomitant development projects in the Persian Gulf siphoned off from Sudan its best professional and skilled workers, who were lured by high wages abroad only to create a "brain drain" at home. The Nimeiri regime did not prove successful in breaking this cycle of persistent economic decline.

The Rise of Muslim Fundamentalism

In the elections of 1965, the Islamic Charter Front, a political party that espoused the principles of the Muslim Brotherhood (Ikhwān al-Muslimīn), received only an insignificant portion of the popular vote. But the election roughly coincided with the return from France of Ḥasan al-Turābī, who assumed the leadership of the party, renamed the Islamic National Front (NIF). Turābī methodically charted the Brotherhood and the NIF on a course of action designed to seize control of the Sudanese government despite the Muslim fundamentalists' lack of popularity with the majority of the Sudanese people. Tightly disciplined, superbly organized, and inspired by the resurgence of Islam in the Middle East, the Muslim Brotherhood consciously sought to recruit disciples from the country's youth. It was relentlessly successful, and by the 1980s the Muslim Brotherhood and the NIF had successfully infiltrated the country's officer corps, the civil service, and the ranks of secondary-school teachers.

Despite its relatively small size, the Muslim Brotherhood began to exert its influence, which did not go unnoticed by President Nimeiri, whose SSU had failed to galvanize popular support. In the face of deteriorating relations with both the southern Sudanese and the traditionalists of the Ummah-Mahdī grouping, Nimeiri turned increasingly to the Muslim Brotherhood for support. He appointed Turābī attorney general and did not object to the latter's designs for a new constitution based partly on Islamic law, the Sharīʿah. In September 1983 Nimeiri modified the nation's legal codes to bring them into accord with Islamic law. This measure was bound to be resisted by the Christians and animists of the southern Sudan. Moreover, Nimeiri was coming to accept the arguments of the Muslim Brotherhood and other northern political groups that the Addis Ababa Agreement had been a mistake. In June 1983 Nimeiri unilaterally divided the southern region again into three provinces, thereby effectively abrogating the Addis Ababa Agreement.

Civil War

Even before the official demise of the agreement, the civil war between the African Christians of the south and the

Muslim Arabs of the north had resumed with even greater ferocity than before. There had been sporadic uprisings in the south since the signing of the Addis Ababa Agreement in 1972, but they had been quickly suppressed. In May 1983, however, an army battalion stationed at Bor mutinied and fled into the bush under the leadership of Colonel John Garang de Mabior. The rebels had become disenchanted with Nimeiri and his government, which was riddled with corruption and was contemptuous of southerners. Led by Garang, the ranks of the Bor garrison, which had taken up sanctuary in Ethiopia, were soon swollen by discontented southerners determined to redress their grievances by force of arms under the banner of the Sudanese People's Liberation Army (SPLA) and its political wing, the Sudan People's Liberation Movement (SPLM).

Nimeiri's Overthrow and Its Aftermath

Although Nimeiri at first sought to crush the rebels by military force, his deployment of the Sudanese army only succeeded in disrupting the distribution of food, which, when coupled with drought and diminished harvests, created widespread famine in the southern Sudan. Without popular support, Nimeiri found himself facing a successful armed rebellion in the south and growing criticism in the north over the rigour with which he sought to carry out the corporal punishments prescribed under Islamic law. In response, Nimeiri softened his hard-line policies: he annulled the state of emergency that he had invoked five months earlier, he rescinded the tripartite division of the south, and he suspended the more brutal aspects of the Islamic courts. But these futile gestures were too late. Nimeiri was overthrown in a bloodless coup in April 1985 by his chief of staff, Gen. ʿAbd al-Raḥmān Siwar al-Dahab. Although the new military government held elections in 1986 that returned Ṣādiq al-Mahdī as prime minister, the next three years were characterized by political instability, indecisive leadership, party manipulations resulting in short-lived coalitions, and abortive attempts to reach a peaceful settlement with the SPLA. These years of indecision came to an end on June 30, 1989, when a Revolutionary Command Council for National Salvation led by Lieut. Gen. Omar Ḥasan Aḥmad al-Bashir seized power.

The Emergence of the National Islamic Front

The Revolutionary Command Council (RCC) was in fact the vehicle for the NIF. Bashir and his colleagues realized that, as a minority with little popular support, they would have to resort to harsh measures to curtail the educated elites who had been instrumental in organizing populist revolutions in the past. With a ruthlessness to which the Sudanese were unaccustomed, the RCC imprisoned hundreds of political opponents, banned trade unions and political parties, silenced the press, and dismantled the judiciary. The RCC sought to prosecute the war in the south with vigour, inhibited only by the deterioration of the national economy. With the support of the NIF, the Muslim Brotherhood, and a brutally efficient security system, the most unpopular government in the modern history of Sudan remained firmly in power as the country entered the last decade of the 20th century.

The confidence of the RCC and its supporters in the Muslim Brotherhood enabled Bashir to reintroduce Islamic law, including corporal punishment, in March 1991 and emboldened the government to support Iraq in the Persian Gulf War. Both these acts isolated Sudan not only from the West but from its Arab neighbours as well (although the Libyan government was supportive). The economy continued to deteriorate, precipitated by this isolation and also by civil war in the south, fallen productivity, and rampant inflation. There were widespread shortages of basic commodities, particularly in the sensitive urban areas, creating disturbances which were mercilessly suppressed. In the south the army continued to lose towns to the SPLA, but it managed to hold the three provincial capitals of Malakāl, Wāw, and Juba. Unable to defeat the SPLA on the field of battle, the government armed and unleashed an Arab militia against their traditional African rivals, principally the Dinka. Moreover, it consistently ignored pleas for food and obstructed the efforts of Western humanitarian relief agencies to provide food aid. Caught between two armies, plundered by the Arab militia, and scourged by a persistent drought, countless Africans fled to northern towns and cities or sought sanctuary in Ethiopia. Thousands perished fleeing the endemic East African famine or in the camps for the displaced, where they received no relief from the RCC-led government, which was determined to crush the SPLA as the initial step in a policy to Islamize the non-Muslims of the southern Sudan.

The RCC ruled until 1993; that year it oversaw the transition from military rule to a civilian government. Nonetheless, it was a civilian government in which the NIF was securely in power, as the RCC appointed Bashir to the presidency of the new government before disbanding. The first presidential and legislative elections since the 1989 coup were held in 1996; Bashir won the presidency and was also reelected in 2000. The ostensible transformation of the government continued with a 1998 referendum in which a new constitution was overwhelmingly approved. The introduction of multiparty politics in 1999, although viewed with pessimism by many, also seemed to support the transition to a more democratic approach to government. The partial suspension of the new constitution later that year, however, tempered optimism, as it appeared Sudan was clinging to an authoritarian regime. Also that year, Sudan began to export oil, providing the opportunity to bring in much-needed revenue to the country's blighted economy.

Two children at a camp for displaced persons near Al-Fāshir, in the Darfur region of The Sudan, 2006. Ramzi Haidar—AFP/Getty Images

Meanwhile, the civil war continued to rage. Numerous cease-fires, agreements, and peace discussions occurred during the 1990s and in the early years of the 21st century but yielded very little success. The government of Sudan and rebels eventually signed a peace agreement in January 2005, giving hope that the conflict that had ravaged the country since the early 1980s was finally over. The peace agreement provided for a new constitution and outlined new measures for sharing power, distributing wealth, and providing security in the country. It also allowed for a separate administration for southern Sudan and stipulated that a referendum on independence for that region would be held in six years—key issues for the rebels.

A separate conflict that remained unresolved centred on the Darfur region in western Sudan. The conflict began in 2003 when rebels launched an insurrection to protest what they contended was the Sudanese government's disregard for the western region and its non-Arab population. In response, the government equipped and supported Arab militias (Janjaweed) to fight against the rebels in Darfur. The militias, however, also terrorized the civilians in the region and prevented

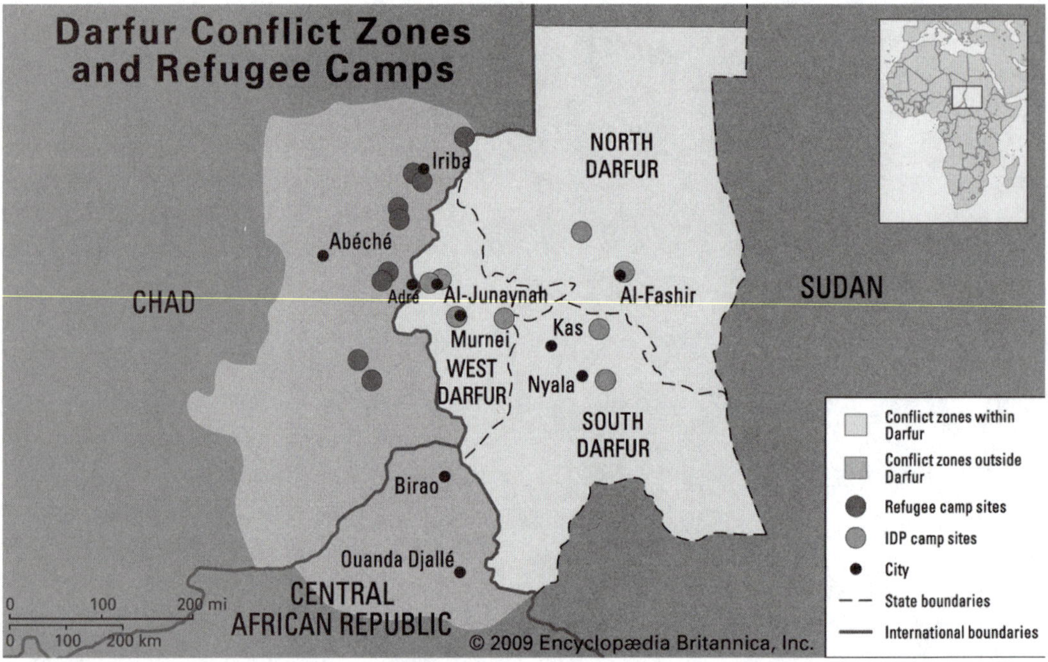

Map showing Darfur-related conflict zones and campsites for refugees and internally displaced peoples (IDPs) in The Sudan, Central African Republic, and Chad, 2008.

international aid organizations from delivering much-needed food and medical supplies. Despite a 2004 cease-fire and the presence of African Union (AU) troops that followed, by 2007 the conflict and resulting humanitarian crisis had left hundreds of thousands of people dead and more than two million displaced, internally as well as externally, as they were forced to flee from the fighting. On July 31, 2007, the United Nations Security Council authorized a joint UN-AU peacekeeping mission (UNAMID) to replace the AU mission, although UNAMID troop deployment did not begin until 2008.

In July 2008 an International Criminal Court (ICC) prosecutor alleged that Bashir, as president of Sudan, bore criminal responsibility for the crisis in Darfur. The prosecutor accused Bashir of orchestrating genocide, war crimes, and crimes against humanity in the region and sought a warrant for his arrest; the Sudanese government denied the charges and proclaimed Bashir's innocence. On March 4, 2009, the ICC issued an arrest warrant for Bashir on charges of war crimes and crimes against humanity but not genocide. The warrant marked the first time that the ICC sought the arrest of a sitting head of state.

CHAPTER 10

Tunisia

Tunisia is located along the Mediterranean coast of northern Africa. The modern-day country became independent in 1956. The capital is Tunis.

EARLY HISTORY

Tunisia was called Ifrīqiyyah in the early centuries of the Islamic period. That name, in turn, comes from the Roman word for Africa and the name also given by the Romans to their first African colony following the Punic Wars against the Carthaginians in 264–146 BCE. Following the decline of Rome, the region was ruled briefly by the Vandals and then the Byzantine Empire before being conquered by the Arabs in 647 CE. Although the Arabs initially unified North Africa, by 1230 a separate Tunisian dynasty had been established by the Ḥafṣids. Muslim Andalusians migrated to the area after having been forced out of Spain during the Reconquista, particularly following the defeat of the Muslim kingdom of Granada in 1492. By 1574, Tunisia was incorporated into the Ottoman Empire, whose control of the region, always tenuous, had all but dissolved by the 19th century.

Tunisia is the smallest of the Maghrib states and consequently the most cohesive. By the beginning of the 19th century, virtually all of its inhabitants spoke Arabic. The vast majority of the population was Muslim, with a small Jewish minority. A single major city, Tunis, dominated the countryside both politically and culturally. Tunis itself was located near the site of the ancient city-state of Carthage. More easily controlled from within than any other Maghrib country, Tunisia was also more open to the influence of people and ideas from abroad. Roman Africa, for example, was the most intensively Christianized portion of North Africa, and Ifrīqiyyah was later more quickly and more thoroughly Islamicized.

A small state with limited resources, Tunisia nonetheless managed to retain considerable autonomy within the framework of the larger empires that frequently ruled it from afar. This status was achieved, for example, under the ʿAbbāsids in the 9th century and later under the Ottomans. Tunisia's geographic and historical legacy helped prepare it for the shocks it received in the 19th century as a land caught between an expanding Europe and a declining Ottoman Empire. Yet, relatively autonomous though it was, Tunisia would prove to be as vulnerable economically as it was militarily.

THE GROWTH OF EUROPEAN INFLUENCE

In 1830, at the time of the French invasion of Algiers, though Tunisia was officially a province of the Ottoman Empire, in reality it was an autonomous state. Because the principal military threat had long come from neighbouring Algeria, the reigning bey of Tunisia, Ḥusayn, cautiously went along with assurances from the French that they had no intention of colonizing Tunisia. Ḥusayn Bey even accepted the idea that Tunisian princes would rule the cities of Constantine and Oran. The scheme, however, had no chance of success and was soon abandoned.

Tunisia's security was directly threatened in 1835, when the Ottoman Empire deposed the ruling dynasty in Libya and reestablished direct Ottoman rule. Thereafter, the vulnerable *beylik* (principality) of Tunis found itself surrounded by two larger powers—France and the Ottoman Empire—both of which had designs on Tunisia. From that time until the establishment of the French protectorate in 1881, Tunisian rulers had to placate the larger powers while working to strengthen the state from within.

Aḥmad Bey, who ruled from 1837 to 1855, was an avowed modernizer and reformer. With the help of Western advisers (mainly French), he created a modern army, navy, and related industries. Conscription was also introduced, to the great dismay of the peasantry. More acceptable were Aḥmad's steps to integrate Arabic-speaking native Tunisians fully into the government, which had long been dominated by *mamlūk*s (military slaves) and Turks. Aḥmad abolished slavery and took other modernizing steps intended to bring Tunisia more in line with Europe, but he also exposed his country to Europe's infinitely greater economic and political power. His reforms negatively affected the already stagnant economy, which led to greater debt, higher taxes, and increased unrest in the countryside.

The next bey, Muḥammad (1855–59), tried to ignore Europe, but this was no longer possible. Continued civil disturbances and corruption prompted the British and French to force the bey to issue the Fundamental Pact (ʿAhd al-Amān; September 1857), a civil rights charter modeled on the Ottoman rescript of 1839.

The final collapse of the Tunisian *beylik* came during the reign of Muḥammad al-Ṣādiq (1859–82). Though sympathetic to the need for reforms, Muḥammad was too weak either to control his own government or to keep the European powers at bay. He did, in 1861, proclaim the first constitution (*dustūr*; also *destour*) in the Arabic-speaking world, but this step toward representative government was cut short by runaway debt, a problem exacerbated by the government's practice of securing loans from European bankers at exorbitant rates.

When the principal minister, Muṣṭafā Khaznadār (who had served from the earliest days of Aḥmad Bey's reign), attempted to squeeze more taxes out of the hard-pressed peasants, the countryside rose in a revolt (1864). This uprising almost overthrew the regime, but the government ultimately suppressed it through a combination of guile and brutality.

Though Tunisia went bankrupt in 1869 and an international financial commission—with British, French, and Italian representatives—was imposed on the country, there was one last attempt to reform Tunisia from within and thus avoid complete European domination. It was made during the reformist ministry of Khayr al-Dīn (1873–77), one of the most effective statesmen of the 19th-century Muslim world. However, enemies from within and European intrigues from without conspired to force him from office. The final blow to Tunisia's sovereignty came at the Congress of Berlin in 1878, when Britain acquiesced to France's control of Tunisia.

On the pretext that Tunisians had encroached on Algerian territory, France invaded Tunisia in 1881 and imposed the Treaty of Bardo, which sanctioned French military occupation of Tunisia, transferred to France the bey's authority over finance and foreign relations, and provided for the appointment of a French resident minister as intermediary in all matters of common interest. This action provoked an uprising in southern Tunisia during which France attacked and captured Sousse in July 1881, took Kairouan in October, and seized Gafsa and Gabès in November. After the death of Muḥammad al-Ṣādiq, his successor, ʿAlī, was forced to introduce administrative, judicial, and financial reforms that the French government considered useful. This agreement, known as the Convention of Al-Marsa, was signed in 1883 and solidified French control over Tunisia.

THE PROTECTORATE

Tunisia became a protectorate of France by treaty rather than by outright conquest, as had been the case in Algeria.

Officially, the bey remained an absolute monarch: Tunisian ministers were still appointed, the government structure was preserved, and Tunisians continued to be subjects of the bey. The French did not confiscate land, convert mosques into churches, or change the official language. Nevertheless, supreme authority was passed to the French resident general.

Under French guidance, Tunisia's finances were soon stabilized and modern communications established. Though France never overtly seized land nor displaced the population—both of which had occurred in Algeria—the most fertile portions of northern Tunisia, comprising the Majardah valley and the Sharīk Peninsula, were passed on to other European countries. Valuable phosphate mines began operating near Gafsa in the south, and vegetables were cultivated and exported from the Majardah valley after French and Italian colonists had become established there.

By the 1890s a small French-educated group—the members of which came to be called "Young Tunisians"—began pushing for both modernizing reforms based on a European model and greater participation by Tunisians in their own government. The group's conduct during the protectorate, however, was cautious and reserved. Their major weapon became the newspaper *Le Tunisien*, a French-language publication founded in 1907. With the printing of an Arabic edition in 1909, the Young Tunisians simultaneously educated their compatriots and persuaded the more liberal French to help move Tunisia toward modernity.

Even this moderate protonationalism was subject to repressive measures by the French in 1911–12. Little nationalist activity took place during World War I (1914–18), but the first attempt at mass political organization came during the interwar period, when the Destour (Constitution) Party was created (the party was named for the short-lived Tunisian constitution of 1861). In 1920 the Destour Party presented the bey and the French government with a document that demanded that a constitutional form of government be established in which Tunisians would possess the same rights as Europeans. The immediate result was the arrest of ʿAbd al-ʿAzīz al-Thaʿālibī, the Destour leader. Two years later the aged bey, Muḥammad al-Nāṣir, requested that the program of the Destour be adopted or he would abdicate. In response, the resident general, Lucien Saint, surrounded the bey's palace with troops, and the demand was withdrawn. Saint thus introduced restrictive measures, together with minor reforms, that pacified Tunisian sentiment and weakened the nationalist movement for several years.

In 1934 a young Tunisian lawyer, Habib Bourguiba, and his colleagues broke with the Destour Party to form a new organization, the Neo-Destour, which aimed at spreading propaganda and gaining mass support. Under Bourguiba's vigorous leadership, the new party soon supplanted the existing Destour Party and its leaders. Attempts by the French

Young Tunisians

The Young Tunisians was the name of a Tunisian political party headed by Ali Bash Hamba and Bashir Sfar. Formed in 1907 by young French-educated Tunisian intellectuals in opposition to the French rule in Tunisia, the party demanded complete Tunisian control of the government and administration of the country and full citizenship rights for both Tunisians and Frenchmen. The party attracted a following among the young, educated, professional Muslims, but the liberal attitudes and European ways of its members alienated the common people.

In 1911 the Young Tunisians protested against Italy's invasion of neighbouring Muslim Tripolitania. In Tunisia itself, massive protests against French registration of a Muslim cemetery as public property ended in violent riots and killings; boycotts and labour strikes were called against Italian-owned companies in Tunis. The French responded by exiling the leaders of the party, including Ali Bash Hamba and Abd al-Aziz ath-Thaalibi (1912), and driving the Young Tunisians underground. At the end of World War I they emerged again as activists in the Tunisian nationalist movement and, led by ath-Thaalibi, reorganized themselves (1920) into the Destour Party.

to suppress the new movement only fueled the fire. The Neo-Destour began to gain more power and influence after the arrival of the Popular Front government in France in 1936. When the Popular Front government collapsed, repression was renewed in Tunisia and was met with civil disobedience. In 1938 serious disturbances led to the arrest of Bourguiba and other leaders of the party, which was then officially dissolved.

WORLD WAR II

At the outbreak of war in 1939, Neo-Destour leaders, though still untried, were deported to France. However, they were released by the Nazis in 1942 following the German occupation of Vichy France, and, since Hitler regarded Tunisia as a sphere of Italian influence, he handed them over to the fascist government in Rome. There the leaders were treated with deference, the fascists hoping to gain support for the Axis. Bourguiba steadily refused to cooperate. In March 1943 he made a noncommittal broadcast, and the Neo-Destour leaders were finally allowed to proceed to Tunis, where the reigning bey, Muḥammad al-Munṣif (Moncef), formed a ministry of individuals who were sympathetic to Destour.

The assumption of power by the Free French after the Nazi retreat produced complete disillusionment for the Neo-Destour cause. The bey was deposed, while Bourguiba, accused of collaboration with the Nazis, escaped imprisonment by fleeing in disguise to Egypt in 1945. Still, a vigorous campaign of propaganda for Tunisian independence continued, and, in view of the emancipation of the eastern Arab states and later of neighbouring Libya, the French felt compelled to make concessions. In 1951 the French permitted a government with nationalist sympathies to take office—of which the secretary-general of the Neo-Destour, Salah Ben Youssef, became a member—and Bourguiba was allowed to return to Tunisia. When the newly formed government wished to establish a Tunisian parliament, however, further repressions ensued; Bourguiba was exiled, and most of the ministers were put under arrest. This resulted, for the first time, in outbreaks of terrorism. Nationalist guerrillas began to operate in the mountains, virtually paralyzing the country.

In July 1954 the French premier, Pierre Mendès-France, promised to grant complete autonomy to Tunisia, subject to a negotiated agreement. Bourguiba returned to Tunisia and was able to supervise the negotiations without directly participating. In June 1955 an agreement

Habib Bourguiba (far right), reviews Tunisian troops in May of 1956. AFP/Getty Images

was finally signed by the Tunisian delegates—though it imposed strict limits in the fields of foreign policy, education, defense, and finance—and a mainly Neo-Destour ministry was formed. Salah Ben Youssef denounced the document, saying it was too restrictive, and refused to attend a specially summoned congress that unanimously supported Bourguiba. In response, he organized a brief armed resistance in the south that was quickly repressed. Ben Youssef fled the country to escape imprisonment; he was assassinated in 1961.

INDEPENDENCE

The French granted full independence to Tunisia in an accord that was reached on March 20, 1956, and Bourguiba was chosen prime minister. The rule of the beys was subsequently abolished, and on July 25, 1957, a republic was declared, with Bourguiba as president.

Domestic Development

After independence was granted, the Neo-Destour Party (from 1964 to 1988 the Destourian Socialist Party; from 1988 the Democratic Constitutional Rally [known by its French acronym RCD]) ensured that Tunisia moved quickly with reforms, most notably in the areas of education, the liberation of women, and modifications to the legal system. Economic development was slower, but the government paid considerable attention to the more impoverished parts of the country. In 1961 Ahmad Ben Salah took charge of planning and finance. His ambitious efforts at forced-pace modernization, especially in agriculture, were foiled, however, by rural and conservative opposition. Expelled from the party and imprisoned in 1969, Ben Salah escaped in 1973 to live in exile. His fall brought a move in the government toward more conservative alignment.

In 1975 the Chamber of Deputies unanimously bestowed the presidency for life on the sick and aging Habib Bourguiba, who centralized power under his progressive but increasingly personalized rule. Hedi Amira Nouira, noted for his financial and administrative skills, became prime minister in November 1970, but his government failed to resolve the economic crisis or address growing demands for reform from liberals in his own party. A decade later, the ailing Nouira was replaced by Muhammad Mzali, who made efforts to restore dissidents to the party and by 1981 had granted amnesty to many who had been jailed for earlier disturbances. In addition, he persuaded Bourguiba to accept a multiparty system (although only one opposition party was actually legalized).

The outcome of the elections in November 1981 was disappointing to those who sought political liberalization. The National Front, an alliance of the Destourian Socialist Party and the trade union movement, swept all 136 parliamentary seats, a result received with cynicism and dismay by the opposition. Meanwhile, an Islamist opposition was developing around the Islamic Tendency Movement (Mouvement de la Tendance Islamique [MTI]). By 1984 Bourguiba had perceived an Islamist hand behind riots and demonstrations protesting rising prices. In response, he sent in the army and initiated a fierce campaign against the MTI. Bourguiba's long rule, widely popular in its early years except among traditionalist groups, had provoked an increasing but passive opposition among Tunisians. Bourguiba, long in declining health, became unable to mask his autocratic tendencies. National elections in 1986 were boycotted by the major opposition parties, and the National Front once again carried the vote. In November 1987, amid widespread unrest and growing Islamist support, Bourguiba was declared mentally unfit to rule and was removed from office. He was succeeded by Gen. Zine al-Abidine Ben Ali, whom he had appointed as prime minister a month earlier.

President Ben Ali promised political liberalization and a transition to

Supporters of Tunisian Pres. Zine al-Abidine Ben Ali hold placards at the start of the presidential election campaign, 2009. Fethi Belaid—AFP/Getty Images

democracy. His early reforms attempted to restore a national consensus; one of these, the National Pact signed in 1989, drew together the ruling party, the legal opposition, the Islamists, and all the national organizations. Many political parties were legalized, with the exception of the MTI (renamed Al-Nahḍah ["The Renaissance"] in 1988), but the 1989 national elections still failed to introduce a multiparty competition. The president gained 99 percent of the vote, and the RCD won all 141 seats in the legislature. Local elections in 1990, boycotted by opposition parties, were also swept by the ruling party. Following early local electoral victories by Algerian Islamists in 1990 and Islamist opposition to the First Persian Gulf War (1990–91), the government began to crack down on Islamist political activity.

Although the government initially eased press controls and released political prisoners, the opposition soon became disillusioned with the new regime. Subsequently, the government turned against secular opposition, and it has since been criticized for its abuse of human rights and its reliance on military and security forces. Piecemeal electoral reforms have failed to produce any genuine form of power sharing or transfer of power away from the president or his party (Ben Ali won reelection in 1994, 1999, 2004, and 2009, each time by an overwhelming margin). Similarly, the media and national organizations and associations have lost much of what little autonomy they wrested from the state, and Ben Ali's regime has increasingly been subject to accusations of authoritarianism. The government, for its part, has claimed that democratization must be a gradual process that cannot be allowed to destabilize or inhibit the processes of economic liberalization and social consolidation. The implementation of bicameral legislature in 2005 was given as a step toward political liberalization.

Foreign Relations

Foreign relations under Habib Bourguiba were dominated by his personal conviction that Tunisia's future lay with the West and, in particular, with France and the United States. There were, nonetheless, some early crises, including a French bombing raid on the Tunisian village of Sakiet Sidi Youssef (Sāqiyat Sīdī Yūsuf) in 1958, during which France claimed the right to pursue Algerian rebels across the border; the Bizerte incident of 1961, concerning the continued military use of that port and airfield facility by France; and the suspension of all French aid in 1964–66 after Tunisia abruptly nationalized foreign-owned landholdings. These difficulties aside, Tunisia's relations with France have been improving, as have relations with the United States, despite some tensions with the latter over its involvement in the First Persian Gulf War and its policies toward the developing world. Alignment with the West was never allowed to interfere with positive trade policies with developing countries and what was then the Soviet bloc.

Rather than balance East against West, Bourguiba maximized Tunisia's advantages by maintaining good relations with both and thereby reduced the country's dependency on either one. Bourguiba's pragmatism also extended to the Arab world. Rejecting ideological constraints, he argued for the Arab recognition of Israel and Arab unity based on mutually advantageous cooperation rather than political integration.

Under Ben Ali, Tunisia has followed much the same path. The need for regional security and the desire to advance economic interests, especially trade and foreign investment, has guided foreign policy. With the uncertain future and stability of the Arab Maghrib Union, Tunisia has increasingly concentrated efforts on developing bilateral economic agreements with other Arab states, on promoting the Arab League's Arab Free Trade Area, and in advancing regional economics. An agreement with the European Union, which came into effect in 1998, has also tied Tunisia's economy and security to the Mediterranean community. Attempts to diversify trading links have led to closer ties with the East and Southeast Asia, and strong ties with the United States remain a linchpin in Tunisia's ability to present itself as a stable, reliable, and moderate state. Tunisia has been keen on supporting international organizations, in particular the United Nations, which it has viewed as the protector of smaller states and the defender of international law.

CHAPTER 11

WESTERN SAHARA

Western Sahara is a territory located on the Atlantic coast of northwestern Africa. Neighbouring Morocco claims the territory as its own, although that claim is not internationally recognized. A group of the Western Sahara's indigenous inhabitants fighting for independence named the territory the Saharan Arab Democratic Republic and formed a government-in-exile in the 1970s.

Little is known of the prehistory of Western Sahara, although Neolithic (New Stone Age) rock engravings in Saguia el-Hamra and in isolated locations in the south suggest that it was occupied by a succession of hunting and pastoral groups, with some agriculturists in favoured locales, prior to a gradual process of desertification that began about 2500 BCE. By the 4th century BCE there was trade between Western Sahara and Europe across the Mediterranean; the Phoenicians sailed along the west coast of Africa in this period. The Romans also had some contact with the Saharan peoples. By medieval times this part of the Sahara was occupied by Ṣanhajāh Berber (Amazigh) peoples who were later dominated by Arabic-speaking Muslim Bedouins from about 1000 CE.

In 1346 the Portuguese discovered a bay that they mistakenly identified with a more southerly Río de Oro, probably the Sénégal River. The coastal region was little explored by Europeans until Scottish and Spanish merchants arrived in the mid-19th century, although in 1476 a short-lived trading post, Santa Cruz de Mar Pequeña, was established by Diego García de Herrera, a Spaniard. In 1884 Emilio Bonelli, of the Sociedad Española de Africanistas y Colonistas ("Spanish Society of Africanists and Colonists"), went to Río de Oro bay and signed treaties with the coastal peoples. Subsequently, the Spanish government claimed a protectorate over the coastal zone. Further Spanish penetration was hindered by French claims to Mauritania and by partisans of Sheikh Māʾ al-ʿAynayn, who between 1898 and 1902 constructed the town of Semara at an inland oasis. Cape Juby (Ṭarfāyah) was occupied for Spain by Col. Francisco Bens in 1916, Güera was occupied in 1920, and Semara and the rest of the interior were occupied in 1934.

In 1957 the territory was claimed by Morocco, which itself had just reached independence the previous year. Spanish troops succeeded in repelling Moroccan military incursions into the territory, and in 1958 Spain formally united Río de Oro and Saguia el-Hamra into a Spanish province known as Spanish Sahara. However, the situation was further complicated by newly independent Mauritania's claims to the province in 1960, and in 1963 huge phosphate deposits were discovered at Bu Craa in the northern portion of the Spanish Sahara, which made the province a potentially economically valuable prize for any country that could firmly establish possession of it. Mining of the deposits at Bu Craa began in 1972.

Decades of social and economic change caused by drought, desertification, and the impact of the phosphate discoveries resulted in an increase in national consciousness and anticolonial sentiment. A guerrilla insurgency by the Spanish Sahara's indigenous inhabitants, the nomadic Saharawis, sprang up in the early 1970s, calling itself the Popular Front for the Liberation of Saguia el-Hamra and Río de Oro (Polisario Front). The insurgency led Spain to declare in 1975 that it would withdraw from the area. Faced with consistent pressure from Morocco and Mauritania and itself undergoing a period of domestic uncertainty, Spain agreed to the partition of Western Sahara between the two countries despite a World Court ruling that Morocco's and Mauritania's legal claims to the Spanish Sahara were tenuous and did not negate the right to self-determination by the Saharawis. Morocco gained the northern two-thirds of the area and, consequently, control over the phosphates; Mauritania gained the southern third. Sporadic fighting developed between the Polisario Front, which was supported by and based in Algeria, and the Moroccan forces. In 1976 the Polisario Front declared a government-in-exile of what it called the Saharan Arab Democratic Republic (a government recognized by some 70 countries), and it continued to raid Mauritanian and Moroccan outposts in Western Sahara.

Mauritania bowed out of the fighting and reached a peace agreement with the Polisario Front in 1979, but in response Morocco promptly annexed Mauritania's portion of Western Sahara.

Polisario Front commandos run to take up positions during a June 1988 air raid drill. AFP/ Getty Images

Morocco fortified the vital triangle formed by the Bu Craa mines, Laayoune, and Semara while the Polisario Front guerrillas continued their raids. A United Nations (UN) peace proposal in 1988 specified a referendum for the indigenous Saharawi to decide whether they wanted an independent Western Sahara under Polisario Front leadership or whether the territory would officially become part of Morocco. This peace proposal was accepted by both Morocco and the Polisario Front, and the two sides agreed to a cease-fire in 1991. As a UN administrative and peacekeeping force arrived in Western Sahara to prepare to conduct the referendum, however, Morocco moved tens of thousands of "settlers" into the territory and insisted that they have their voting qualifications assessed. This drawn-out procedure, which involved questions regarding the definition of who among the traditionally nomadic Saharawis would be entitled to cast a ballot, continued throughout the 1990s and into the early 21st century. Meanwhile, Morocco continued to

Protestors for Western Sahara independence at the European Union-Morocco summit in Granada, Spain, Mar. 7, 2010. AFP/Getty Images

expand its physical infrastructure in Western Sahara despite widespread protests against its presence in the areas under its control. Efforts to mediate the crisis also continued into the 21st century, including the 2009 approval by the UN Security Council for informal talks to take place between Morocco and the Polisario Front, after previous rounds of talks in 2007 and 2008 had been unsuccesful.

During this time the Polisario Front continued its campaign despite a number of setbacks. Among the challenges were defections from the organization and a reduction in support by its primary backer, Algeria, as that country was forced to concentrate on its own internal problems. Algeria's diplomatic campaign on behalf of Saharawi self-determination, however, continued unabated. By 2001 tens of thousands of Western Saharans, including numerous Polisario Front soldiers, had relocated to semipermanent refugee camps in Algeria.

Conclusion

Northern Africa is a region of long, complex, and varied histories. The countries of the Maghrib had a long history of resistance to outside forces and successfully overcame Punic, Roman, and Christian invasions. It was not until the 7th and 8th centuries CE that the Maghrib was conquered, when Arab forces invaded and were victorious. They imposed on the native peoples both the religion of Islam and the Arabic language, and thus absorbed the Maghrib into the Muslim world, where the countries of the Maghrib—Algeria, Morocco, and Tunisia—remain today. Despite this absorption, most of the native peoples in the Maghrib have managed to preserve their cultural identity throughout the centuries.

The histories of Egypt and Sudan are closely intertwined, yet each country also has unique aspects of its historical past. Egypt's long historical continuity is marked by a succession of major religions, cultural trends, and foreign powers. Today it is a leader of the Arab world and, despite its location on the African continent, is more often associated with the countries of the Middle East than with its African neighbours. For many centuries Egypt's history included that of Sudan, although that country also has a singular history of its own. Given its location, Sudan has long served as an arena for interaction between the cultural traditions of Africa and those of the Mediterranean world. The impact of its historical interactions are evident even today as Sudan straddles two worlds within one country: northern Sudan is dominated by Islam and the Arabic language and is closer to the Mediterranean world, while southern Sudan is instead influenced by sub-Saharan African languages and cultures. Indeed, as the first decade of the 21st century drew to a close, it was not clear if northern and southern Sudan would remain united, or if the country would divide into two separate entities.

Owing to the fact that the modern-day country of Libya comprises three historical regions—Tripolitania in the northwest, Cyrenaica in the east, and Fezzan in the southwest—Libya's history is likewise diverse. For much of Libya's early history, both Tripolitania and Cyrenaica were more closely linked with neighbouring territories than with one other. For several centuries, the Ottoman authorities recognized them as separate provinces. In the early 20th century, however, the regions were unified to form a single colony under Italian rule, which gave way to the modern-day country of Libya.

An examination of the histories of countries of northern Africa makes evident a pattern of shared as well as distinct experiences. This pattern is also evident today, in both the experiences of each country and the challenges that they face in the 21st century.

Glossary

abrogate To abolish by authoritative action.

amphora Ancient vessel form used as a storage jar and one of the principal vessel shapes in Greek pottery, a two-handled pot with a neck narrower than the body.

antedate To precede in time; to come or happen before.

a priori Relating to or derived by reasoning from self-evident propositions.

bey Provincial governor in the Ottoman Empire.

caliph A successor of Muhammad as temporal and spiritual head of Islam—used as a title.

citadel A fortress that commands a city.

college An organized body of persons engaged in a common pursuit or having common interests or duties.

colon A colonial farmer or plantation owner.

cooptation Absorption, assimilation.

delimit To fix or define the limits of.

desiccate To dry up.

dey A ruling official of the Ottoman Empire in northern Africa.

efflorescence Blossoming.

epitaph An inscription on or at a tomb or a grave in memory of the one buried there.

exarch A Byzantine viceroy.

grand vizier Chief minister.

hinterland A region lying inland from a coast.

hominin Any member of the family Hominidae, especially extinct near-relatives of modern man.

Homo erectus Extinct species of the human lineage, perhaps a direct ancestor of human beings (*Homo sapiens*).

imamate The office of an imam, any of the various rulers that claim descent from Muhammad and exercise spiritual and temporal leadership over a Muslim region..

immutable Not capable of or susceptible to change.

interdict To destroy, damage, or cut off (as an enemy line of supply) by firepower to stop or hamper an enemy.

internecine Of, relating to, or involving conflict within a group.

isthmus Narrow strip of land connecting two large land areas otherwise separated by the sea.

megalith A very large, usually rough stone used in prehistoric cultures as a monument or building block.

multifarious Diverse.

mutable Prone to change; inconstant.

neologism A new word, usage, or expression.

oligarchy Government by the few.

pasha A man of high rank or office (as in Turkey or northern Africa).

pieds noirs (French: "black feet") A European settler born in French North Africa, especially Algeria.

praetorian Household troops of the Roman emperors.

prefect In ancient Rome, any of various high officials with primarily judicial and administrative responsibilities.

proconsul A governor of military commander of an ancient Roman province.

promontory A prominent mass of land overlooking or projecting into a lowland or body of water.

prosaic Everyday, ordinary.

proximate Very near.

quay A structure built parallel to the bank of a waterway for use as a landing place.

stela A usually carved or inscribed stone slab or pillar used for commemorative purposes.

supersession The act of being superseded; to be displaced.

suzerainty Overlordship

tumulus artificial mound or hillock, especially the type built over an ancient grave.

usurp To seize and hold (as office, place, or powers) in possession by force or without right.

wilāyah Province; administrative division.

Bibliography

Broad coverage of all aspects of northern Africa may be found in Trevor Mostyn and Albert Hourani (eds.), *The Cambridge Encyclopedia of the Middle East and North Africa* (1988). A useful survey is Richard Lawless and Allan Findlay (eds.), *North Africa: Contemporary Politics and Economic Development* (1984). Two annual publications, *The Middle East and North Africa* and *Africa Contemporary Record*, contain updated essays on the countries of northern Africa. Useful atlases include Gerald Blake, John Dewdney, and Jonathan Mitchell (eds.), *The Cambridge Atlas of the Middle East and North Africa* (1987); and Moshe Brawer (ed.), *Atlas of the Middle East* (1988). Paula Youngman Skreslet, *Northern Africa: A Guide to Reference and Information Sources* (2000), is an annotated bibliography that provides invaluable assistance for those pursuing a more in-depth study of the subject.

The monumental work by Stéphane Gsell, *Histoire ancienne de l'Afrique du Nord*, 8 vol. (1913–28), remains indispensable as an exhaustive account of the history of the Maghrib to 44 BCE. B.H. Warmington, *Carthage*, 2nd ed. rev. (1969), is a standard history of Phoenician Carthage for both specialist and general readers; J.B. Rives, *Religion and Authority in Roman Carthage from Augustus to Constantine* (1995), is also useful. A.H. Merrils, *Vandals, Romans, and Berbers: New Perspectives on Late Antique North Africa* (2004), provides insight into this period.

The entire period of Arab domination in North Africa is discussed in Jamil M. Abun-Nasr, *A History of the Maghrib in the Islamic Period* (1987, reprinted 1990). Works on specific periods include David Stephan Powers, *Law, Society, and Culture in the Maghrib, 1300–1500*, (2002); and Julia Ann Clancy-Smith, *North Africa, Islam, and the Mediterranean World: From the Almoravids to the Algerian War* (2001). Lucette Valensi, *On the Eve of Colonialism: North Africa Before the French Conquest* (1977; originally published in French, 1969), offers solid interpretation that dispels old myths about the French colonial era. Magali Morsy, *North Africa, 1800–1900: A Survey from the Nile Valley to the Atlantic* (1984), is innovative in treating all of northern Africa as a single region. Roger Benjamin, *Orientalist Aesthetics: Art, Colonialism, and French North Africa, 1880–1930* (2003), reflects on the cultural effects of French influence in the region. More recent political, economic, and social developments are covered by I. William Zartman and William Mark Habeeb, *Polity and Society in Contemporary North Africa* (1993); and Bruce Maddy-Weitzman and Daniel Zisenwine, *The Maghrib in the New Century: Identity, Religion, and Politics* (2007).

References specific to historical and contemporary Egypt include *Egypt*

Almanac (2003), a publication by Egypto-File that is articulate, accurate, and amply furnished with statistics and historical information; Jaromir Malek (ed.), *Egypt: Ancient Culture, Modern Land* (1993), surveys Egypt's geography, history, government, and culture; Barbara Watterson, *The Egyptians* (1997), a well-written overview of Egypt from the Stone Age to modern times; T.G.H. James, *Egypt: The Living Past* (1992), which also stresses the continuity of ancient and modern Egypt, with colour photographs; and Glenn E. Perry, *The History of Egypt* (2004). Useful publications that focus primarily on Sudan include John Obert Voll and Sarah Potts Voll, *The Sudan: Unity and Diversity in a Multicultural State* (1985), which provides basic information on the land, people, economy, and history; and G.M. Craig (ed.), *The Agriculture of the Sudan* (1991), a regional survey that also includes much information on the country's physical geography, people, economy, administrative and social conditions, and cultural life. Peter Woodward, *Sudan, 1898–1989: The Unstable State* (1990); and Robert O. Collins, *A History of Modern Sudan* (2008), provide useful overviews of Sudan's modern history.

INDEX

A

'Abd al-'Azīz, 112, 159, 160
Abdelkader, 59, 64, 66, 69, 111
Abd el-Krim, 61, 114, 118
Addis Ababa Agreement, 149, 150, 151
African Union (AU), 106, 155
Alexander the Great, 10, 18, 83
Alexandria, 37, 83, 84, 93
Algeria
civil war in, 78–81
colonial rule in, 66–68
early history of, 63
foreign relations of, 81–82
French conquest of, 64–66
as independent nation, 75–82
and movement for independence, 70
and nationalist movements, 68–69
Algerian Manifesto, 70
Algerian War of Independence, 70, 71–75, 117
'Alwah, 131, 132, 133
Amazigh (Berber), 3, 32, 38, 51, 63, 113, 114, 115, 116, 117, 118, 121, 166
Anglo-Egyptian Condominium Agreements, 85, 143
Anglo-Egyptian Treaty (1936), 90, 91, 144, 146
Anya Nya, 147, 149
Arab Bureaus, 67
Arab conquest of North Africa, 3, 36, 37, 38–41, 109
Arabian Peninsula, 4
Arabic language, 3, 4, 147
Arab-Israeli wars, 91, 92, 94, 96, 97, 104
Arab League, 91, 96, 98, 103
Arab-Nubian relations, 13
Arianism, 33, 35
assassinations, 38, 93, 97, 98, 116
Aswān, 126, 128, 129, 132
Aswān High Dam, 93
authoritarianism, 99, 142, 147, 152, 164

B

Baal Hammon, 13
Banghāzī, 18, 37, 100, 107
barbarians, 33, 34
Barbarossa, Khayr al-Dīn, 55
Barbary States, 3
Baring, Evelyn (Lord Cromer), 84, 85, 86
Bedouins, 4, 62, 166
Ben Bella, Ahmed, 71, 72, 76
Bendjedid, Chadli, 77, 78, 81
Berber resistance (to Arab rule), 41–42
Berber (Amazigh), 3, 38, 40, 41, 42, 43, 44, 46, 47, 48, 49, 50, 51, 54, 114, 166
Boumedienne, Houari, 76, 77, 79, 81, 82
Bourguiba, Habib, 61, 62, 72, 159, 160, 161, 162, 163, 164, 165
Byzantine Empire, 34–37, 40, 84, 156

C

Carthage
and the Greeks of Cyrenaica, 16–18
and human sacrifice, 13, 15
religion and culture of, 13–14
and Rome, 14–16
Carthaginian Period
Carthaginian supremacy, 7–9
Phoenician settlements, 6–7
political and military institutions, 12
subject peoples, 11
trade, 9–10
wars outside Africa, 10–11
Casablanca, 112, 113, 116, 122, 124, 125
Casablanca Conference, 115
Ceuta, 47, 112, 118, 120

Chad, 102, 105, 107
Christianity, 29–32, 33, 37, 109, 131, 133, 134, 138
Christian kingdoms, 131–133
Christians, 4, 30, 31, 32, 33, 52, 53, 55, 66, 84, 99, 137, 138, 139, 150
civil wars, 20, 27, 79–81, 94, 105, 149, 150–154
Cleopatra Selene, 18, 20
communists, 75, 148
Coptic Christians, 97, 99
Cyrenaica, 3, 5, 6, 16–18, 21, 34, 37, 38, 40, 48, 61, 62, 100, 102, 103, 104
Cyrene, 17, 18, 37, 102

D

Damascus, 38, 66
Darfur, 127, 128, 135, 137, 139, 140, 154, 155
demonstrations (political), 70, 76, 91, 94, 97, 114, 125, 144, 147, 148, 163
Destour Party, 61, 159, 160, 161, 162
Dinshawāy Incident, 85, 86
Donatism, 31, 32
Donatus, 30, 31
Dunqulah, 131, 132, 134

E

Egypt
- British occupation of, 84–88
- and constitutional monarchy, 88–92
- early history of, 83–84
- Republic of, 92–99

Egyptian-Sudanese relations, 135
Entente Cordiale, 61, 85
European colonialism, 54, 58–61, 66–68, 69, 71, 100, 102, 113, 114, 120
European Union (EU), 82, 165

F

Fārūq I, King, 89, 90, 91, 92
Fāṭimids, 43, 44, 46–48, 84
Fez, 20, 44, 47, 50, 51, 54, 112
Fezzan, 62, 103
French Algeria, 63–70, 72
Fu'ād I, King, 88–92
Fundamental Pact, 59, 158
Funj, 133, 134, 135

G

Gafsa, 5, 158, 159
Gaiseric, 33, 34
Gaulle, Charles de, 70, 73, 75
Granada, 53, 54, 156
Grand Mosque of Tunis, 46
Great Britian, 59, 61, 84, 85, 87, 88, 89, 90, 91, 93, 106, 112, 136, 142–144, 146, 158
Greeks, 1, 6, 7, 8, 9, 10, 12, 13, 16, 17, 37
Green March, 123

H

Hannibal, 14, 15, 16
Hassan II, King, 81, 106, 121, 122, 123, 124, 125
Herodotus, 9
human sacrifice, 13, 15

I

Idrīs I, 44
Idrīs II, 44
Idris, King (Sīdī Muḥammad Idrīs al-Mahdī al-Sanūsī), 61, 103
international aid, 94, 97, 98, 103, 121, 152, 155, 164
Islamic Jihad, 97
Islamic Salvation Front (FIS), 78, 70, 81
Islamists, 77, 79–81, 99, 122, 162, 163, 164
Israel, 91, 92, 93, 94, 95, 96, 98, 104, 105, 122, 165

J

Janjaweed, 128, 154
Jews/Judaism, 4, 37, 57, 105, 109, 115, 120, 122
Juhaynah, 132

K

Kabylia uprising, 66, 67
Karamanli, Aḥmad, 57
Khalīfah (ʿAbd Allāh ibn Muḥammad), 117, 120, 139, 140–142, 143, 148
Khartoum, 126, 131, 135, 136, 137, 140, 144, 145, 147, 148
Kush, 127, 128, 129, 131, 132

L

Lagu, Joseph, 149
Libya
  and the discovery of oil, 103–106
  early history of, 100–102
  economic sanctions against, 107–108
  as independenct nation, 103–108
  Italian colonization of, 100, 102, 103
  Ottoman rule of, 102
  and Qaddafi regime, 106–108
Libyan Desert, 21, 35, 62, 105
Luxor, 99

M

Maghrib, 1, 3, 4, 5, 18, 23, 24, 27, 32, 35, 36, 37, 38, 40, 41, 42, 43, 44, 46, 47, 48, 49, 50, 51, 52, 53, 54, 55, 57, 58, 73, 82, 122, 156, 157
Mahdiyyah, 139–143
Mamlūks, 84, 132, 157
Marrakech, 49, 50, 51, 54, 112
Masinissa, King, 16, 19, 20, 23
Mauritania, 4, 82, 120, 123, 167
Mecca, 49, 124
Melilla, 47, 112, 117, 118, 120
Meroe, 129, 131
Messali Hadj, Ahmed, 61, 69, 71
monarchies, 57, 62, 81, 88–92, 103, 105, 106, 110, 121, 123–125
Morocco
  and decline of traditional government, 111–112
  early history of, 109–111
  foreign policy of, 122
  French protectorate of, 113–115
  French zone in, 115–117
  independence of, 120–122
  Spanish zone in, 117–120
  and Western Sahara, 122–123
Mubārak, Ḥosnī, 97, 98, 99
Muhammad, Prophet, 41, 44, 47, 131, 139
Muslim Brotherhood, 91, 92, 93, 97, 150, 152
Muslim dynasties
  Aghlabids, 42, 43, 44, 46, 47
  Almohads, 48, 49, 50, 51, 52
  Almoravids, 48, 49, 50, 51, 52
  Fāṭimids, 43, 44, 46–48
  Idrīsids, 44
  sharifians, 54–55, 110
  Umayyads, 40, 42, 47, 49
  Zīrids, 46–48

N

Napoleonic wars, 57, 64
Nasser, Gamal Abdel, 92, 93, 94, 95, 97, 146
nationalist movements, 68–69
National Liberation Front (NLF), 61, 69
Neolithic culture, 5, 6
Nile River, 85, 127, 128, 129, 131, 132, 133, 136, 137, 139, 142, 143, 147, 149
nomads, 4, 18, 22, 29, 34, 35, 36, 48, 51, 131, 132, 134, 167, 168
Nubia, 126–129, 131, 132, 134, 135
Numidia, 12, 18, 19, 20, 21, 23, 29, 30, 31, 32, 33

O

oil (petroleum), 62, 77, 81, 82, 100, 102, 103–104, 105, 106, 149, 150, 152
Organization of African Unity, 81
Organization of Petroleum Exporting Countries (OPEC), 81
Ottoman Empire, 54, 55, 59, 64, 84, 87
Oujda, 111

P

Phoenicians, 6, 7, 9, 27, 166
piracy, 55, 56, 57
Polisario Front, 123, 167, 168, 169
political parties, 61, 71, 73, 77, 78, 79, 88, 89, 90, 92, 93, 97, 99, 103, 115, 116
Pomaria, 22
Ptolemies, 18, 20, 37, 83
Punic Wars, 11, 14, 16, 19, 156

Q

Qaddafi, Muammar al-, 62, 104, 105, 106, 107, 108, 122, 145, 146, 147, 148, 150, 151, 159, 160, 162, 163, 164
Qur'an, 4, 49, 50, 70, 134

R

Rabat, 23, 72, 109, 113, 114, 117, 125
Red Sea, 1, 127, 129
refugees, 19, 44, 68
religious fundamentalism, 125, 150–155
Roman North Africa
  administration and defense of, 21–23
  and the Byzantine Period, 34–37
  Christianity in, 29–32
  economy of, 25–27
  and the later Roman Empire, 27–29
  and Roman Cyrenaica, 37
  Romanization in, 32–33
  urban life in, 23–25
  Vandal conquest of, 33–34
Rustamids, 43

S

Sādāt, Anwar el-, 95, 96, 97, 98
Saguia el-Hamra, 81, 123, 166, 167
Sahara, 1, 3, 5, 8, 61, 62, 81, 82, 102, 113, 117, 121, 122, 123, 127, 166, 167, 168, 169
Saharawis, 167, 168
Sanūsiyyah, 61, 62, 100, 102, 103
Scipio Africanus the Elder, 15, 16
Sharīk Peninsula, 8, 13, 25, 159
Shīʿite/Shīʿite Islam, 44, 46, 47, 48
Sicily, 6, 7, 10, 11, 12, 14, 15, 34, 46, 50
Sidon, 6
Sinai Peninsula, 85, 93, 94, 96, 98
Sitifis, 22, 23, 25, 27, 29
Six-Day War (War of Attrition), 94, 104
slave trade, 136, 137, 138, 139
socialism, 77, 78, 93, 105, 121
Southern Sudan Liberation Movement (SSLM), 149
Soviet Union, 93, 94
Spain, 6, 7, 9, 10, 12, 15, 19, 32, 33, 41, 44, 47, 49, 50, 51, 52, 53, 59, 61, 109, 112, 113, 117, 118, 120, 123, 156, 167
Stone Age society, 3–6
sub-Saharan Africa, 54, 110
Sudan
  and ancient Egyptian influence, 126–127
  and ancient Nubia, 126–129
  and the Anglo-Egyptian Condominium, 143–146
  and Christian and Islamic influence, 129–135
  and civil war, 150–151
  and Egyptian-Ottoman rule, 135–138
  and Islam, 132–133, 134–135
  and the kingdom of Kush, 127–129

and the Mahdiyyah, 139–143
Republic of, 146–155
Suez Canal, 1, 86, 88, 94
Suez Canal Company, 93
Sufism, 50, 52, 54, 55, 56, 64, 134, 139
Sunni Islam, 42, 44, 46, 109

T

Tangier, 9, 20, 41, 44, 53, 73, 111, 112, 113, 115, 116, 117, 118, 120
terrorism, 75, 99, 161
Tlemcen, 22, 40, 50, 51, 52, 53, 55, 111
trade, trans-Saharan, 8, 43, 44, 48, 57
treaties, 14, 64, 167
Tripoli, 8, 54, 57, 58, 100, 107
Tripolitania, 3, 27, 29, 32, 33, 34, 36, 37, 41, 42, 43, 50, 52, 53, 62, 100, 102, 103, 104, 160
Tuareg, 32
Tunis, 40, 46, 53, 56, 59, 61, 64, 72, 156, 157, 160
Tunisia
domestic development in, 162–164
early history of, 156–157
European influence in, 157–158
foreign relations of, 164–165
independence of, 162–165
Tyre, 6, 7, 13

U

UN Emergency Force (UNEF), 93, 94
United Nations (UN), 71, 91, 94, 105, 165, 168
United States of America, 93, 94, 96, 97, 105, 106, 107, 120, 122, 164, 165
Utica, 7, 8, 10, 15, 21, 24

V

Vandals, 33–34

W

Wafd, 87, 88, 89, 90, 91, 92
Western Sahara, 62, 81, 82, 121, 122–123, 166–169
World War I, 62, 68, 70, 87, 91, 102, 113, 114, 118, 160
World War II, 61, 62, 70, 71, 90, 91, 100, 102, 103, 115, 144, 160

Y

Yom Kippur War, 96, 97
Young Algerians, 61, 68
Young Tunisians, 61, 159, 160

Z

Zanātah, 48, 51
Zīrids, 46–48